Create Macromedia® Flash™ Movies

Check the Web for Updates:

To check for updates or corrections relevant to this book and/or CD-ROM visit our updates page on the Web at **http://www.prima-tech.com/updates**.

Send Us Your Comments:

To comment on this book or any other PRIMA TECH title, visit our reader response page on the Web at **http://www.prima-tech.com/comments**.

How to Order:

For information on quantity discounts, contact the publisher: Prima Publishing, P.O. Box 1260BK, Rocklin, CA 95677-1260; (916) 787-7000. On your letterhead, include information concerning the intended use of the books and the number of books you want to purchase.

Create Macromedia® Flash™ Movies

Dan Ransom,
Mary Kelly Donahue
& Julie Meloni

A DIVISION OF PRIMA PUBLISHING

PRIMA TECH

A Division of Prima Publishing

Prima Publishing, colophon, and In a Weekend are registered trademarks of Prima Communications, Inc. PRIMA TECH is a trademark of Prima Communications, Inc., Roseville, California 95661.

Publisher: Stacy L. Hiquet
Associate Marketing Manager: Jennifer Breece
Managing Editor: Sandy Doell
Acquisitions Editor: Lynette Quinn
Project Editor: Estelle Manticas
Technical Reviewer: Christian Hughes
Copy Editors: Laura Gabler, Hilary Powers
Interior Layout: William Hartman
Cover Design: Prima Design Team
Indexer: Johnna VanHoose-Dinse

ISBN: 0-7615-2866-0

Library of Congress Catalog Card Number: 00-106666

Printed in the United States of America

00 01 02 03 04 II 10 9 8 7 6 5 4 3 2 1

For Donna
—DR

To my finest work ever, my son Jacob
—MKD

ACKNOWLEDGMENTS

I'd like to take this opportunity to thank all the people who've helped this book come together: Estelle, Hilary, Kim, Lynette and the rest of the hard-working people at Prima Tech. Thanks for going beyond the normal call of duty and pulling this book out from the brink of the surreal. Thanks Christian for your very thorough technical review and comments. Of course I also need to thank my fellow authors Mary Kelley Donahue and Julie Meloni, as well as all the others responsible for getting the book to the printer, including Layout Artist Bill Hartman, Indexer Jonna VanHoose-Dinse, and all of the manufacturing staff.

—Dan Ransom

Thanks to Julie for getting me the gig; I appreciate your faith in my abilities. Thanks to both Estelle and Lynette for all your patience and assistance, not to mention the cookies! Thanks always to Kate for the countless little things every day. A special thanks to Shona for your unending support. It means the world to me. Thanks to my Mom and Dad for all things. I love you always.

—Mary Kelley Donahue

AUTHOR BIO

As a developer and designer of Web pages, **Dan Ransom** currently helps maintain over a dozen Internet domains. When he is not creating Flash movies Dan specializes in cross-browser HTML, JavaScript, and DHTML. He lives in Sacramento and plays the harmonica, badly.

Mary Kelley Donahue is the Creative Director for i2i Interactive, a multimedia company located in Campbell, CA. A graduate of Stanford University with an Honors degree in History, Mary has put those useful skills to work in the multimedia business since 1985. Her spare time is filled with participating in an ever-widening variety of sports and activities with her eight-year old son, working in the yard with the family, and getting outside as much as possible (to escape the computer lurking in the other room).

Julie Meloni has been developing Web-based applications since the Web first saw the light of day, and remembers the excitement surrounding the first GUI Web browser. She would like to list all of the activities she does in her spare time, but she hasn't had any spare time in five years, so that would be a short list.

CONTENTS AT A GLANCE

CONTENTS

SUNDAY AFTERNOON
All About Animation

SUNDAY EVENING
Creating Your Final Project 225

INTRODUCTION

Flash movies are all over the place. From e-mail greeting cards to movie trailers and Web sites, people are creating entertaining and interactive movies with Macromedia Flash 5. Now it's your turn! Flash allows you to create movies with animations, interactivity, and sound, and use them for entertainment, as interfaces for a Web site or presentation, or just as a fun way to spend a weekend. The best part is that these fancy-schmancy movies are incredibly simple to create.

One of the reasons so many animators are turning to Flash to create their movies is that the basics of the application are so easy to learn. While the Flash 5 program can be quite complex at the higher levels, it remains simple to use for beginners. The remarkable people at Macromedia have managed to implement the best of both worlds: a quick learning curve with detailed complexity. This book will both walk you through the basics and hint at the complexity.

Macromedia has provided a tool to create effective and engaging movies containing graphics, audio, animation, interactivity, and much more. You're here to learn the basics of this behemoth application via this set of short sessions filled with precise instructions and examples.

What This Book Is About

When you first open Flash 5, you'll notice it's a big, complex, and fairly scary-looking application. At least, that's what I thought when I first opened it. The sessions in this book will target key sections of the application and teach you the basics of their use, with the goal of showing you that it's not such a scary business after all.

For example, sessions focus on how to use the tools, the panels, and the timeline, as well as what the heck a *stage* is, and so on. By the end of these sessions, you'll have scratched the surface of the Flash 5 features and will be able to poke around on your own without trepidation, or you'll be able to read an advanced book without your eyes glazing over when you hit the more difficult concepts.

Who Should Read This Book?

If you have never used Flash before (any version) and you want to learn how to make cool animated movies, then you should read this book. No assumptions are made regarding your skill set, just that you want to learn a new tool and you can follow instructions. The instructions will lead you toward completing examples, with or without any creative abilities.

Obviously, if you have creative abilities your completed movies will be more artistic than if you don't. However, even a lack of ability to match colors should not preclude you from diving right into this book. You can still make the application do what it should—the focus here is on application usage and not so much on design theory.

If you have used Flash before to any great extent, this book is probably too simplistic for you. If you can already use the individual tools and you understand the concepts of basic animation and movie publishing, you should probably move on to a more advanced book.

What You Need to Begin

The Flash 5 application is available for both Windows and Macintosh operating systems, and evaluation versions for both platforms are on this book's CD-ROM. Fundamentally, the application works the same on both platforms. Shortcut keys and some menu items may be different between platforms, and will be noted in the text.

You can find instructions for installing Flash 5 in Appendix B of this book.

Besides a computer, the Flash 5 application, this book, and your willingness to learn, there's one optional piece of the puzzle: a graphical Web browser. You do not need to be connected to the Internet while working with the Flash application, but having a Web browser is helpful for viewing the help files included with Flash 5. The two leading browsers are from Netscape (http://www.netscape.com/) and Microsoft (http://www.microsoft.com/). Version 4.0 or higher of either browser is recommended, and these browsers can be downloaded from the company Web sites.

If you are interested in adding Flash movies to your Web pages, you should know that this book does not cover the specifics of accessing the Internet or uploading your movies to your Web site via FTP. This book *does* cover the concept of creating published files for viewing in a Web browser, but specific functionality and troubleshooting is between you and your Internet Service Provider.

How This Book Is Organized

This book is divided into seven sessions, beginning on Friday evening and continuing into Sunday evening. You should be able to complete each session within two to four hours. The following overview hits the highlights of each session:

- **Friday Evening: Getting Started with Flash 5.** Covers the basics of the application, including how to access the help system and how to open and save a movie project file. The first few tools in the toolbox are introduced during this session.
- **Saturday Morning: Drawing Simple Shapes.** You'll receive an introduction to each drawing tool in the Flash toolbox: the Pencil, Line, Pen, Oval, Rectangle, Brush, and Eraser. With each description, you'll follow step-by-step instructions to use the tool to produce a specific shape or object.
- **Saturday Afternoon: Manipulating Shapes, and Other Odds and Ends.** This session teaches you how to work with existing objects created by the tools you learned about in earlier sessions. For example, you'll play with modifying straight lines in a square to make a wacky polygon, and with scaling an object to make it fit better in your movie. Also in this session you'll learn the basics of publishing your movie for viewing outside the application.
- **Saturday Evening: Design Basics.** This session gives you a break from the brain-benders and spends a lot of time talking about very basic design theory, such as using colors to communicate a message effectively. You'll also learn how colors are defined, and how to create your own custom colors, fills, and gradients.
- **Sunday Morning: Scenes, Layers, and Your Library.** Back in the groove of learning complicated things, this session takes you through your object library and shows you how to use scenes and layers while creating your movie. When using scenes and layers, you're separating your complex movie into small, easily modifiable elements. This is an extremely important concept, as it enables you to go back and make changes to your movies without tearing your hair out at two o'clock in the morning.

- **Sunday Afternoon: All about Animation.** This session takes you through various types of animation, using text, shapes, and colors to show you how to perform motion-based or fluid animation.
- **Sunday Evening: Creating Your Final Project.** Your final project is the culmination of everything you've learned in the preceding sessions. This session will have you create an interface with basic interactivity that will let a user play a number of animated movie clips.

Special Features of This Book

This book uses a number of icons and typographical conventions to make it easier on you as you work through each session. These icons are used to call your attention to notes, tips, cautions, additional resources on the Web, and resources included on the CD-ROM. Here are examples of what you'll see:

Notes are little bits of information specific to what you're doing within each session. They'll provide relevant information you may find useful as you work your way through the Flash 5 application.

Tips offer hints, tricks, and wacky ideas to apply as you continue your learning process.

Cautions warn you of potential hazards and other pitfalls that typically cause beginners to run screaming from the computer, vowing never to work with this application again. We'll have none of that!

FIND IT ON THE WEB

This icon marks resources located on the Web that may be helpful to you as you continue to work with Flash.

ON THE CD

This icon marks resources or tools located on the CD-ROM, such as the example movies used in each session.

FRIDAY EVENING

Getting Started with Flash 5

- Getting Help with Flash 5
- Creating a New Movie
- Open an Existing Movie
- Introducing the Toolbox

So it's Friday night and you don't have anything better to do than sit around and learn how to create dynamic, interactive movies. Gee, that doesn't sound too bad—imagine how impressed your friends will be on Monday!

Flash has really made an impact in the world of animation. The easy-to-learn interface and time saving tools allow even novice animators to produce high-quality and entertaining movies. In fact, a number of animated shows got their start as Flash movies, including the crude but popular *South Park* television series. You may never see your movies on TV, but with a little time and a bit of practice you could certainly amuse your family with a cartoon impression of Grandpa or impress your co-workers with your multi-media slideshow presentation.

By now you've read the Introduction and installed Flash 5 on your computer, right? Maybe you've even opened the application and poked around in it for a few minutes. If you were like me the first time I opened the application, you got scared and closed it—there sure are a lot of strange windows, menus, and toolboxes! Do not fear, gentle reader—I got over my fear and eventually wrote this book. You, too, will find that in this case, the bark is worse than the bite.

In this Friday Night session, you'll become familiar with some of the menus and tools of the Flash 5 application. This session may not be terribly exciting, but you will get a good, solid foundation for moving forward.

In this session, you'll learn how to:

- Use the offline Help system
- Identify the menus, tools, and panels
- Start a new movie and open an existing movie
- Use the selection tools and modifiers
- Use the text tools and panels

Getting Help with Flash 5

I hope that this book will answer the majority of your questions about Flash, but if you come up against something you don't understand, don't panic: Macromedia does a wonderful job of including Help systems and tutorials in its products. Those included with the Flash application are infinitely helpful, and warrant an introduction.

1. Open your Flash application by double-clicking the Flash 5 icon.
2. Select the Help menu item from the menu bar (see Figure 1.1).

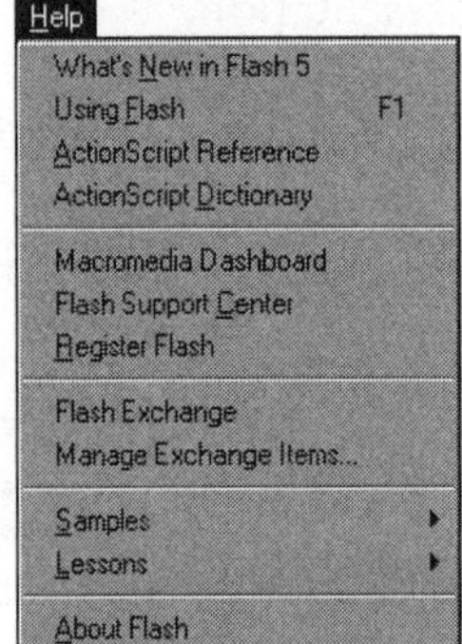

Figure 1.1

The Flash 5 Help menu

You will see the following options:

- **What's New in Flash 5.** This option opens an informational page (without connecting to the Internet) all about the new features of Flash 5. Requires a Web browser.

- **Using Flash**. This option opens the Flash Help system (without connecting to the Internet). Requires a Web browser.
- **ActionScript Reference**. This option opens the ActionScript Reference system (without connecting to the Internet). Requires a Web browser.
- **ActionScript Dictionary**. This option opens the ActionScript Dictionary (without connecting to the Internet), which is a bare-bones manual for ActionScript functions. Requires a Web browser.

These Help pages require that you have chosen to install the Flash 5 Plug-In for your default browser.

- **Macromedia Dashboard.** A window within the Flash 5 application that contains content sent by Macromedia, updated often by connecting to Macromedia through the Internet. You can connect manually, or you can have your Dashboard automatically update itself.
- **Flash Support Center.** Connects to the Flash Support Center Web site. Requires a Web browser and an active connection to the Internet.
- **Register Flash.** Presents a way to keep your program up to date with all the latest updates and bug fixes from Macromedia. You can connect manually, or have your Dashboard automatically update itself. Dashboard requires that you be connected to the Internet.
- **Samples.** This option opens a submenu of included sample files provided by Macromedia.
- **Lessons.** This option opens a submenu of included step-by-step lessons provided by Macromedia.
- **About Flash.** This option opens the About Flash dialog box, showing the application's credits and your registration information.

Using the Flash 5 Help System

To start using the Help system, select Help, Using Flash from the menu bar. Your Web browser will launch, although you will not need to connect to the Internet.

Windows Users:

You can also access the Help system by pressing the F1 key on your keyboard.

Inside your Web browser window you should see the Start page of the Macromedia Flash 5 Help system (see Figure 1.2).

Once inside the Help system, use the links on the lower-left side to select a main topic. If that topic has subtopics, they will appear when you click on the topic name.

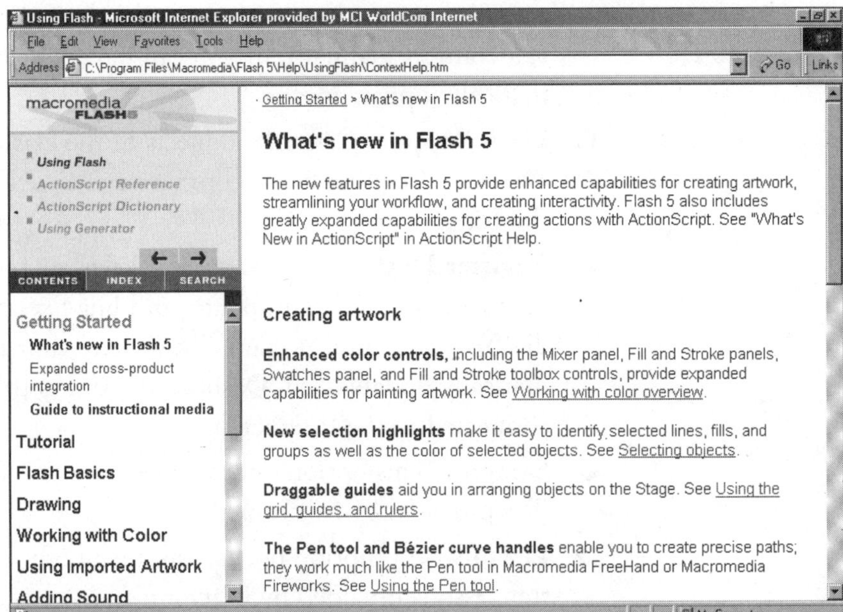

Figure 1.2

The start page of the Macromedia Flash 5 Help system

Navigation topics are displayed according to their importance, with subtopics displayed in smaller type than main topics. Subtopics within subtopics are smaller still.

When you select a subtopic, the text for that topic will appear in the body area, on the right side of your Web browser window.

Try it out, after starting the Help system.

1. Select the Flash Basics topic. The menu will refresh, showing numerous subtopics, such as "Flash basics overview," "The Flash workflow," "About vector and bitmap graphics," and "The Flash work environment."
2. Select the "Flash basics overview" subtopic.
3. The body area will display the text for the "Flash basics overview" subtopic (see Figure 1.3).

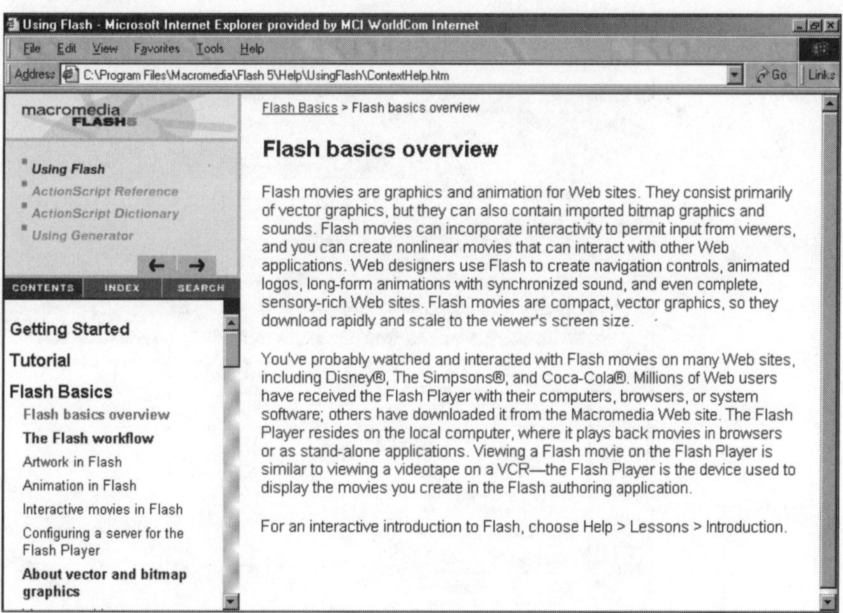

Figure 1.3

The "Flash basics overview" subtopic

Using the Macromedia Lesson Topics

In addition to a great Help system, Macromedia includes several interactive lessons within the Flash 5 application. Each lesson is a short primer on a topic, such as drawing, using buttons, or simple animation. If you need a quick refresher on a topic, these interactive lessons can help. You can access these lessons by selecting Help, Lessons from the menu bar, then selecting a specific lesson from the submenu. When you select a lesson, such as the drawing lesson (02 Drawing.fla), it will appear in your work area. See Figure 1.4 for an example.

These lessons are fully functioning Flash movies, meaning that buttons and animation elements will work while you are viewing the lesson within your work area. To move forward or backward in the lesson, press the left or right arrows that are found in the lower-right corner of the movie.

To end a lesson, select File, Close from the menu bar and the file will close.

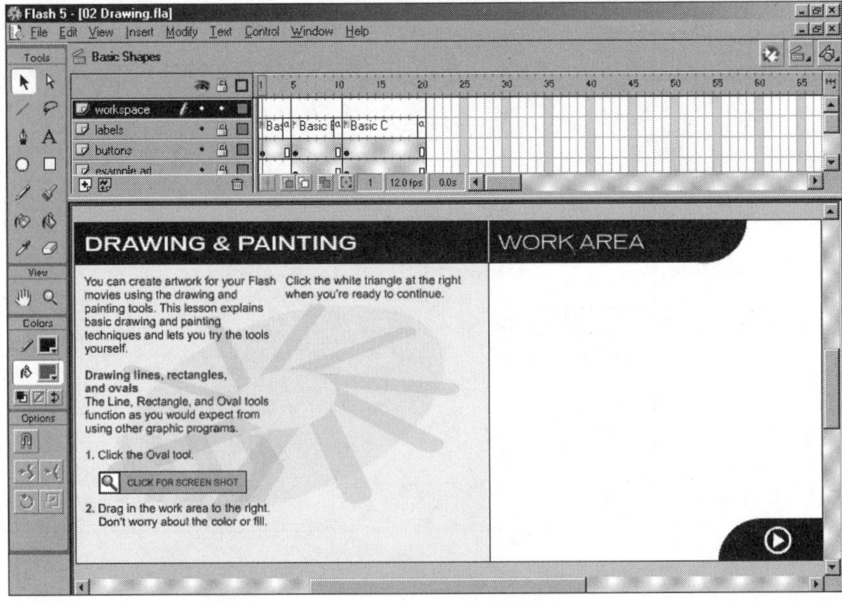

Figure 1.4

The drawing lesson

You can use the Ctrl+W (Command + W on the Mac) key combination to close an open file.

Using the Macromedia Sample Files

Macromedia also includes several sample movies with the Flash 5 application. You can use these sample movies as templates for your own projects or as examples of new effects. Access these movies by selecting Help, Samples from the menu bar, then select a specific movie from the submenu. When you select a sample, such as the Dice sample, its project file will appear in your work area as shown in Figure 1.5.

To view the sample in action, select Control, Test Movie from the menu bar. This action will export the project to a Flash movie file, then display the movie within the application.

Figure 1.5

The Dice sample project

You can use the Ctrl+Enter (Command + Return on the Mac) key combination to quickly test a movie (see Figure 1.6).

Figure 1.6

The Dice sample movie

When you use the Test Movie command within your authoring environment, all buttons, text fields, animation, and other Flash features are active—there's no need to export the file and view it through your Web browser. In the Dice example, you can press the Roll Dice button to make the movie run (it rolls the dice).

To close the movie file, select File, Close from the menu bar and the file will close. Repeat the step to close the project file. You may be asked to Save Changes if you made any clicks or movements within the project file. Go ahead and select Yes.

Now that you've been introduced to the Help system and Macromedia's sample files, I'm sure you're ready to start using the Flash tools on your own. In the next section, you'll learn how to create a new movie and modify some basic parameters.

Creating a New Movie

It's time to create your first Flash movie. Are you ready to get started? I am. Don't expect too much at first, though, you've got a whole weekend ahead. Your movies will get steadily better as you progress through the sessions.

Creating a new movie is as simple as selecting File, New from the menu bar. You'll use the File menu quite a bit—for creating new movies, opening, saving, and closing existing movies, and exiting the application. Following are all of the options under the File menu:

- **New.** Creates a new, empty movie.
- **Open.** Opens an existing movie.
- **Open as Library.** Opens an existing movie and makes its elements available to the current movie as a library.
- **Open as Shared Library.** Opens a library from another movie and makes its library available to the current movie as a shared library.
- **Close.** Closes the current movie.
- **Save.** Saves the current movie.
- **Save As.** Saves the current movie with a different name.
- **Revert.** Returns the current movie to its last saved version.
- **Import.** Allows you to insert sound, graphics, and other files into your current movie.
- **Export Movie.** Exports the current movie to an optimized Flash movie, a QuickTime movie, an animated GIF, or another animated file type.
- **Export Image.** Exports the current movie display to a nonanimating (static) image file.

- **Publish Settings.** Allows you to adjust numerous settings before you publish your movie, such as image quality, movie looping, and so on.
- **Publish Preview.** Mimics the publishing process by opening a temporary file and loading your movie, "published" according to the current saved settings.
- **Publish.** Creates the "final" version of the movie and supporting files, based on the current saved settings.
- **Page Setup.** Defines printing options, should you wish to print the frames in your movie.
- **Print Preview.** Displays a preview of the printed frames in your movie based on the current saved settings.
- **Print.** Prints the frames of your movie based on the current saved settings.
- **Send.** Available only on the PC, this option allows you to compose and send an e-mail message with the current movie as an attachment.
- **Recent File List.** Displays a list of recently used files.
- **Exit.** Closes the application and all open movies. This option is Quit on the Mac.

Don't be concerned if some of these terms are confusing. As the lessons progress, you'll be introduced to the menu items you need to use. You may get through this entire book without ever using a few of the menu items—there are a lot of them, and I don't think I've used every single one!

It's time to get started. Create a new, empty movie by selecting File, New from the menu bar. Figure 1.7 shows you this first step.

You can use the Ctrl+N (Command + N on the Mac) key combination to open a new movie.

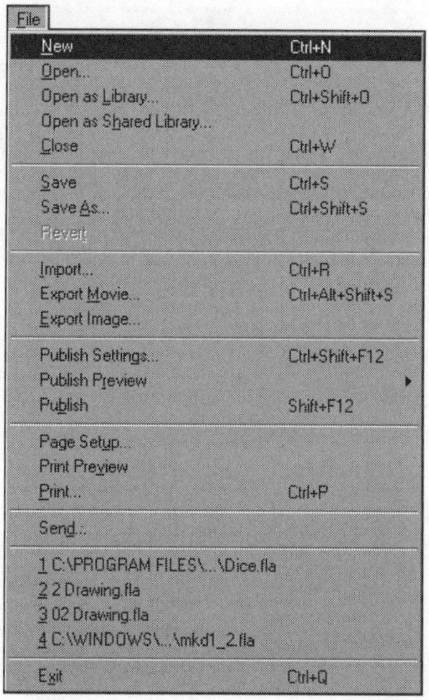

Figure 1.7

Create a new movie using the menu bar

When the new movie is created, a large white square is placed within the application window, like that in Figure 1.8. This white square is called the *stage.* The stage, appropriately, is where your movie will be performed. On the stage you'll color, draw, place graphics, type text, and perform other tasks related to the appearance of your movie. The gray area around the stage is also part of your work area, but nothing in the work area will appear in your movie, unless it is explicitly placed on the stage. Consider the gray area "backstage"; it's just a prep area for elements that haven't made it to the stage yet.

This empty movie may not be that impressive, but it's a start. Depending on your screen resolution and monitor size, you may only see a small bit of the stage itself. Obviously, seeing only a small bit of your canvas when trying to paint a masterpiece won't be very helpful, so now you'll learn the basic steps for controlling your work area.

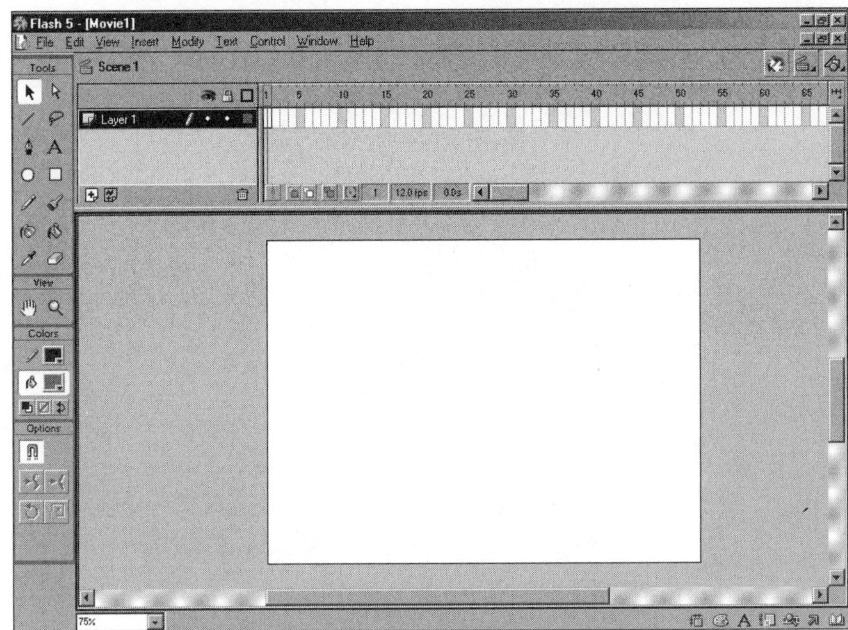

Figure 1.8

A new, empty movie

Modifying Basic Movie Elements

The first step in taking control of your work area is to modify the stage size, using the Modify menu. You'll use the Modify menu more in later sessions, as you learn to flip, rotate, group, and place elements within your movie. But there's no time like the present to learn about its options.

- **Instance.** Toggles the Instance Properties Panel, allowing you to control the properties of the selected instance. An instance is an occurrence of a symbol.
- **Frame.** Toggles the Frame Properties Panel, allowing you to control the properties of the selected frame, such as its name, associated sounds and animation, and so on.
- **Layer.** Opens the Layer Properties dialog box, allowing you to control the properties of the current layer, such as its name, type, and so on.

- **Scene.** Toggles the Scene Properties Panel, allowing you to modify the name of the current scene.
- **Movie.** Opens the Movie Properties dialog box, allowing you to control the overall properties of the current movie, such as its size and units of measurement used.
- **Smooth.** Softens curves in the selected line or object.
- **Straighten.** Makes small straightening adjustments to the selected line or curve.
- **Optimize.** Reduces the number of curves in a selected element. This technique can actually reduce the size of the Flash movie.
- **Shape.** Opens a submenu that offers the Convert Lines to Fills, Expand Fill, and Soften Fill Edges options.
- **Trace Bitmap.** Opens the Trace Bitmap dialog box, allowing you to modify specific settings before transforming a bitmap graphic into a vector graphic. This option is covered in more detail in Appendix A.
- **Transform.** Opens a submenu that allows you to apply transformations to an item, such as scaling and rotating the item.
- **Arrange.** Opens a submenu that allows you to modify the "stacking order" of items (which is in front, which is on the bottom, and so on).
- **Frames.** Opens a submenu that allows you to modify frames within the current timeline.
- **Group.** Groups together one or more selected elements. Grouped elements can be moved and manipulated all at once.
- **Ungroup.** Ungroups a previously grouped object.
- **Break Apart.** Takes an object and breaks it into individual shapes, lines, or other individual, editable elements.

Now that your head is spinning with all these modification options, just focus on the size attributes of your new movie. You'll learn about most of the other modification options soon enough.

Select Modify, Movie from the menu bar, as shown in Figure 1.9.

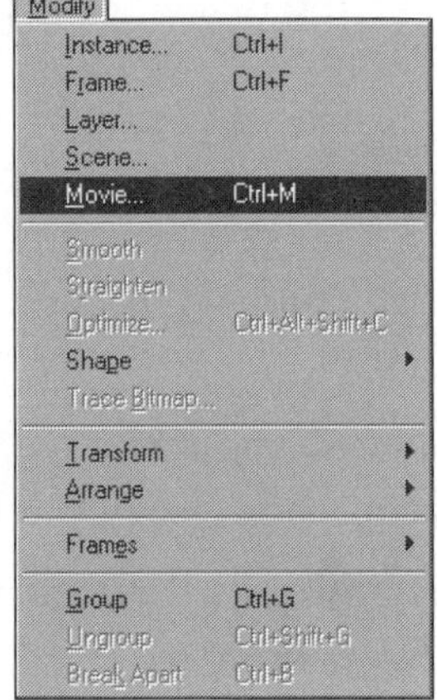

Figure 1.9

Display the Movie Properties dialog box using the menu bar

You can also use the Ctrl+M (Command + M on the Mac) key combination to open the Movie Properties dialog box.

The Movie Properties dialog box will open (see Figure 1.10). This dialog box allows you to select basic sizing and measurement options for your movie.

Figure 1.10

The default values of the Movie Properties dialog box

Usually, you'll keep all of the default values except the dimensions of the movie. However, it's good to know what modification options you have.

The first option is the Frame Rate, which defaults to 12 fps (frames per second). This rate is perfectly normal, and there's no real reason to change it unless you want your movie to fly by very quickly or to animate at a snail's pace. I don't recommend either. A slow movie is boring, and a movie with a high frame-per-second rate will cause your computer to grind to a halt, unless you have a faster, more expensive computer than I do.

The next modification options are for the width and height of your movie stage. The minimum width or height is 18 pixels and the maximum for either width or height is 2,880 pixels.

Changing the width and height are the primary modifications you'll make to a new movie. For now, change both the width and height of the current stage to 300 pixels, then click OK. Your stage will resize automatically.

This resized stage should be easier to work with, since you are now able to see the entire canvas.

If you just need your movie to fit better on your stage, and you don't want to modify its overall size, use the drop-down list box in the lower left of the application window to select a percentage such as 50 percent or even 25 percent, as in Figure 1.11. Your viewable area will scale accordingly, while leaving the movie size intact.

Play around with the Movie Properties dialog box to become familiar with your sizing options before moving on to the next section. The stage should be a comfortable size for you; you're going to be spending a lot of time there.

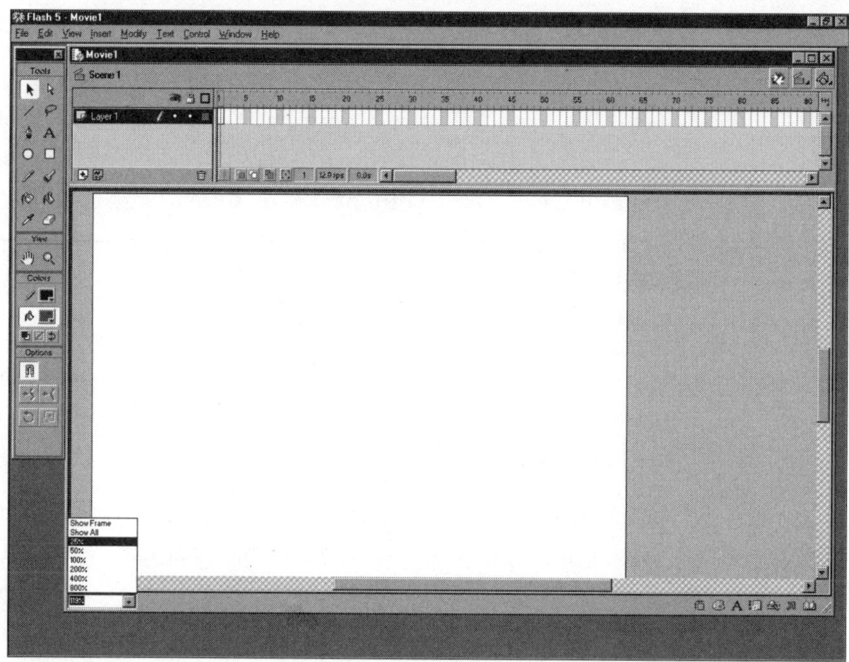

Figure 1.11

Adjusting the stage view percentage

Open an Existing Movie

In this section, all you'll do is open a sample file from the CD-ROM included with this book. This sample file is an example of the most basic type of Flash movie. It is nothing more than text on a colored background. This sample file will also be used in the next section, when you'll start using the toolbox.

To open an existing movie, select File, Open from the menu bar. A dialog box will appear prompting you to navigate around the file system until you find the target file.

Follow these steps to open the sample file:

1. Put this book's CD-ROM in your CD-ROM drive.
2. Select File, Open from the menu bar.

3. In the Open dialog box, navigate through the folders on the CD-ROM, and open the session1 directory.
4. Highlight the sample_s1.fla file, as shown in Figure 1.12. Files with an extension of .fla are the source files for the Flash movie, or the files in which you make all your changes.

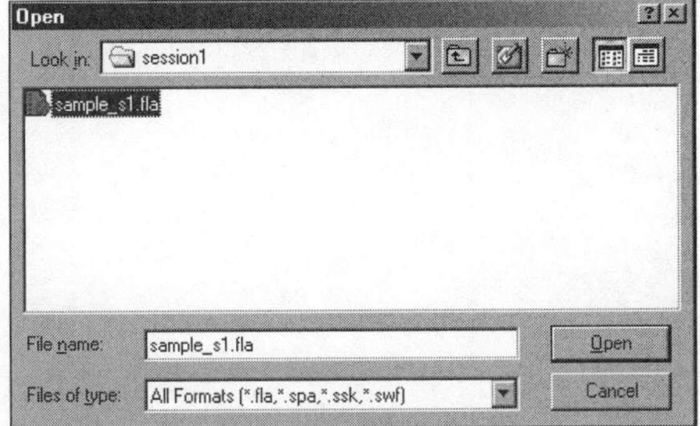

Figure 1.12

Select the target file

5. Click Open to open the sample_s1.fla file. Your workspace will show the sample_s1.fla file open on your stage, as in Figure 1.13.

I've made this sample file terribly unappealing on purpose. Now that you've opened it, the next section will show you how to select and delete all of the different parts of the movie, using the selection tools.

Take a Break

Step away from the computer and grab a quick bite to eat. After dinner you'll learn all about one of the most important utilities in Flash: the toolbox. You'll also create your first Flash 5 movie!

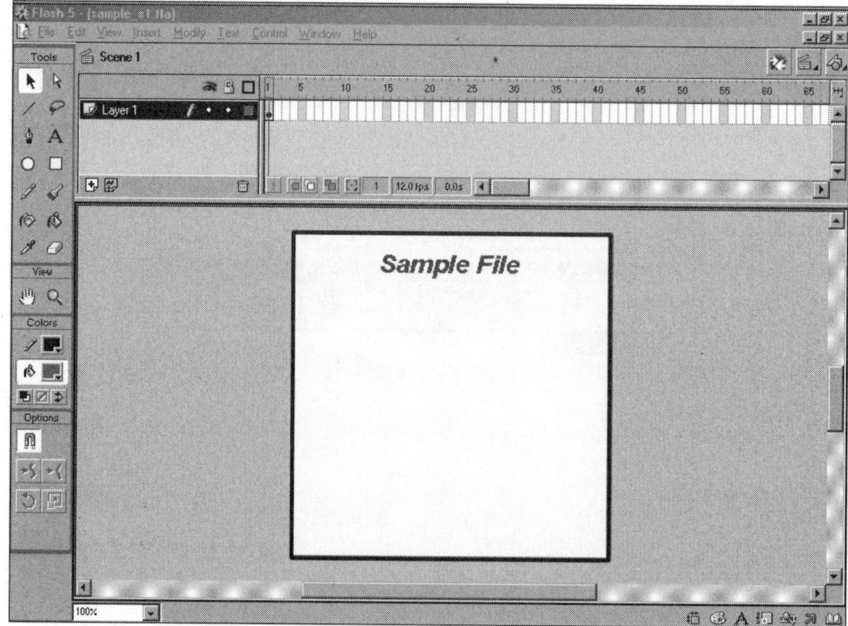

Figure 1.13

The sample_s1.fla file, opened on your stage

Introducing the Toolbox

No more boring "open file, close file" instructions—it's time to get familiar with the toolbox! This element of the Flash application contains all of the tools you'll need for drawing, coloring, selecting, and moving objects in your movies. You should familiarize yourself with the toolbox—it's one of the most important utilities. Figure 1.14 shows the toolbox.

There are four sections in the toolbox:

- **Tools Section**. Contains drawing, painting, text, and selection tools.
- **View Section**. Contains the hand and zoom tools, for panning and zooming in a selection.
- **Colors Section**. Contains items used for modifying the stroke and fill colors of selections.
- **Options Section**. Contains tool-specific modifiers; when a tool is selected, any options associated with it appear in this area.

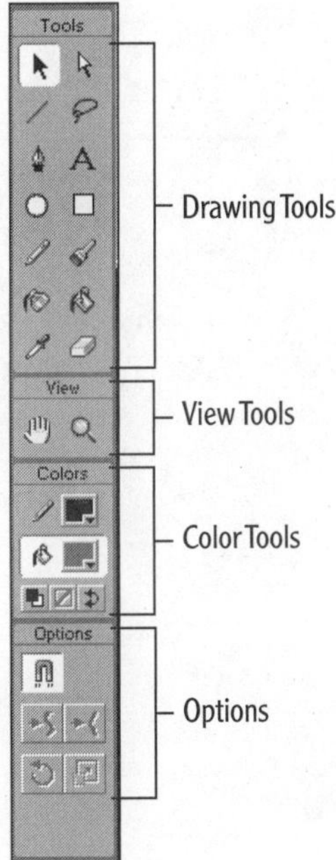

Figure 1.14

The Flash 5 toolbox

When a tool is selected, any modifiers for that tool are displayed. Sometimes, a modifier will be grayed out or not selectable until another action is performed. Often, a modifier will be grayed-out until an item on the stage is selected.

Continuing in the tradition of not overwhelming you with descriptions of each and every tool, the remainder of this session will introduce you to just two tools: the Arrow tool (used for selecting and moving elements) and the Text tool (used for typing and placing text on the stage).

Using the Arrow Tool

The Arrow tool is the default tool, meaning it is preselected for you when you open the application. In Figure 1.15, you can see how the toolbox looks when the Arrow tool is selected.

If the Arrow tool is not the tool you're currently using, you can switch to it simply by clicking the Arrow tool button. Your mouse pointer will look like an arrow when the Arrow tool is active.

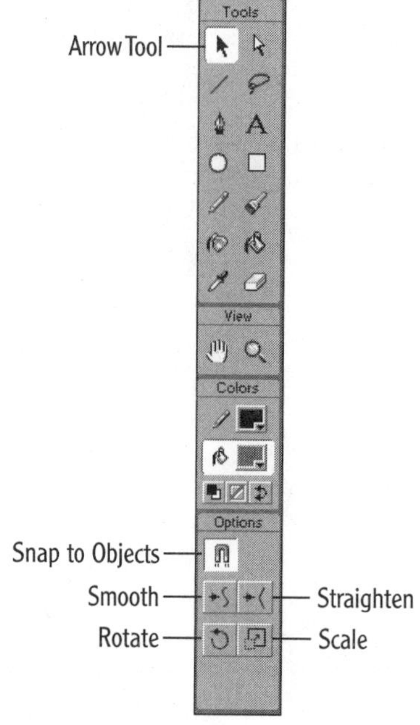

Figure 1.15

The toolbox with the Arrow tool selected

Don't confuse the Arrow tool with the Subselect tool. The Arrow tool is the solid black arrow on the left side of the toolbar.

The modifiers for the Arrow tool are:

- **Snap to Objects.** If selected, any element you place on the stage will "snap" in place, using a grid mechanism to determine where the "place" is.
- **Smooth.** If you select the Smooth modifier when a line or shape is selected on the stage, the lines will automatically smooth out.
- **Straighten.** If you select the Straighten modifier when a line or shape is selected on the stage, any crooked area in your lines will automatically straighten out.

- **Rotate.** If selected when an object is selected on the stage, the Rotate bounding outline (dotted box) will appear around the object, allowing you to rotate that object any which way you want.
- **Scale.** If selected when an object is selected on the stage, the Scale bounding outline will appear around the object, allowing you to scale the object to any size you want.

You should still have the sample_s1.fla file open and on your stage. If you have closed this file, please select File, Open from the menu bar and reopen the file. Now you'll use the Arrow tool to completely dissect this sample file!

Throughout the next couple of sessions I'll only show the stage area of the screen in the figures, so that you can see up close what I'm talking about.

Select and Delete Objects

Using the Arrow tool, click on the horizontal black line at the top of the sample file. The line should become dotted, as shown in Figure 1.16. The dotted lines or objects indicate that the element has been selected.

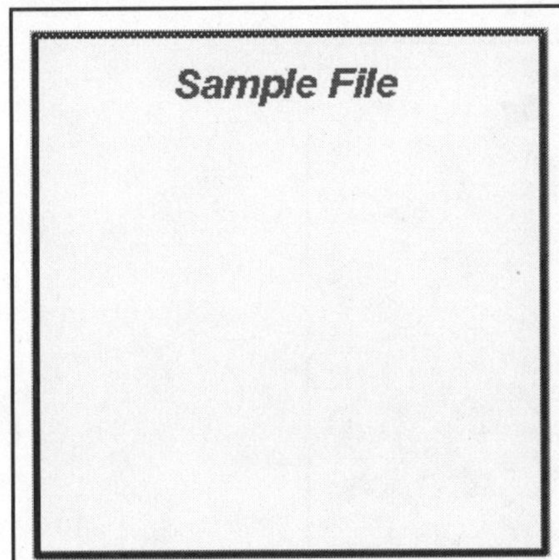

Figure 1.16

Sample movie with top horizontal line selected

Delete the selected line by pressing the Delete button on your keyboard. The top horizontal line should disappear.

Repeat this process for the two vertical black lines, with one exception: select them both before pressing the Delete button.

1. Click on one of the vertical black lines.
2. Press the Shift button on your keyboard.
3. With the Shift button still pressed, click on the other vertical black line.
4. Release the Shift button. Both lines will be selected.
5. Press the Delete button on your keyboard. Both vertical lines will disappear.

The next deletion that you'll do is to get rid of the yellowish background. Click with the Arrow tool anywhere in the yellow space to select the entire background. The background will be dotted to show that it is selected, as in Figure 1.17.

Press the Delete button on your keyboard. You will be left with a white area containing purple text at the top and a single black horizontal line at the bottom. In the next section, you'll do some rotating and scaling of the remaining elements. Keep the sample file open, in its current state.

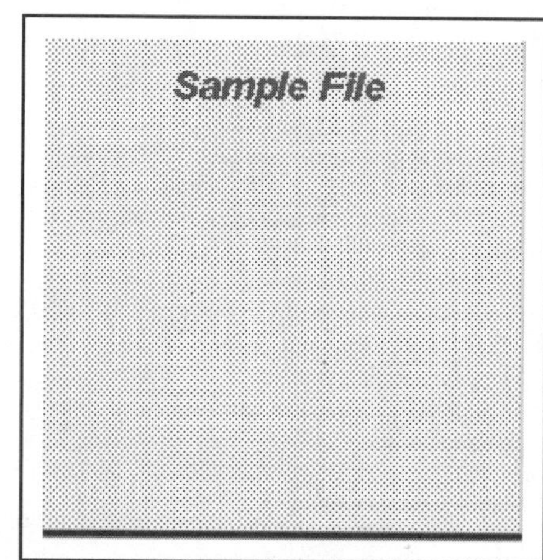

Figure 1.17

Sample movie with background selected

Select and Rotate Objects

To begin working with the Arrow tool modifiers, follow these steps as an example:

1. Using the Arrow tool, click on the horizontal black line at the bottom of the sample file.
2. Click the Rotate modifier in the toolbox. The horizontal line will now have a bounding outline around it, as in Figure 1.18.

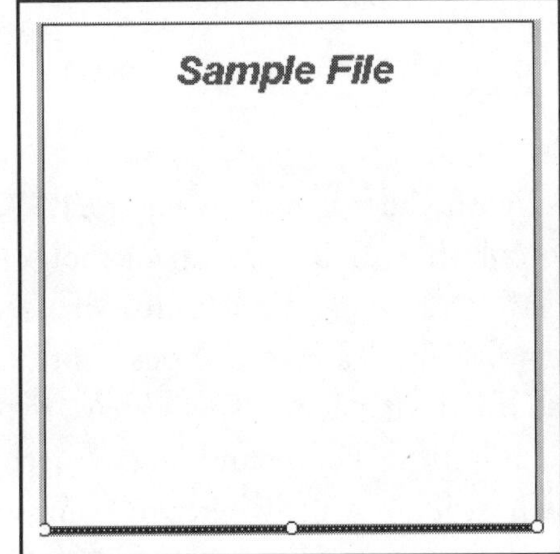

Figure 1.18

Sample movie with Rotate bounding outline surrounding a line

3. To begin rotating the line, click on one of the circles at the end of the line. These circles are handles by which you can grab an object.
4. With your mouse button still pressed, drag one of the handles toward the center of the object. You will see the line move at an angle.
5. Release the mouse button at some point. In Figure 1.19, I have dragged the left handle halfway to the center and released it. The position of your line may differ.
6. You will see that although you have released the mouse button, the bounding outline still surrounds the line. Click your mouse button anywhere on the stage to apply the position of the line.

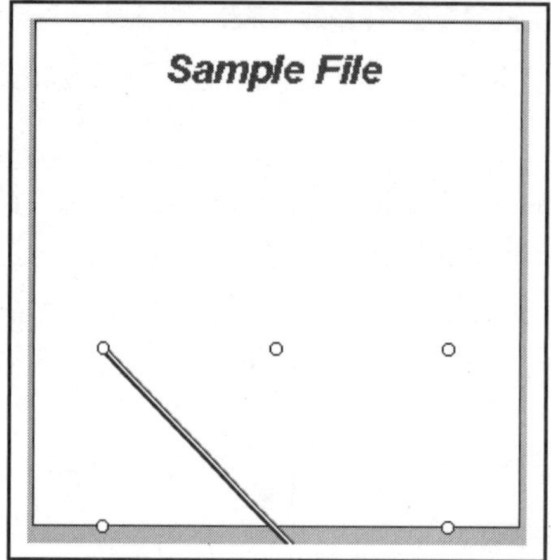

Figure 1.19

Line rotated on the stage

If your line is partially off the stage, as in Figure 1.19, simply click the line with the Arrow tool, then drag it with your mouse until it is entirely within your stage. Flash creates an outline of the shape that you can position on the stage. Until you release your mouse button the old position will still be visible, so that it may look like you have two lines! Don't fear, you only have one, but this "before-and-after" mechanism helps you determine if the new position is really where you want to place the object. You can see an example of this in Figure 1.20.

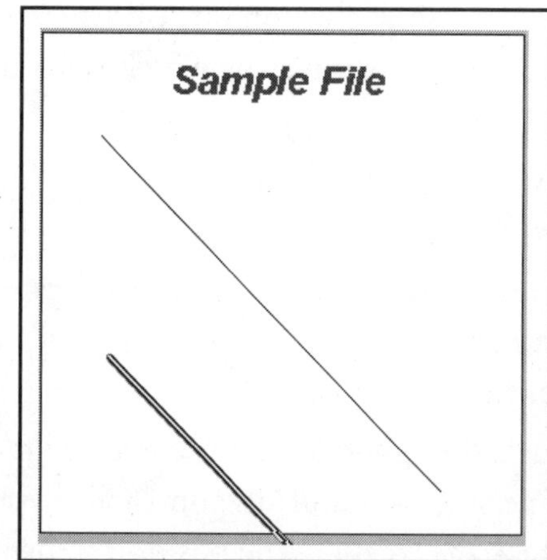

Figure 1.20

When you move an object on the stage, it appears that there are two objects, until you release the mouse button.

To apply the new position, simply release your mouse button anywhere else on the stage.

Using the Rotate modifier isn't the only way to rotate an object. You could also select Modify, Transform from the menu bar, then select Rotate to get the bounding outline, or select Rotate 90° CW or Rotate 90° CCW to let the application automatically rotate by 90 degrees either way.

Select and Scale Objects

Now that you've deleted or rotated objects in the sample movie, you'll use the purple text to learn about the Scale modifier.

1. Using the Arrow tool, click anywhere on the purple text. The entire text box will be selected.
2. Press the Scale modifier in the toolbox. The text box will now have a bounding outline around it (see Figure 1.21).
3. To begin scaling the text, click on one of the squares. These are handles by which you can grab an object.

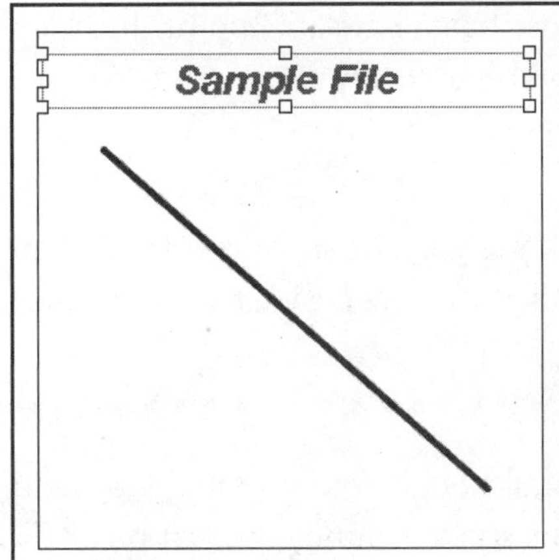

Figure 1.21

The Scale bounding outline surrounding a text box

4. With your mouse button still down, drag one of the handles upward or downward, or even from left to right. You will see the box become larger and the text within it will stretch evenly (scale).
5. An outline of the box has been created, displaying the new size. Until you release your mouse button, the old position will be visible, so that it may look like you have two text boxes. You can see an example of this in Figure 1.22, as I dragged the handles downward.

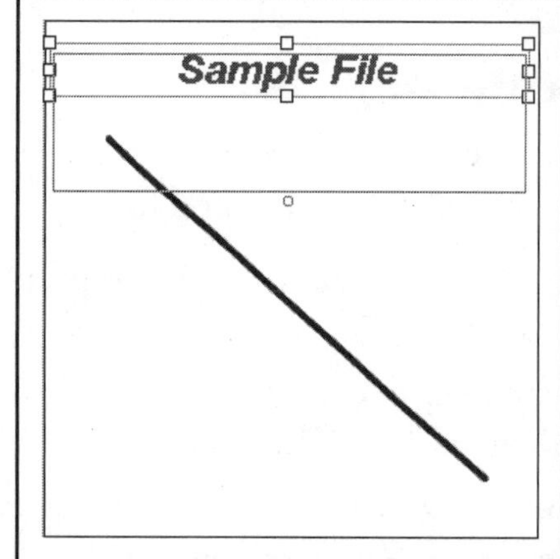

Figure 1.22

Appearance of two text boxes when scaling on the stage

6. Release the mouse button at some point. In Figure 1.23, I have dragged the center handle on the lower horizontal line toward the bottom of the screen. The position of your text box may differ.

Holding down the Shift key as you scale an object will cause Flash to maintain the proportions of the drawing. In other words the width will be adjusted to the same percentage that the height is.

7. You will see that although you have released the mouse button, the bounding outline still surrounds the text box. Click your mouse button anywhere on the stage to apply the modifications.

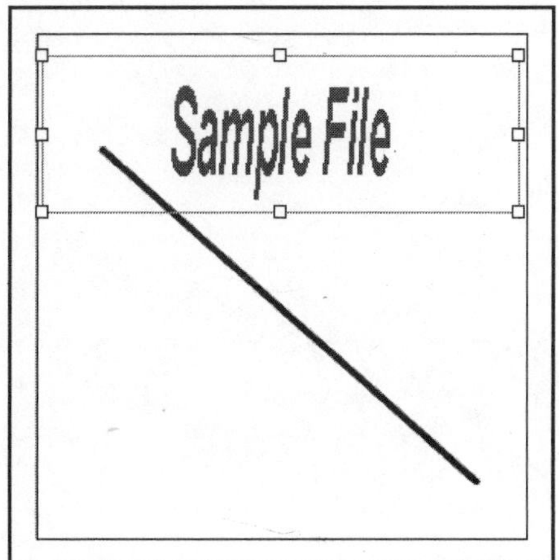

Figure 1.23

Text scaled on the stage

In the next section, you'll be working from a fresh stage, so you can close the sample movie by selecting File, Close from the menu bar. You may save the file if you wish, by selecting File, Save As from the menu bar and giving the file a new name and location when prompted by the dialog box. Or you can close without saving by selecting File, Close.

Using the Text Tool

The Text tool is used to place text in your movie. You can use the Text tool in conjunction with the Character Panel to add text of any size, font, or color. In Figure 1.24, you can see how the toolbox looks when the Text tool is selected. If the Text tool is not the current tool you're using, you can switch to it simply by pressing the Text tool button in the toolbox (the "A").

You'll notice that unlike the Arrow tool, the Text tool has no modifiers in the options area of the toolbox! Instead, the Text tool uses a *panel,* or a floating area that contains modifiers. You can keep panels open while you work, move them around, or hide them completely.

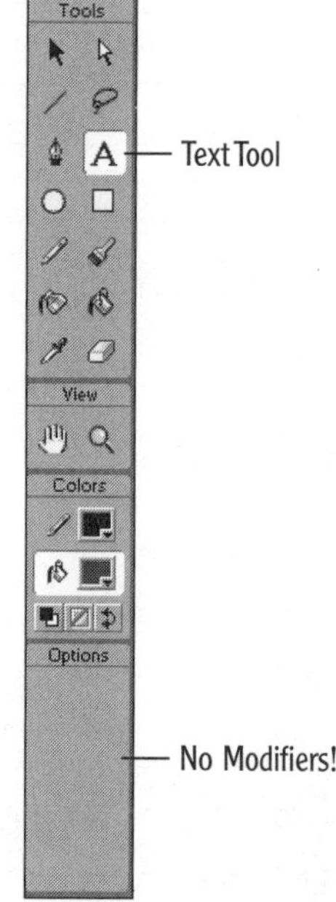

Figure 1.24

The toolbox with the Text tool selected

You can access panels in a number of ways. You can select Window, Panels, [Name of Panel] from the menu, or you can use the buttons in the Launcher at the lower right of your application window (see Figure 1.25).

NOTE

You can also use Flash 5's shortcut keys to launch some panels. See Appendix C for some of the more useful shortcut keys.

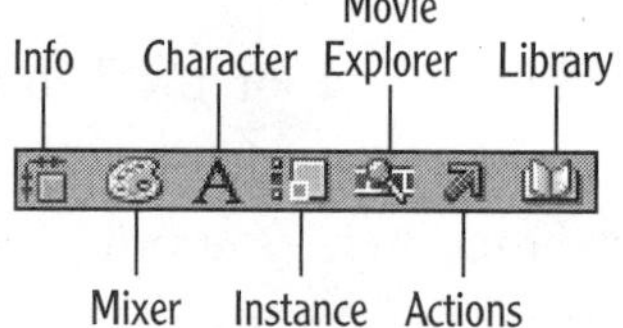

Figure 1.25

Panels in the Launcher

Using the Character Panel

Figure 1.26 shows the Character Panel. Check to see if it is already open, otherwise go ahead and use the Launcher to open the Character Panel.

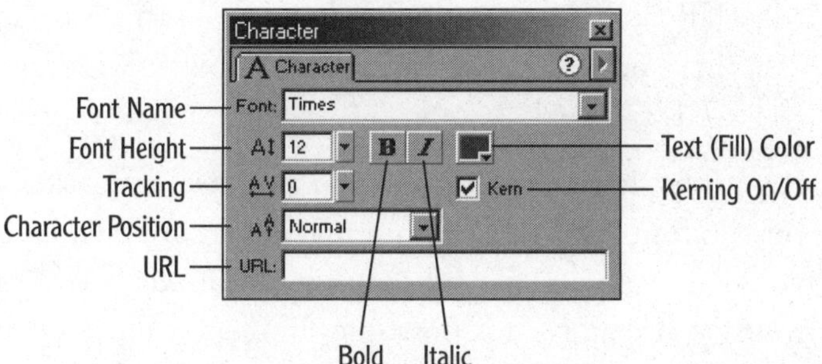

Figure 1.26

The Character Panel

The Character Panel contains the modifiers for font type, size, and color:

- **Font.** Use the pull-down list of fonts to select the font you wish to use for a particular area of selected text. If a font is available for use by Flash, it will be listed in the pull-down menu. As you use the pull-down menu, you'll see an example of the actual font, which is useful when you don't have the font committed to memory!
- **Font Height.** You can either type a number in the text box or use a slider to select a point size of a font.
- **Text (Fill) Color.** Select the font color modifier to display a palette of colors. After the color palette is displayed, you can pick one of the colors for use when typing text.
- **Bold.** When pressed, changes the style of the selected text to bold.
- **Italic.** When pressed, changes the style of the selected text to italics.
- **Tracking.** Used to adjust the spacing between selected characters or chunks of text.
- **Character Position.** Controls the appearance of type, in relation to the baseline: normal, superscript (above), or subscript (below).

- **Kern.** Toggle the check box on or off to use the built-in kerning features of the font in use. Kerning controls the default spacing between characters.
- **URL.** When a block of text is selected, you can assign a hyperlink (URL) to it by typing that location in this box. When the viewer clicks on hyperlinked text, their browser window will open to the URL assigned.

Regarding fonts in Flash 5, you can use any TrueType, Postscript, or bitmap fonts installed on your machine. However, if you attempt to open your *.fla project file on another machine, one without your specific fonts, you could run into some problems. The font in your project file will display properly on multiple machines if you use one of the three device fonts supplied with the Flash 5 application: _sans, _serif, and _typewriter.

Adding Text to Your Movie

Start fresh and open a new movie before learning to use the Text tool. Select File, New from the menu bar, then use the Movie Properties dialog box to create a stage that fits comfortably in your workspace.

Next, create and modify a new block of text.

1. Select the Text tool from the toolbox.
2. Open the Character Panel from the Launcher, and press the Color modifier. The color palette will appear.
3. Select a color by moving your mouse pointer over the colors, then clicking once to select the target color. You can see an example of this in Figure 1.27, where the selected color (in this case, a lovely blue) is outlined in white.
4. Select a font from the Font Names pull-down menu. I'm using Copperplate Gothic Bold in this example, but feel free to choose a font that you like.

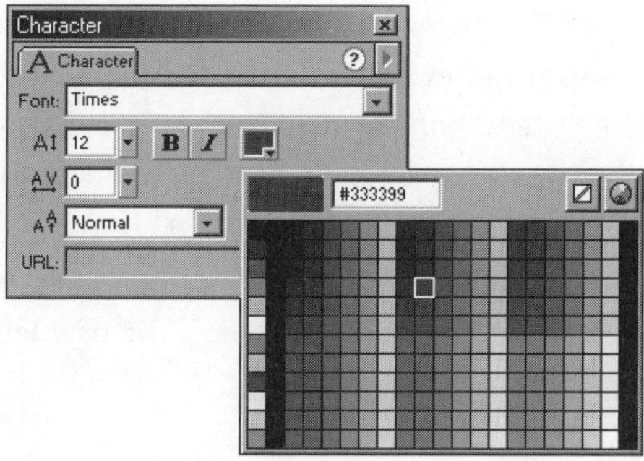

Figure 1.27

The text color palette, with a lovely blue selected

5. Select a font size from the Font Size pull-down menu. My font size is 18 points in this example, but again, pick a size that fits your needs.
6. Click your mouse anywhere on the stage, and type some words (your name, your dog's name, or whatever you want). As you type, text magically appears! The text box extends in width as you type (see Figure 1.28).

Figure 1.28

Some blue text typed in the text box

7. If you need to go back and edit text—say, for example, if you're a bad typist—it's no problem. Click with the Text tool inside the text box, and highlight with your mouse those characters you want to change. For an example, see Figure 1.29, where I needed to change the letter "R" (it should have been a "Y").
8. To change the highlighted letter (or letters), just type your new ones. The old letters will be deleted as the new letters are typed.

Figure 1.29

Highlight a portion of text, then edit.

Creating a Fixed-Width Text Box

Sometimes, instead of creating a free-flowing text box, you may need to create a fixed-width text area. With a fixed-width text block, as its name implies, you create a field of a particular width. As you type, the text will wrap at the ends of lines, and new lines of the same width will be added so that the text fits properly. Fixed-width text can be helpful when creating multi-column text, like in a magazine or newspaper. Also fixed-width text can be easier to position within a background image.

Follow these steps to create a fixed-width text box in your movie. I have continued using the same project file as in the previous section, so my free-flowing text field and my fixed-width text box are on the same stage.

1. Click your mouse button anywhere on the stage, then drag to create a box of the desired width.
2. Release your mouse button. Your fixed-width text field might appear something like that shown in Figure 1.30.

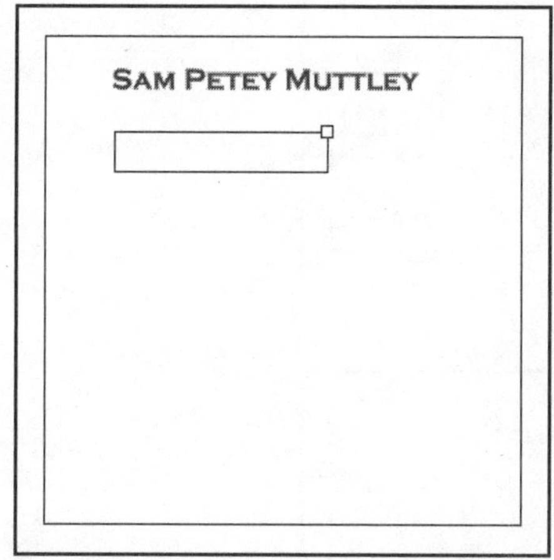

Figure 1.30

A new fixed-width text field

3. Select the Text tool from the toolbox.
4. Open the Character Panel from the Launcher, then select a color from the color picker.
5. Select a font.
6. Select a font size.
7. Back in the stage, start typing some text. Notice how the text wraps automatically within the width you defined (see Figure 1.31).

If you don't like the width of the field after you've started typing text, you can still change it. Simply click on the square in the upper-right corner of the text box. This is called a *resize handle*; it allows you to grab the text box and resize it. Add some width to your text box, like I have in Figure 1.32, by dragging the resize handle to the right. The text will automatically adjust to fit within the new size.

You can do even more with your text fields using the Paragraph Panel.

Figure 1.31

Adding text to a fixed-width text field

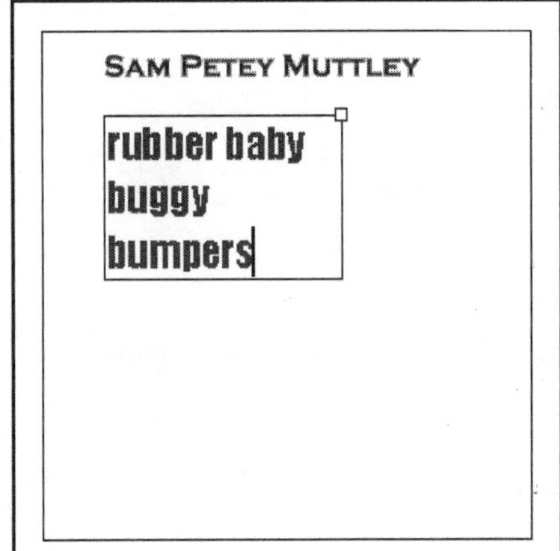

Figure 1.32

Resized fixed-width text field

Using the Paragraph Panel

The Paragraph Panel is not part of the Launcher, so to open it, go to Window, Panels, Paragraph in the menu bar.

The Paragraph Panel allows you to set justification, indentation, and margins for your selected text.

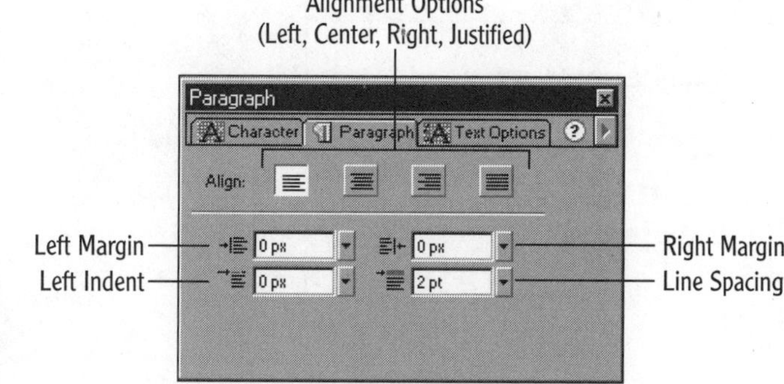

Figure 1.33

The Paragraph Panel

- **Alignment Options.** Select a button to align your text to the left, right, center, or full justification.
- **Left Margin.** You can either type a number in the text box or use a slider to select a margin width, in pixels, from the left edge of the text box.
- **Right Margin.** You can either type a number in the text box or use a slider to select a margin width, in pixels, from the right edge of the text box.
- **Left Indent.** You can either type a number in the text box or use a slider to select an indent width, in pixels, from the left edge of the text box. A negative value will create a hanging first line.
- **Line Spacing.** You can either type a number in the text box or use a slider to select the line spacing, in pixels. Line spacing controls the vertical room between lines of text.

Try centering the text within your text block by highlighting all of it using your mouse button, then selecting the center alignment button from the Paragraph Panel. The text will automatically align itself as shown in Figure 1.34.

You can also change the margins and line spacing within a fixed-width text field by selecting the indent or margin buttons in the Paragraph Panel. Go ahead and try them out on your own.

Figure 1.34

Text centered within a fixed-width text field

One more tidbit of information before it's time to close up shop for this session. You can move a text block, just like any other object, by pressing the Arrow tool in the toolbox, then clicking on the text area and dragging the element to its new location.

What's Next

In the next session, you'll learn all about the drawing tools. You'll create simple shapes and drawings and use the Stroke Panel to adjust border size, color, and effect.

SATURDAY MORNING

Drawing Simple Shapes

- Introducing the Drawing Tools
- Using the Pencil Tool
- Using the Line Tool
- Using the Pen Tool
- Using the Oval and Rectangle Tools
- Using the Brush Tool
- Using the Eraser Tool

I hope you've had a good night's sleep and are ready to dive into the wonderful world of drawing tools. You've already learned about two of the main tools in the toolbox, Arrow and Text, but there are several more that are readily available to you.

Flash 5 makes it easy for anyone to create shapes and simple drawings. Many a great Flash movie has been created using nothing more than geometric shapes. As you become more familiar with the application, you will discover that these simple shapes are the basis of Flash 5's drawing power. By simply manipulating rectangles and ovals, you can create a vast array of complex drawings.

The name of the game for this session is drawing simple shapes, and filling them in with color. But no one can draw a perfect circle. The people at Macromedia realize this, and that's why they include many modifiers to the drawing tools, which help straighten those lines, curve those curves, and generally make your life a lot easier.

In this session, you'll learn how to

- Use the Pencil, Line, Pen, Brush, Oval, and Rectangle tools to do some drawing
- Use the Eraser tool to erase what you've drawn

Introducing the Drawing Tools

Michelangelo's David wasn't carved from marble by telepathy. If you want to create art, you're going to need to know the tools of the trade. Instead of a mallet and chisel, Flash 5 includes a number of somewhat less-strenuous tools. Collectively, these are called *drawing tools*.

This session focuses on the main drawing tools:

- **Pencil**. Used to draw lines and shapes, as if drawing with a real pencil.
- **Line**. Used to draw perfectly straight lines.
- **Pen**. Used to draw precise straight lines or curves.
- **Oval and Rectangle**. Used to draw basic geometric shapes.
- **Brush**. Used to create brushlike strokes, as if painting with a brush.

At the end of the session, you'll also learn about the Eraser tool. Think of it as a catharsis.

Clicking on its button in the toolbox activates each drawing tool. Tools in a toolbox? What will those wacky developers at Macromedia come up with next?

Using the Pencil Tool

You use the Pencil tool just as you use a real pencil—to draw free-form lines. *Free-form* basically means "however you draw it, that's how it looks." Luckily, there are basic modifiers that can "fix" free-form lines drawn with the Pencil tool.

In Figure 2.1, you can see how the toolbox looks when the Pencil tool is selected. If the Pencil tool is not the current tool you're using, you can switch to it simply by clicking the Pencil tool button in the toolbox.

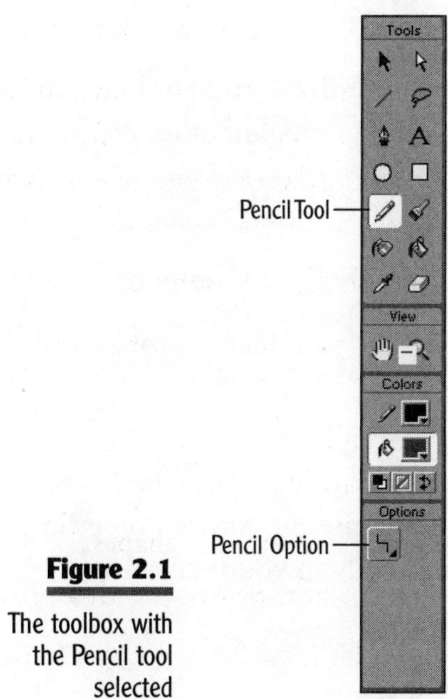

Figure 2.1

The toolbox with the Pencil tool selected

When you switch to the Pencil tool, you see one modifier. However, if you press the single modifier button, a submenu appears as shown in Figure 2.2, containing the drawing modes for the Pencil tool.

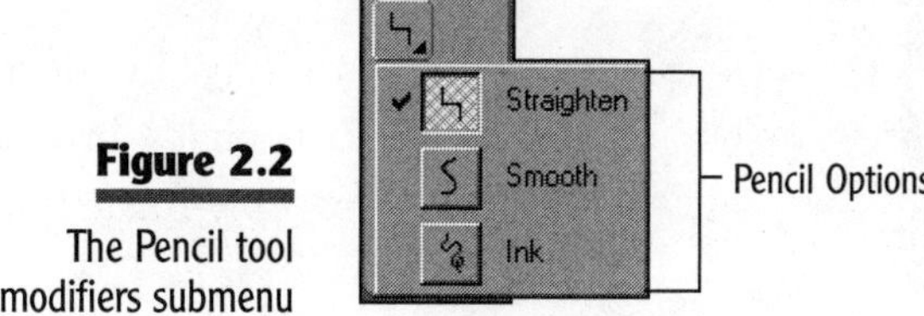

Figure 2.2

The Pencil tool modifiers submenu

These modes are

- **Straighten**. The default drawing mode; draws straight lines, and automatically "perfects" shapes close to triangles, ovals, circles, and rectangles.
- **Smooth**. Draws smooth, curved lines.
- **Ink**. Draws in a true freehand fashion, with no computer assistance.

Creating Lines and Shapes

Start fresh and open a new movie before learning to use the Pencil tool. Select File, New from the menu bar, then use the Movie Properties dialog box to create a stage that fits comfortably in your workspace.

1. Select the Pencil tool from the toolbox.
2. Select the Straighten drawing mode.
3. Press the color swatch next to the stroke color button to open the color picker, shown in Figure 2.3.

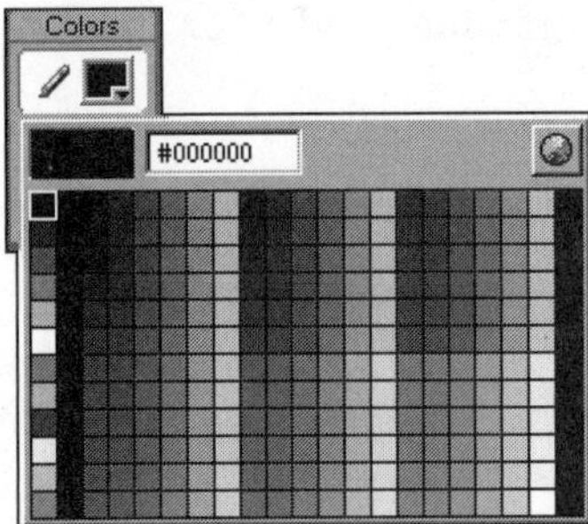

Figure 2.3

The stroke color picker selected

4. Select a stroke color from the color picker by moving your mouse pointer over the colors, then clicking once to select the target color. I picked a nice purple color, but feel free to choose any color you like.
5. Place your mouse pointer somewhere over the stage, and click and hold your mouse button to indicate a starting point.
6. Drag your mouse to draw your line or shape, and if it's not straight, watch it straighten!

When you use the Straighten modifier, Flash keys in on points in your line and interprets what should be straightened. You can see a few hard angles in the sample line I drew, in Figure 2.4.

You may be thinking, "What if I want a thin line, or a textured line, or some line that doesn't have this default width or look?" Simple! Just use the Stroke Panel.

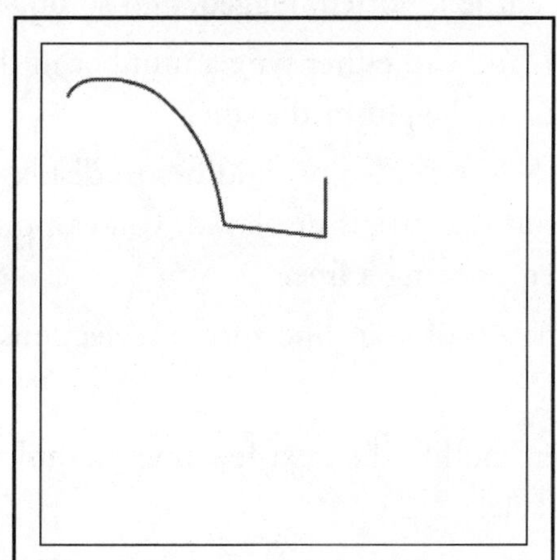

Figure 2.4

Stage with a sample straightened line drawn

Using the Stroke Panel

The Stroke Panel is accessed by selecting Window, Panels, Stroke from the menu bar. Go ahead and open the Stroke Panel (see Figure 2.5) to see what you can modify.

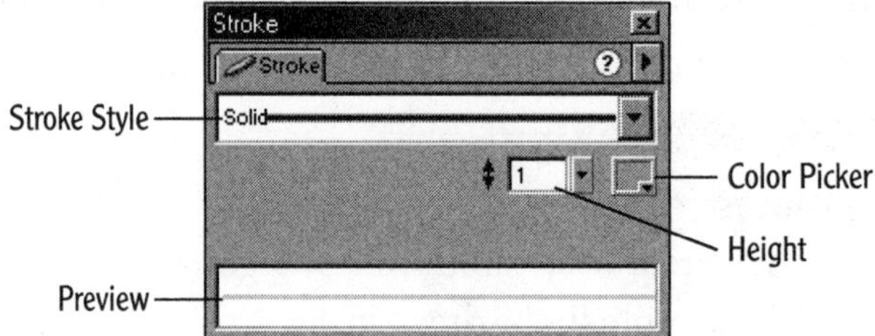

Figure 2.5

The Stroke Panel

The Stroke Panel contains line-specific modifiers:

- **Stroke Style**. A drop-down menu of several stroke styles, such as solid, hairline, dashed, dotted, ragged, and so on.
- **Stroke Height**. You can either type a number in the text box or use a slider to select the height of the line.
- **Stroke Color**. Select the Color modifier to display a palette of colors. After the color palette is displayed, you can pick one of the colors for use when drawing a line.
- **Stroke Preview**. All of your line-specific selections are previewed in this area.

You'll draw and then modify the next few line examples using the modifiers in the Stroke Panel.

1. Select the Pencil tool from the toolbar, if it's not already selected.
2. Select the Smooth drawing mode from the Options area of the toolbox.

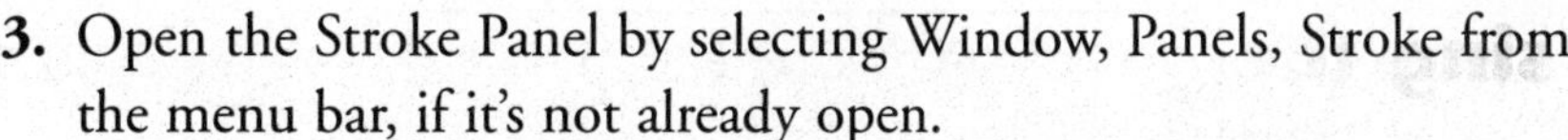

3. Open the Stroke Panel by selecting Window, Panels, Stroke from the menu bar, if it's not already open.
4. In the Stroke Panel, select the "Footprint" stroke (next to last) and a line height of 8.
5. In the Stroke Panel, press the color swatch next to the pencil button to open the color picker, then select a color (see Figure 2.6).

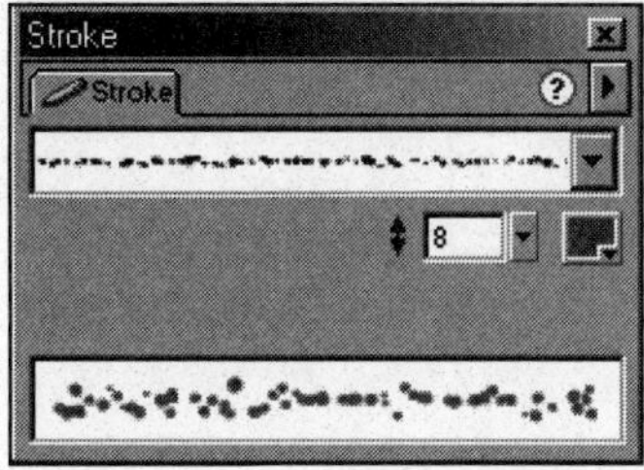

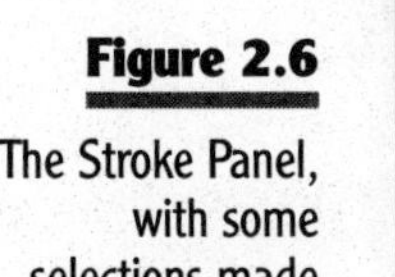

Figure 2.6

The Stroke Panel, with some selections made

NOTE

As you finish making your selections, the preview area of the Stroke Panel should show you a sample of your line. In my case, it shows a footprint-like thick green line.

6. Place your mouse pointer somewhere over the stage, and click and hold your mouse button to indicate a starting point.
7. Drag your mouse to draw your line or shape. It appears thick and solid until you're through drawing and you release your mouse button. When you release the mouse button, the styles you selected in the Stroke Panel are applied.

Unlike the Straighten modifier, when you use the Smooth modifier you won't have any hard angles in your line. You can see the smooth sample line I drew in Figure 2.7.

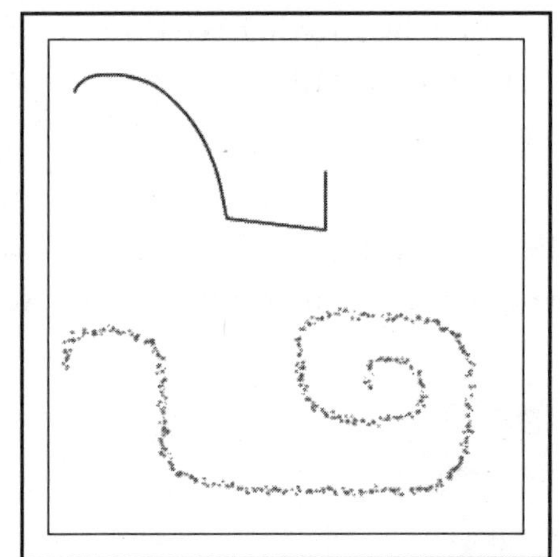

Figure 2.7

Stage with a sample smooth line drawn

Using the Ink Modifier

The Ink modifier is used to draw freehand lines. Flash does not adjust the line as with the Straighten and Smooth options.

The last line example is drawn using the Ink modifier.

1. Select the Pencil tool from the toolbar, if it's not already selected.
2. Select the Ink drawing mode from the Options area of the toolbox.
3. Open the Stroke Panel by selecting Window, Panels, Stroke from the menu bar.
4. In the Stroke Panel, select the "Dotted" stroke (fourth in the menu) and a line height of 3.
5. In the Stroke Panel, press the color swatch next to the pencil button to open the color picker, then select a color. I picked black this time.
6. Place your mouse pointer somewhere over the stage, and click and hold your mouse button to indicate a starting point.

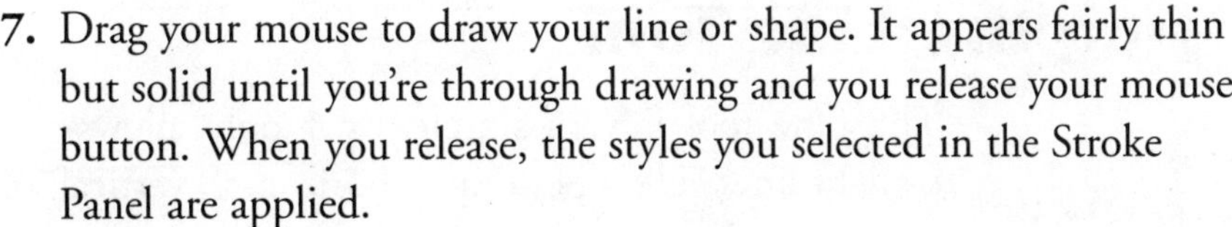

7. Drag your mouse to draw your line or shape. It appears fairly thin but solid until you're through drawing and you release your mouse button. When you release, the styles you selected in the Stroke Panel are applied.

The Ink modifier doesn't apply any modification to your drawn object. You can see the sample jagged shape I've drawn in Figure 2.8.

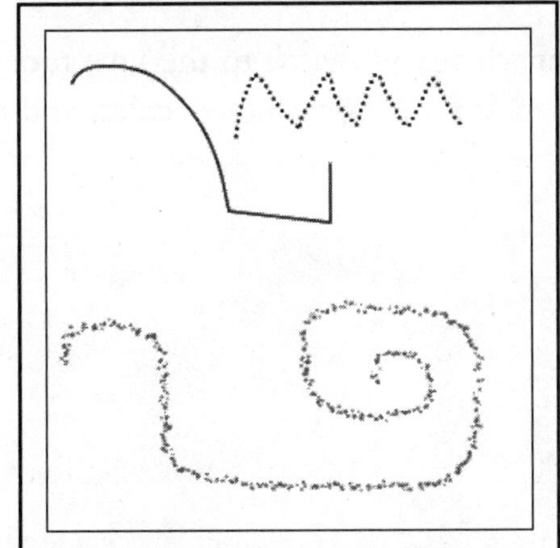

Figure 2.8

Sample jagged shape using the Ink modifier

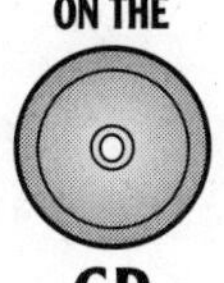

ON THE CD

Black-and-white screen shots don't really help when it comes to showing color, so check out the project file with the sample lines and shapes drawn with the Pencil tool, in the sample_s2.fla file in the session2 folder on the enclosed CD-ROM.

Before moving to the next section, you can save your project file or simply discard it without saving. In the next section, you start a new project file.

Using the Line Tool

The Line tool is very simple, as it only allows you to draw perfectly straight lines. The lines can be horizontal, vertical, or diagonal, but they will be absolutely straight.

In Figure 2.9, you can see how the toolbox looks when the Line tool is selected. If the Line tool is not the current tool you're using, you can switch to it by simply pressing the Line tool button in the toolbox.

No modifiers appear when you switch to the Line tool. Instead, you use the Stroke Panel to modify the appearance, color, and height of the line you want to draw.

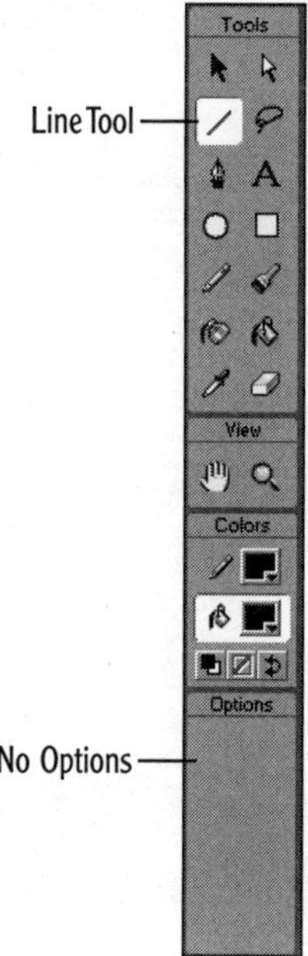

Figure 2.9

The toolbox with the Line tool selected

Drawing Straight Lines

Open a new movie before learning to use the Line tool. Select File, New from the menu bar, then use the Movie Properties dialog box to create a stage that fits comfortably in your workspace.

This first set of lines are horizontal and vertical, intersecting like a plus sign.

1. Select the Line tool from the toolbar.
2. Open the Stroke Panel by selecting Window, Panels, Stroke from the menu bar.
3. In the Stroke Panel, select the "Hairline" stroke.
4. In the Stroke Panel, press the color swatch next to the pencil button to open the color picker, then select a color. I've gone back to the trusty purple color.
5. Place your mouse pointer somewhere over the stage, and click and hold your mouse button to indicate a starting point.
6. Drag your mouse from right to left to draw a perfectly straight horizontal line. When you release your mouse button, the styles you selected in the Stroke Panel are applied.
7. Place your mouse pointer above the center of your horizontal line on the stage, and click and hold your mouse button to indicate a starting point.
8. Drag your mouse from top to bottom to draw a perfectly straight vertical line. When you release your mouse button, the styles you selected in the Stroke Panel will be applied.

Try as you might, those two lines cannot be crooked! Take a look at Figure 2.10 for an example.

Figure 2.10

Straight horizontal and vertical lines forming a plus sign

Drawing a Series of Lines

Next, you will draw a series of lines, eventually forming a "Z" shape. With the free-form drawing tools such as the Pencil tool, you get one shot when drawing a straight line, but with the Line tool if you want to make a "Z," you can draw, then release, three times to make three lines. Try it:

1. Select the Line tool from the toolbar.
2. Open the Stroke Panel by selecting Window, Panels, Stroke from the menu bar, if it's not already open.
3. In the Stroke Panel, select the "Dash" stroke (third from the top) and a line height of 3.
4. In the Stroke Panel, press the color swatch next to the pencil button to open the color picker, then select a color. I selected green.
5. Place your mouse pointer somewhere near the upper-left corner of the stage, and click and hold your mouse button to indicate a starting point.

TIP Holding down the Shift key as you draw a line forces Flash to create the line at an increment of 45 degrees. This makes drawing right angles super simple.

6. Drag your mouse to the right to draw a perfectly straight horizontal line. Release the mouse button to indicate the end point for that line.
7. At the release point, click and hold your mouse button again to indicate a starting point for your new line.
8. Drag your mouse to the lower-left corner of your plus sign. Release the mouse button to indicate the end point for that line.
9. At the release point, click and hold your mouse button again to indicate a starting point for your new line.
10. Drag your mouse to the lower-right corner of your plus sign. Release the mouse button to indicate the end point for that line.

You should now have a sort of "Z" drawn on top of your plus sign (see Figure 2.11).

Before moving to the next section, you can save your project file or simply discard it without saving. In the next section, you'll start a new project file.

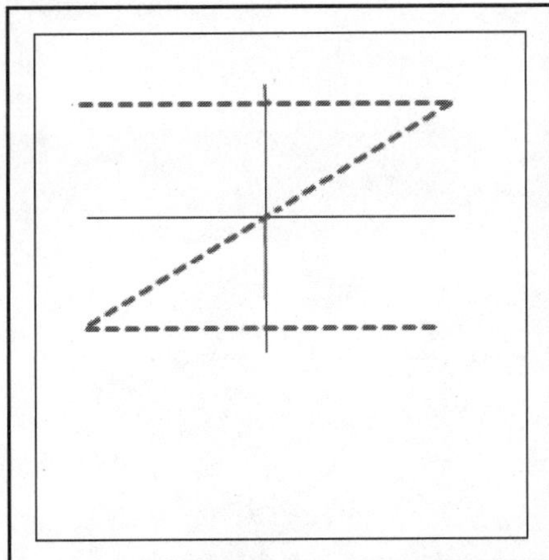

Figure 2.11

More lines!

Using the Pen Tool

The Pen tool is a complex little tool, and it doesn't even have any modifiers! You use the Pen tool to draw a simple line or a series of lines. Each line segment has a starting point and an end point, which are actually handles that you can grab to move the line in various directions, so that you can adjust the curves or angles of your lines. The Pen tool is a bit difficult to learn, but once you get used to it you'll be able to create the smoothest curves and the sharpest angles.

In Figure 2.12, you can see how the toolbox looks when the Pen tool is selected. If the Pen tool is not the current tool you're using, you can switch to it simply by pressing the Pen tool button in the toolbox.

No modifiers appear when you switch to the Pen tool. Instead, you use the Stroke Panel to modify the appearance, color, and height of the line you want to draw.

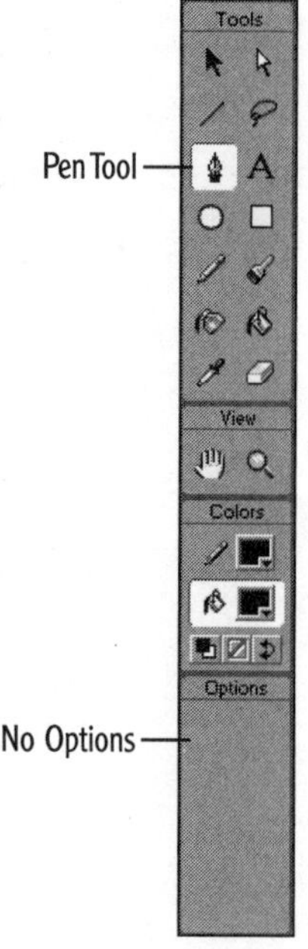

Figure 2.12

The toolbox with the Pen tool selected

Drawing Straight Lines with the Pen Tool

Open a new movie before learning to use the Pen tool. Select File, New from the menu bar, then use the Movie Properties dialog box to create a stage that fits comfortably in your workspace.

This first set of lines show you how the Pen tool actually helps you draw.

1. Select the Pen tool from the toolbar.
2. Open the Stroke Panel by selecting Window, Panels, Stroke from the menu bar, if it's not already open.
3. In the Stroke Panel, select the "Solid" stroke and specify a line height of 3.
4. In the Stroke Panel, press the color swatch next to the pencil button to open the color picker, then select a color. I picked black.
5. Place your mouse pointer over the upper-left corner of the stage and click once to indicate a starting point for the line. You will see a dot appear.
6. Place your mouse pointer over the lower-right corner of the stage and click once to indicate an end point for this line. You will see another dot appear, as well as a line that automatically appears between the two dots (see Figure 2.13).

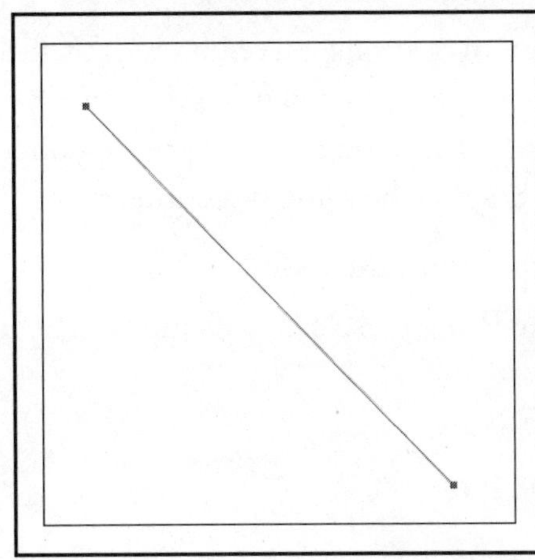

Figure 2.13

A line segment drawn with the Pen tool

7. Place your mouse pointer over the upper-right corner of the stage, directly above the end point of your line and click once. Another line segment is drawn.
8. Click again in the lower-left corner of the stage to connect the line.
9. Finally, click the mouse button near the original starting point, to connect the final line. Select the Arrow tool from the toolbox to finalize your line. Figure 2.14 shows the final lines.

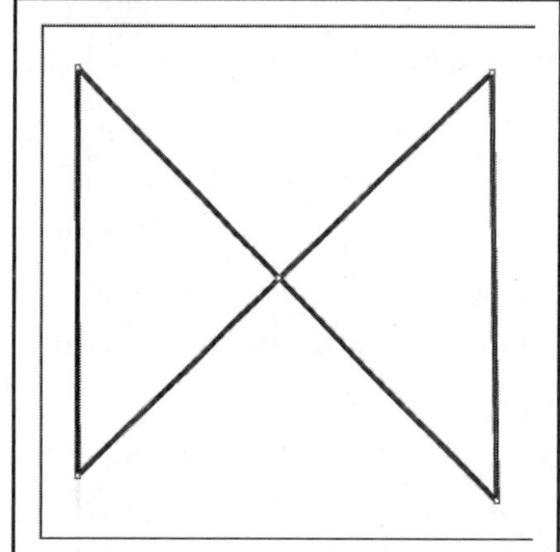

Figure 2.14

Finalized lines

Drawing Curvy Lines with the Pen Tool

You also use the Pen tool to create curved lines. It's a little tricky, but once you get the hang of it, you'll be a pro in no time. Keep this in mind when creating curves with the Pen tool: drag in opposing directions to create an arch or bowl curve, drag in the same direction for an "S" curve.

1. Select the Pen tool from the toolbar.
2. Open the Stroke Panel by selecting Window, Panels, Stroke from the menu bar.

3. In the Stroke Panel, select the "Dashed" stroke and specify a line height of 5.
4. In the Stroke Panel, press the color swatch next to the pencil button to open the color picker, then select a color. I picked red.
5. Place your mouse pointer in an open area of your stage and hold the mouse button down where you want the line to start. Drag your mouse down and to the right a little bit and notice the handles on the line segment appear (see Figure 2.15).

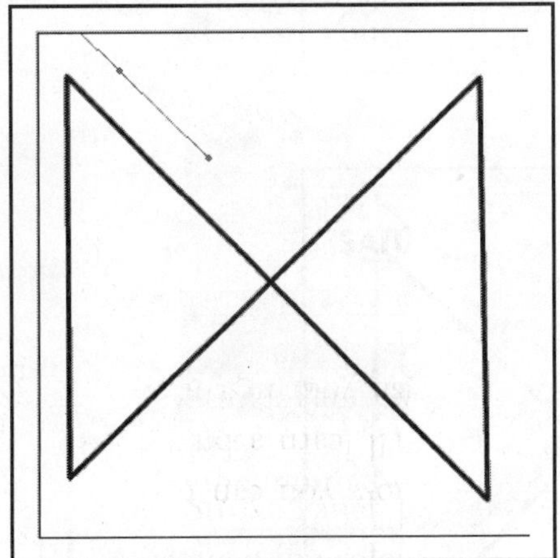

Figure 2.15

Starting to draw a curve

6. Release the mouse button. Move to the right and click your mouse button again to set an end point for this curvy line. The two points automatically connect. Notice in Figure 2.16 that it's not all that curvy, yet.
7. Select the Subselection tool from the toolbox. This tool's button is the white arrow, next to the Arrow tool. With this tool, click once with your mouse on the origination point of the curvy line. A blue line (officially called a *tangent handle*) appears, which you use to drag and create your curve (see Figure 2.17).

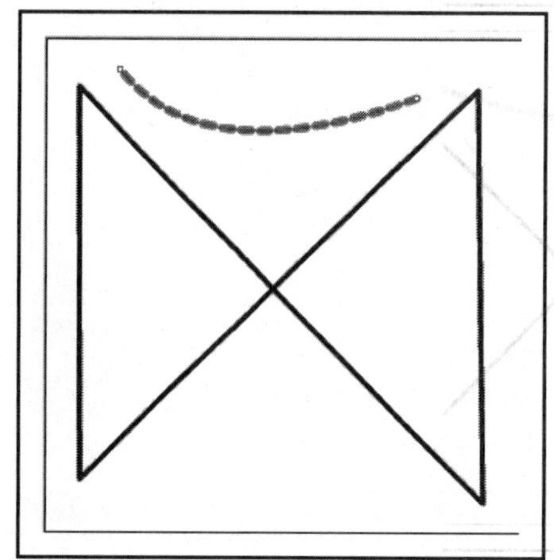

Figure 2.16

Not very curvy, yet

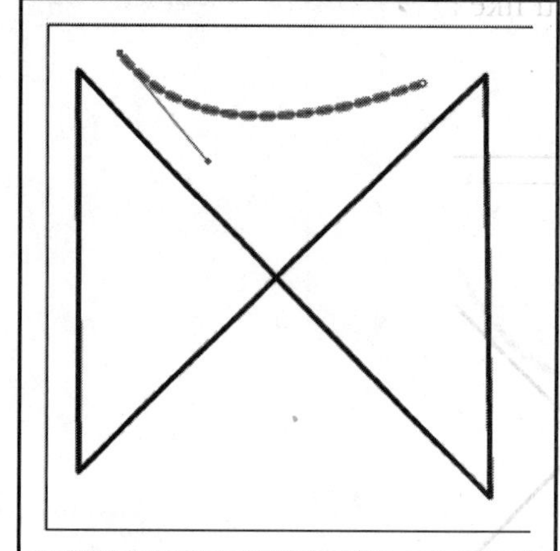

Figure 2.17

Tangent handle appears

8. Click on the end of the tangent handle and drag it to the left or right or up and down. The proposed new curve appears and changes depending on how you move the handle. Figure 2.18 shows the new curve.

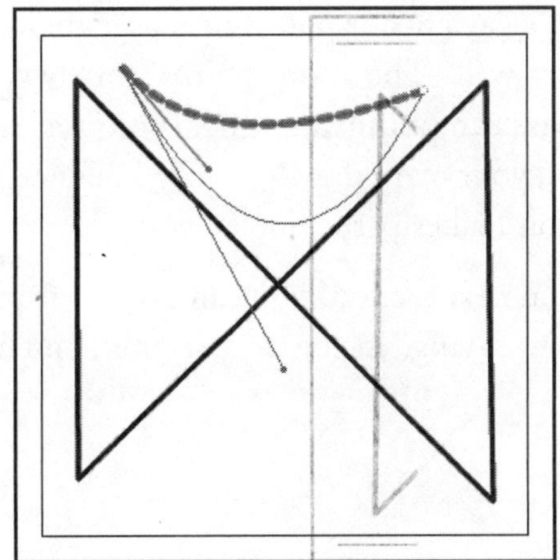

Figure 2.18

Creating the curve

9. Pick a curve you like and release the mouse button (see Figure 2.19).

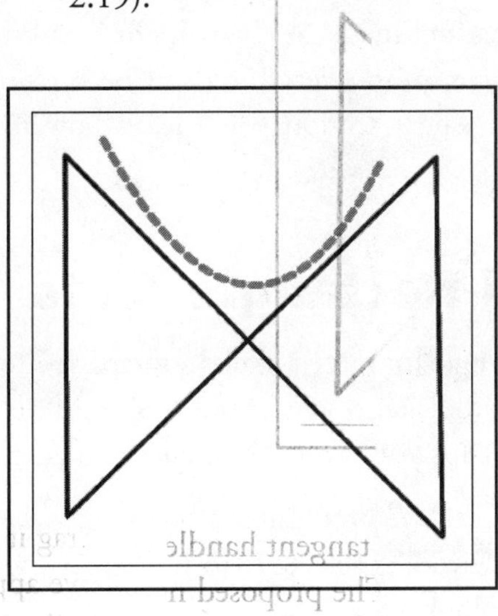

Figure 2.19

The final curve

You can add or take away anchor points or nudge them around using the Subselection tool as well. The more points you have, the more little curves and tweaks you can put in your line. I recommend playing around with the Pen tool on your own, drawing crazy lines and curves, to get the hang of it. Repetition makes perfection!

Before moving to the next section, you can save your project file or simply discard it without saving. In the next section, you'll start a new project file.

Take a Break

Take some time to relax and study the area around you. Look at the walls, desk, chair, people, pets, that cup of Ovaltine you are about to enjoy, or anything else that catches your eye. Try to see the basic shapes out of which all these things are made. A chair might be a bunch of rectangles, a doorknob is a circle; most everything can be broken down into geometric shapes. In the next section you'll learn how to draw these basic shapes.

Using the Oval and Rectangle Tools

The Oval and Rectangle tools are a walk in the park after dealing with the Pen tool. The Oval tool helps you create ovals and perfect circles, while the Rectangle tool helps you create rectangles and perfect squares.

In Figure 2.20, you can see how the toolbox looks when either the Oval tool or the Rectangle tool is selected. To use either tool, simply click on its button in the toolbox.

No modifiers appear when you switch to the Oval tool, but the Rectangle tool has a modifier called *Round Rectangle Radius* (what a name!), which curves the edges of your rectangle or square.

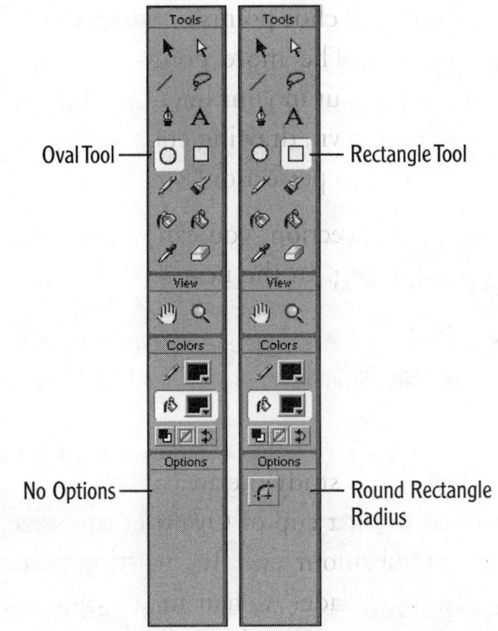

Figure 2.20

Toolboxes with the Oval tool and the Rectangle tool selected

When you draw either of these shapes, you use both the Stroke and Fill Panels. The Stroke Panel modifies the appearance, color, and height of the outline of the shape, while the Fill Panel adds color to the inside of the shape.

Drawing Ovals

Open a new movie before learning to use the next two tools. Select File, New from the menu bar, then use the Movie Properties dialog box to create a stage that fits comfortably in your workspace.

The goal of this section is to draw an oval and then to draw a perfect circle. It's really a piece of cake.

1. Select the Oval tool from the toolbar.
2. Open the Stroke Panel by selecting Window, Panels, Stroke from the menu bar, if it's not already open.

3. In the Stroke Panel, select the "Solid" stroke and a line height of 3.
4. In the Stroke Panel, press the color swatch next to the pencil button to open the color picker, then select a color. I selected black.
5. Open the Fill Panel by selecting Window, Panels, Fill from the menu bar.
6. In the Fill Panel, press the color swatch to open the color picker, then select a color. I selected a nice blue.

Alternatively, you can use the fill and stroke color buttons in the colors section of the toolbox to pick your colors.

7. Place your mouse pointer somewhere over the stage, and click and hold your mouse button to indicate a starting point.
8. Drag your mouse from right to left or up and down. As you drag your mouse, an outline appears, showing the approximation of the oval you're drawing (see Figure 2.21).

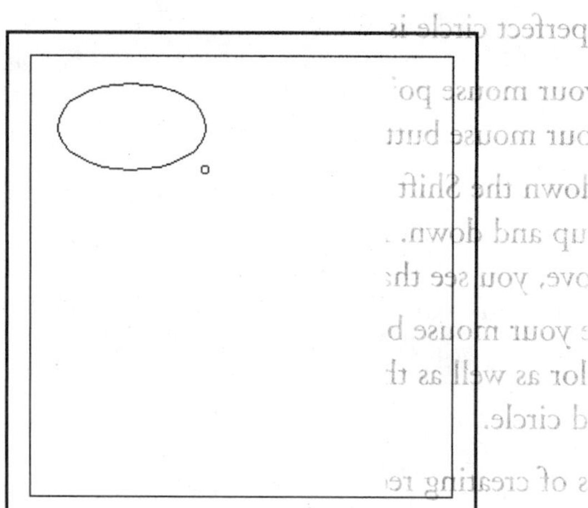

Figure 2.21

Drawing an oval

9. Release your mouse button to create the oval. It should apply the stroke color and style, as well as the fill color. Figure 2.22 shows the finished oval.

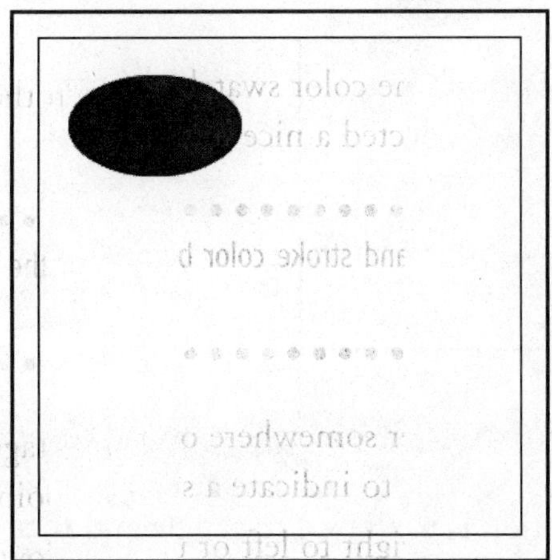

Figure 2.22

A finished oval

Drawing Circles

Drawing a perfect circle is also quite simple.

1. Place your mouse pointer somewhere over the stage, and click and hold your mouse button to indicate a starting point.
2. Hold down the Shift key while dragging your mouse from right to left or up and down. As you drag your mouse and watch the outline move, you see that it's constrained to a perfect circle.
3. Release your mouse button to create the circle with the stroke style and color as well as the fill color applied. Figure 2.23 shows the finished circle.

The process of creating rectangles and perfect squares is quite similar, as you'll soon see.

Figure 2.23

A perfect circle

Drawing Rectangles

The goal of this section is to draw a rectangle and then to draw a perfect square. You also learn how to use the Round Rectangle Radius modifier to create rounded corners.

1. Select the Rectangle tool from the toolbar.
2. Open the Stroke Panel by selecting Window, Panels, Stroke from the menu bar, if it's not already open.
3. In the Stroke Panel, select the "Irregular Line" (third from the bottom) stroke and a line height of 5.
4. In the Stroke Panel, press the color swatch next to the pencil button to open the color picker, then select a color. I selected a green.
5. Open the Fill Panel by selecting Window, Panels, Fill from the menu bar.
6. In the Fill Panel, press the color swatch to open the color picker, then select a color. I selected yellow.
7. Place your mouse pointer somewhere over the stage, and click and hold your mouse button to indicate a starting point.

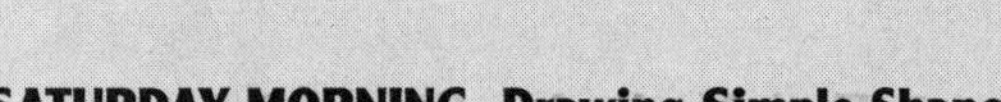

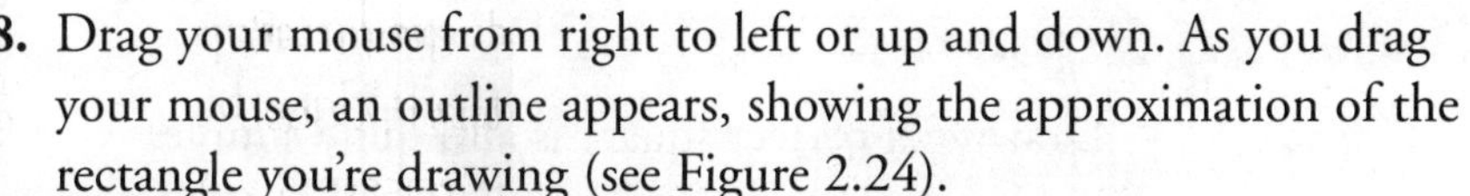

8. Drag your mouse from right to left or up and down. As you drag your mouse, an outline appears, showing the approximation of the rectangle you're drawing (see Figure 2.24).

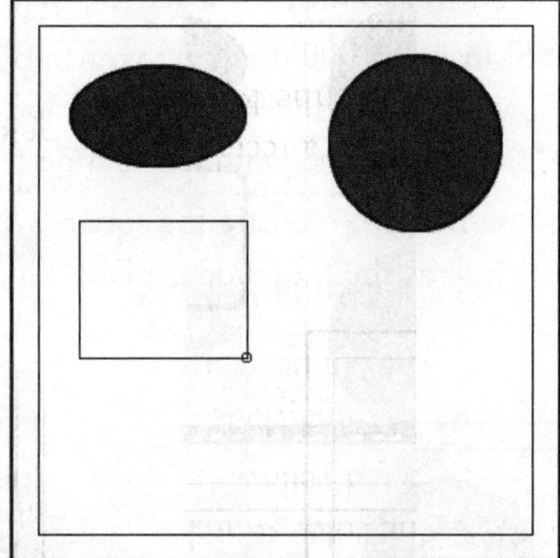

Figure 2.24

Drawing a rectangle

9. Release your mouse button to create the rectangle (see Figure 2.25). It should apply the stroke color and style, as well as the fill color.

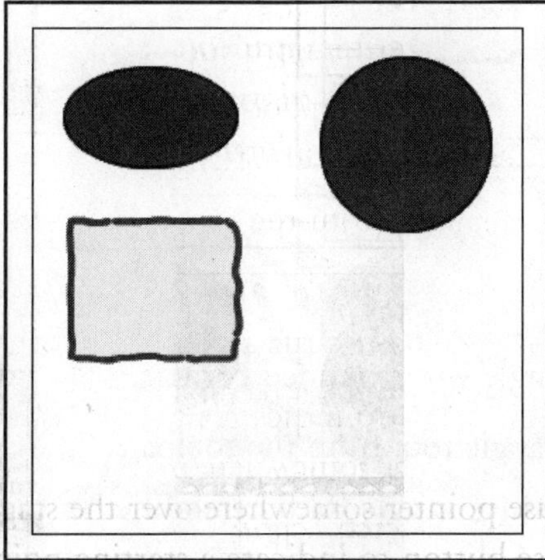

Figure 2.25

A finished rectangle

Drawing Squares

Drawing a perfect square is also quite simple.

1. Place your mouse pointer somewhere over the stage, and click and hold your mouse button to indicate a starting point.
2. Hold down the Shift key while dragging your mouse from right to left or up and down. As you drag your mouse and watch the outline move, you'll see that it's constrained to a perfect square.
3. Release your mouse button to create the square with the stroke style and color as well as the fill color applied. Figure 2.26 shows the finished square.

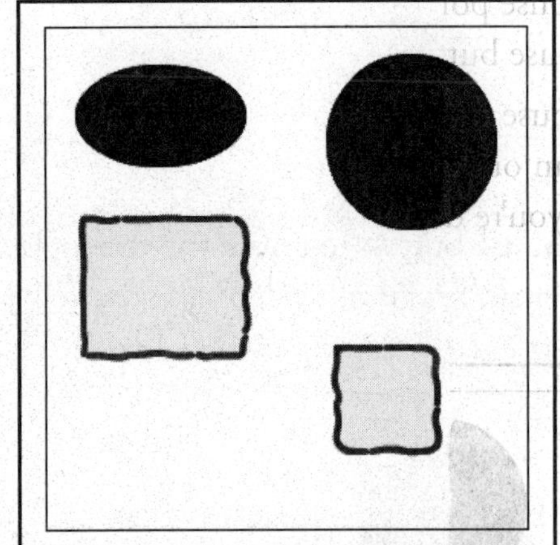

Figure 2.26

A perfect square

Rounded Rectangles

Next, create a rectangle with rounded corners.

1. Select the Rectangle tool from the toolbar.
2. Press the Round Rectangle Radius modifier in the Options section of the toolbox. A dialog box appears, asking you for the corner radius. The higher the number, the more curve you get. Select a reasonable number, such as 12.

3. Open the Stroke Panel by selecting Window, Panels, Stroke from the menu bar.
4. In the Stroke Panel, select the "Solid" stroke and a line height of 5. You can use any stroke style, but it's easier to see the rounded edges with the solid style.
5. In the Stroke Panel, press the color swatch next to the pencil button to open the color picker, then select a color. I've kept the green.
6. Open the Fill Panel by selecting Window, Panels, Fill from the menu bar.
7. In the Fill Panel, press the color swatch to open the color picker, then select a color. I kept the yellow.
8. Place your mouse pointer somewhere over the stage, and click and hold your mouse button to indicate a starting point.
9. Drag your mouse from right to left or up and down. As you drag your mouse, an outline appears, showing the approximation of the rectangle you're drawing, including the rounded edges (see Figure 2.27).

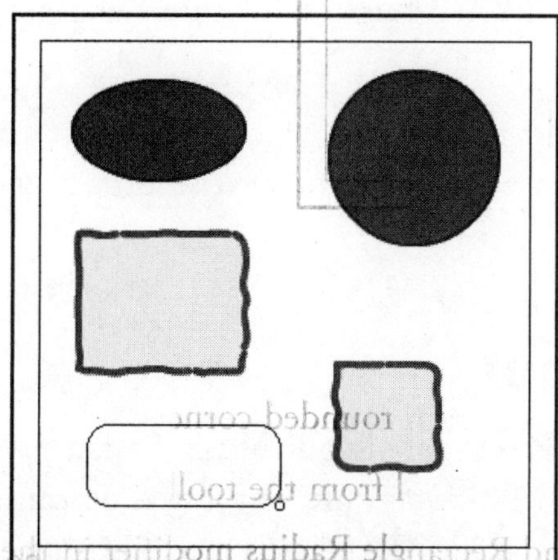

Figure 2.27

Drawing a rectangle with rounded corners

10. Release your mouse button to create the rectangle. It should apply the stroke color and style, as well as the fill color and the rounded edges (see Figure 2.28).

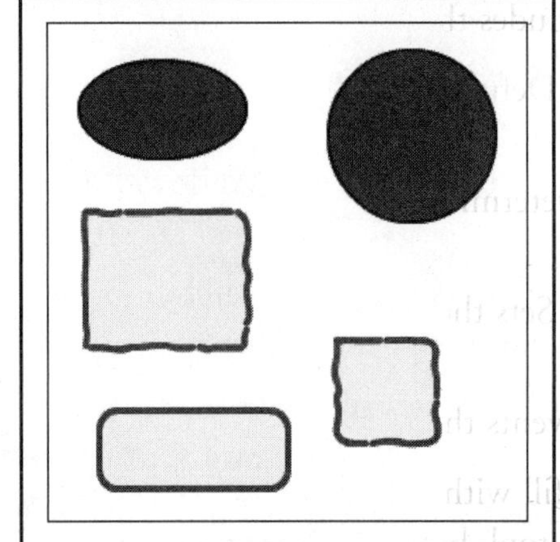

Figure 2.28

A finished rectangle with rounded corners

Go ahead and get a little crazy with some shape drawing practice. Experiment with strokes and fills, and start to get an idea of just what colors don't go with others! You'll learn about colors and gradients in the next session.

Before moving to the next section, you can save your project file or simply discard it without saving. In the next section, you'll start a new project file.

Using the Brush Tool

It's a poor painter who uses only one brush. So far, you have drawn lines using the Pencil and Pen tools only, but just as on canvas, sometimes the job calls for a more specific tool. This is where Flash 5's Brush tool comes in. With the Brush tool you can fill backgrounds, draw rounded lines, create cool calligraphy effects, and much more.

You can think of the Brush tool as the counterpoint of the Pencil tool. The Pencil tool draws strokes only, while the Brush tool draws fills. To adjust the Brush tool you can use the Fill Panel or select a Brush tool option from the toolbox.

The Brush tool includes the following options:

- **Brush Mode**. Defines how the line affects the other elements on the stage.
- **Brush Size**. Determines the width of the line drawn using the Brush tool.
- **Brush Shape**. Sets the shape of the line drawn using the Brush tool.
- **Lock Fill**. Prevents the fill from being edited.

Drawing a simple fill with the Brush tool is a little different than drawing with the Pencil tool, but you should be able to pick it up quickly.

Open a new movie by selecting File, New from the menu bar, then use the Movie Properties dialog box to create a stage that fits comfortably in your workspace.

To draw a simple fill on the stage, follow these steps:

1. Click the Brush tool in the toolbox.
2. Select a Brush Size and Brush Shape in the toolbox.
3. Click and drag on the stage to draw a fill (see Figure 2.29).

By default the Brush Mode is set to normal, but there are a number of other options. The Brush Modes are

- **Paint Normal**. Draws the fill on the stage covering up everything below.
- **Paint Fills**. The fill does not cover any stroke elements on the stage but appears on top of any filled or blank areas.
- **Paint Behind**. The fill only appears on blank areas of the stage.

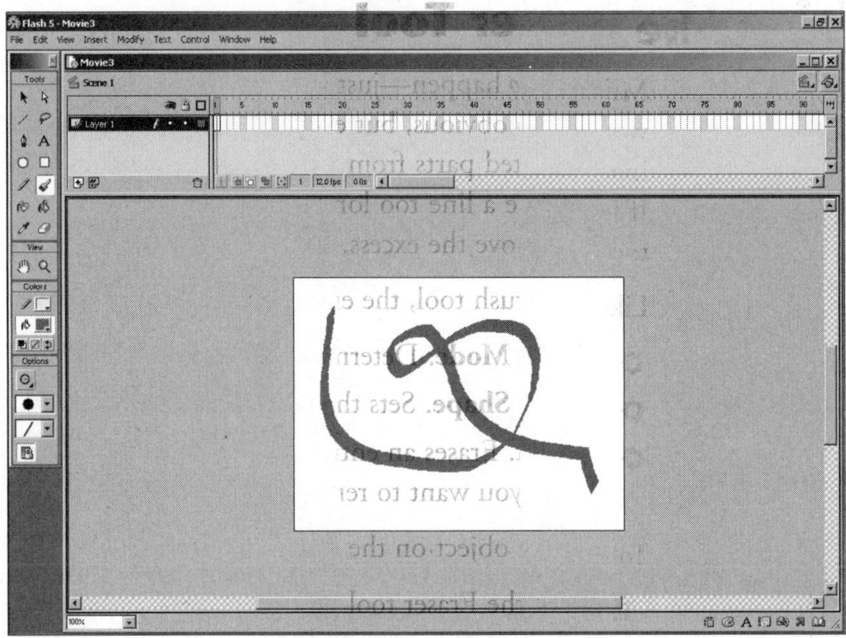

Figure 2.29

Drawing with the Brush tool

- **Paint Selection**. Draws the fill only inside the selected area. If nothing is selected the fill will not appear.
- **Paint Inside**. Paints "inside the lines." The fill only appears inside the object where the fill began.

You can practice drawing with the various Brush Modes by placing an oval with a thick stroke on the stage. Then use the Brush tool with different settings to draw fills on and around the oval. You can see how the fill affects the oval based on the Brush Modes.

You can alter a fill after you have drawn it by using the Fill Panel. The Fill Panel allows you to change not just the fills drawn with the Brush tool, but also other fills such as inside ovals and rectangles. The Fill Panel will be covered in the next session.

Using the Eraser Tool

Mistakes *do* happen—just look at the platypus. Hopefully your mistakes won't be so obvious, but even if they are, you can correct them. Removing unwanted parts from your Flash movie is the job of the Eraser tool. If you make a line too long, or a smile too wide, you can use the Eraser tool to remove the excess.

Like the Brush tool, the eraser tool has a number of options:

- **Eraser Mode**. Determines what parts of the stage are erased.
- **Eraser Shape**. Sets the shape of the eraser.
- **Faucet**. Erases an entire shape. Click on this option, then on the shape you want to remove.

To erase an object on the stage, follow these steps:

1. Click the Eraser tool in the toolbox.
2. Select an Eraser Mode and an Eraser Shape.
3. Click and drag on the stage. An area will be deleted (see Figure 2.30).

By default the Erase Mode is set to normal, but there are a number of other options. The Brush Modes are:

- **Erase Normal**. Deletes anything on the stage.
- **Erase Fills**. Removes only fills.
- **Erase Lines**. Erases only strokes and lines.
- **Erase Selected Fills**. Only deletes the fill inside the selected area. If nothing is selected the Eraser tool does not function.
- **Erase Inside**. Erases "inside the lines." This option only deletes the object where the erase began.

You'll get the hang of the Eraser tool with a little experimentation. Try out the various modes for yourself.

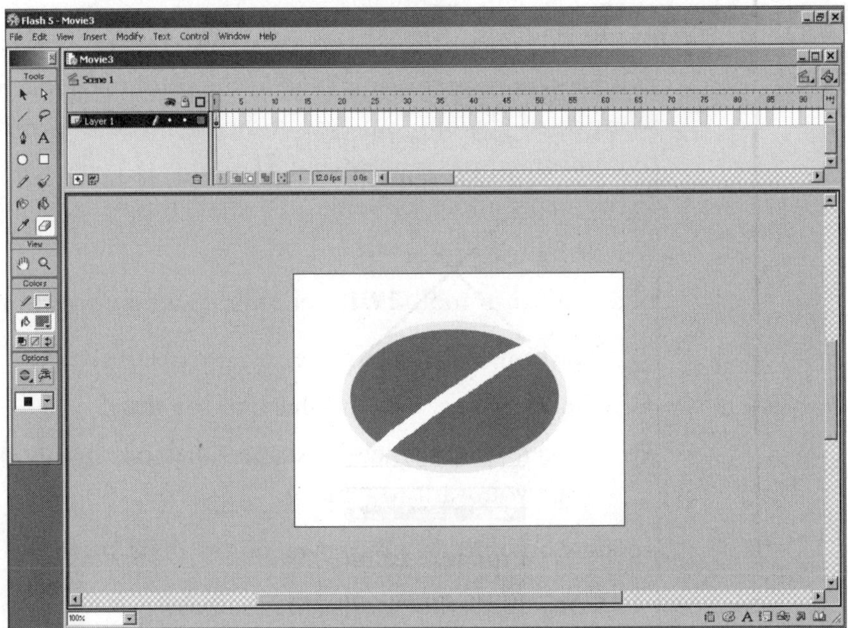

Figure 2.30

Using the Eraser tool

What's Next

This afternoon you'll learn how you can turn these simple shapes into more complex drawings. You'll learn a bit more about what the Arrow tool can do, and you'll publish your first movie. So, grab a quick lunch and hurry back.

SATURDAY AFTERNOON

Manipulating Shapes, and Other Odds and Ends

- Segmenting and Connecting
- More about Segmenting
- Finishing Your Flower Movie
- Publishing a Movie

Take a look at some of the Flash movies on the Internet (Appendix D lists a number of Web sites with Flash movies). You'll notice that Flash movies run the gamut from simple talking triangles to highly detailed, professional quality graphics. From these movies, you can get a good idea of what's possible with Flash 5. But even the most spectacular Flash drawings probably started out as simple shapes. The best Flash animators can manipulate these shapes into spectacular, complex drawings. In this session, I'll show you a little of how this is done.

So far, you've drawn a bunch of simple shapes and added a bit of color to them. Obviously, you want to do more in your Flash movies than just draw some perfect circles sitting next to each other.

To create and manipulate more complex images, you'll work mainly with drawing tools and their modifiers; you'll also learn to edit them if you don't get them just right the first time (and who does?). Since the previous sessions were spent helping you to become familiar with tools and panels, the steps in the next sessions won't be so explicit. If you have trouble finding a particular tool or panel, just look back in the previous sessions for a refresher.

Also during this session, you'll create a little scene and actually publish a movie suitable for viewing online or in stand-alone format. The movie won't do anything except sit there and look pretty, but this is a good time to introduce the basic publishing concepts.

In this session, you'll

- Practice drawing with the Pen tool
- Segment and connect shapes
- Use rotate and skew in a real-life setting

Segmenting and Connecting

Segmenting and *connecting* are high-tech terms that mean "taking chunks away" and "drawing on top of something else," respectively. But, since everyone uses the terms *segmenting* and *connecting,* you should probably know and use those terms, too.

In this session, you will draw a star that will eventually turn into a flower. Also, almost accidentally, you will end up drawing a block of cheese. It may seem odd, but these are good examples of objects that make use of segmenting and connecting.

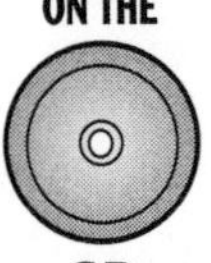

All project files created during this session are also in the session3 folder on the enclosed CD-ROM. For additional information about what's on the CD-ROM, see Appendix E.

Drawing a star is really simple, since you don't actually have to draw anything. There's no dragging with your mouse, trying to get your lines to connect. Remember, from the previous session, that you can use the Pen tool to set points, and the line is created for you. So helpful!

Open a new movie by selecting File, New from the menu bar, and use the Movie Properties dialog box to create a stage that fits comfortably in your workspace.

To draw a star with a different stroke and fill color, follow these steps:

1. Select the Pen tool from the toolbar.
2. In the Stroke Panel, select the "Solid" stroke and specify a line width of 2. Also select a color that you like. I picked a dark red. This is the outline of your star.
3. In the Fill Panel, select "Solid" fill, and pick a color that you like. I picked a fairly non-obnoxious orange.
4. Place your mouse about one-third of the way down from the top of the stage, and click once to indicate a starting point for the line. You will see a dot appear.
5. Place your mouse near the top of the stage and angled toward the right, and click once to indicate the endpoint of the line. You will see another dot appear; a line automatically appears between the two dots (see Figure 3.1).

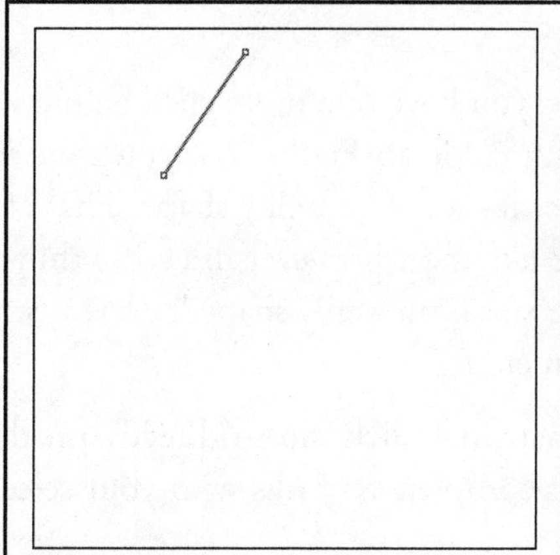

Figure 3.1

Starting to draw your star

Now it's up to you to continue drawing your star. Basically, you need to click your mouse button nine more times, making nine more line segments. Figure 3.2 shows my star after five segments, or just past the halfway point.

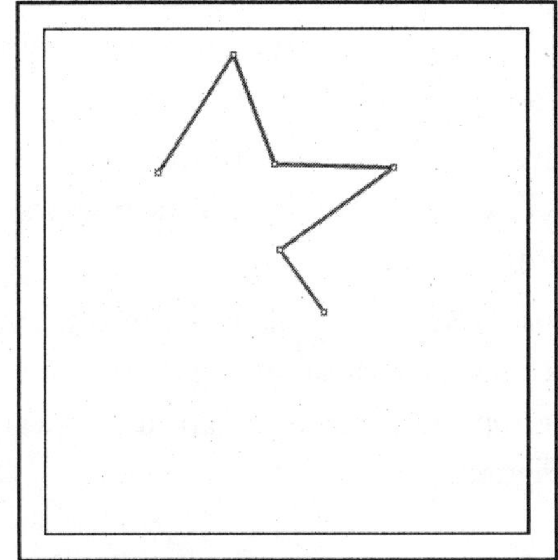

Figure 3.2

Halfway through a star

After nine segments, you have one more click before you finish your star and watch it fill with color. In Figure 3.3, you can see my almost-completed star. Note that it's sort of a funky shape. That's fine: these tools are designed for people like me who never draw the thing correctly the first time around. If your star is unevenly shaped, don't worry—you'll be modifying the lines soon enough.

When you make that final click, do so directly on the original starting point. Your shape is complete and fills with your selected color (see Figure 3.4).

Next, you modify the placement of your object on the stage, in preparation for the transformation from star to flower.

Figure 3.3

Almost finished

Figure 3.4

The completed star

Moving the Object on the Stage

If your drawing isn't in the middle of the stage, put it there before you continue so you will have more room to work in the next section. You have a few options with this object:

- Use your mouse to individually click on each part of your drawing, while holding the Shift key, then move using the Arrow tool.
- Use Ctrl+A (Command + A on Mac) to select all elements on the stage, then move using the Arrow tool.

Trust me, the second option is a lot easier. You can click your mouse 10 times or just once—it's your choice, but the goal is to get all the elements of the object selected, as in Figure 3.5.

Figure 3.5

All elements of the star are selected.

With the Arrow tool, click once in the center of your selected object, and drag the object to the center of the stage. As you drag with your mouse, you will see an outline moving on the stage, like in Figure 3.6. The outline is the proposed new placement of the object.

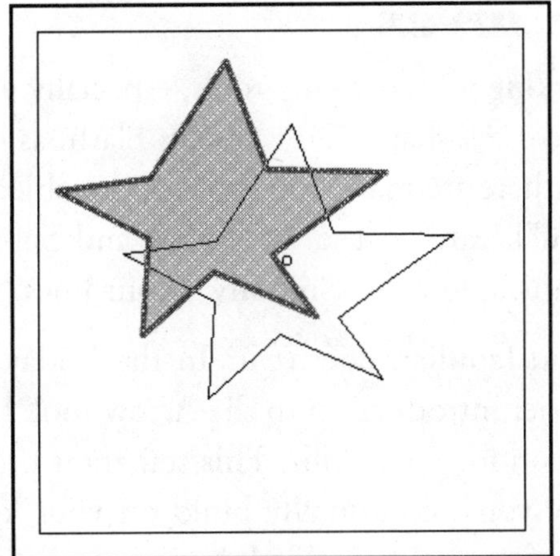

Figure 3.6

Moving the star

When the object is in the center of the stage, release the mouse button and click somewhere else in the application. This action deselects the elements of the object (see Figure 3.7).

Figure 3.7

The star is in the center, deselected.

Now you have more room to work, which will be useful as you modify the lines and curves of your object in the next section.

Tweaking Lines and Curves

Face it—when working with drawing tools, especially with a mouse, you don't always get the exact shape you want. In Flash, as in most good creation applications, there are many ways to edit the objects you've created. In this section, you'll learn to use the Arrow and Subselection tools to tweak (that's a technical term for "modify") your lines.

Yes, this does sound familiar, doesn't it? In the Friday Evening session, you were given a brief introduction to the Arrow tool, but now you have a practical application for your skills. This star transformation exercise is an example of how you'll continually build on your knowledge toward the goal of a strong foundation in Flash basics.

Back to work. Do you still have the sample movie open from the previous section, when you drew the star? If not, go on and open it, or grab the sample from the CD. Save the file with a different name, such as sample_flower.fla. This way, your sample star file will still be intact, although its contents are also present in this new file.

Lengthening Lines

Perhaps you made a squat little star, as I have. You can stretch these points out, using the Subselection tool. This enables the flower-izing you do next.

1. Select the Subselection tool from the toolbox, and click once on a part of the outline of your star. All of the anchor points will appear.
2. Grab the topmost anchor point and drag it to the top of the stage. The point of the star stretches along with it, as in Figure 3.8.
3. Continue stretching your star, until it almost fills your stage (see Figure 3.9).

Are you ready to turn this star into a flower? The next section shows you how to curve the lines so that they eventually look like flower petals.

Figure 3.8

Top of star, stretched

Figure 3.9

Entire star almost fills the stage.

Curving Lines

By the end of this exercise, you'll certainly know how to use your Arrow and Subselection tools! While you used the Subselection tool to stretch your star points, you use the Arrow tool to curve the lines. You'll modify each distinct line that you've drawn.

1. Select the Arrow tool from the toolbox, and place it over the endpoint of one of your lines. Don't click anything just yet.
2. Move your mouse around a little and watch the mouse icon change. If your mouse is over an endpoint or corner, the icon shows up as an arrow plus a corner (right angle). If it's in the middle of a line, the icon is an arrow plus a curve.
3. With your mouse icon showing as an arrow plus a curve, click once and drag your mouse so that the line becomes a nice curve (see Figure 3.10).

Figure 3.10

Turning a line into a curve

Can you see where you're going with this? Each of the straight lines, when curvy, makes your star look a little like a flower. Continue along, curving each of your 10 lines. You may hit a point where your curve doesn't respond all that well, such as that shown in Figure 3.11.

Figure 3.11

A botched curve

No worries! This reaction just means that there are more parts of that particular line that need to be curved. Hover your mouse over the non-curved parts of the line, and if an arrow plus a curve icon appears, just click and drag it outward until you get the appearance you're looking for.

Eventually, you end up with a huge flower-shaped object taking up your stage, as in Figure 3.12.

It's kind of big, isn't it? Maybe too big. Read on for a practical application of the scale feature.

Figure 3.12

The flower takes over the stage.

Scaling Your Object

In the Friday Evening session, you learned to scale objects using the scale modifier of the Arrow tool and dragging the bounding outline until the object is the size you want it. There's another way: enter a scaling percentage and let the application do the work. To scale this flower down to approximately one-third of its current size, follow these steps:

1. Use Ctrl+A (Command + A on Mac) to select all the objects on the stage.
2. Select Modify, Transform, Scale and Rotate from the menu bar. The Scale and Rotate dialog box will appear, as shown in Figure 3.13.

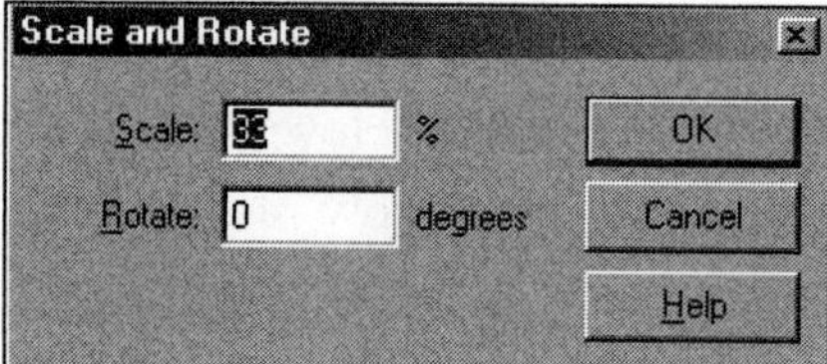

Figure 3.13

The Scale and Rotate dialog box

You can also enter a scaling percentage in the Transform Panel. The Transform Panel, which is opened by selecting Window, Panel, Transform from the menu bar, contains tools for scaling, rotating, and skewing.

3. Enter 33 in the Scale field and 0 in the Rotate field (you aren't rotating anything yet).
4. Press OK and watch your flower scale down to 33 percent of its original size (see Figure 3.14).

Your flower, though lovely, is still missing that colored area in the middle of it which helps unimaginative folks realize that it is, in fact, a flower. What a perfect segue into connecting shapes!

Figure 3.14

A scaled-down flower

Connecting Shapes

It's time to draw one of those perfect circles you learned about in the previous session. First, make sure the flower is not longer selected by clicking on an empty part of the stage with the Arrow tool, and then follow these steps:

1. Select the Oval tool from the toolbar.
2. Open the Stroke Panel and select a stroke, a line width, and a color that you like. I selected the ragged line, with a line width of 8.
3. Open the Fill Panel and select the same color you selected in the Stroke Panel. For each, I used the same dark red that makes up the outline of my flower.

Alternatively, you can use the Fill Color icon in the Colors section of the toolbox to pick your fill color.

4. Somewhere on the stage, but nowhere near your flower object, draw a small circle. Figure 3.15 shows the circle. This circle is eventually going to be plunked into the middle of your flower.

Figure 3.15

The little circle, nowhere near the flower

5. Select the Arrow tool and draw a box around the circle to select all of its parts.
6. Using the Arrow tool, select the circle and move it to the center of your flower. The outline will follow you along as you move your mouse and find that perfect position. When you find it, release your mouse button.
7. Click on an empty area of the stage to deselect the circle. Figure 3.16 shows a hole in the center of the flower.

It looks a wee bit more like a flower now, doesn't it?

The act of releasing your mouse button set the circle's position inside the flower and connected the two shapes. When you move one shape over another, the two shapes automatically connect.

Figure 3.16

Circle in the middle of the flower

Select the elements of the circle again by double clicking the circle, and drag them outside the flower. You see that there's basically a hole in the flower, where the middle part used to be. This is an example of segmenting (see Figure 3.17).

Figure 3.17

Example of segmenting

Use the Undo feature to get your flower back to normal. You can select Edit, Undo from the menu bar or press Ctrl+Z (Command + Z on Mac) to undo the last action.

Save your sample_flower.fla file and set it aside. In the next section, you'll practice the fine art of segmenting objects, then come back to your flower movie at the end of the session.

More about Segmenting

"Making cheese" is actually a lesson about segmenting. Basically, you have a polygon of one color and a bunch of little circles. When you place the circles inside the polygon, they connect. Depending on the color of the circles, they will segment the bottom of the shape when you move them out of the polygon.

Give it a go, by opening the sample file called fun_with_cheese.fla, in the session3 folder on the CD (see Figure 3.18).

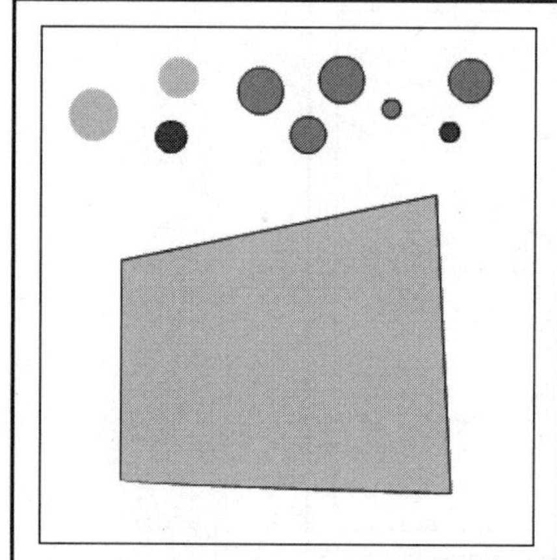

Figure 3.18

Fun with cheese lesson

Double-click each of the circles, and move them inside the polygon then deselect them. It may look something like Figure 3.19 when you're through.

TIP Double-clicking the circles grabs both the outline and the fill.

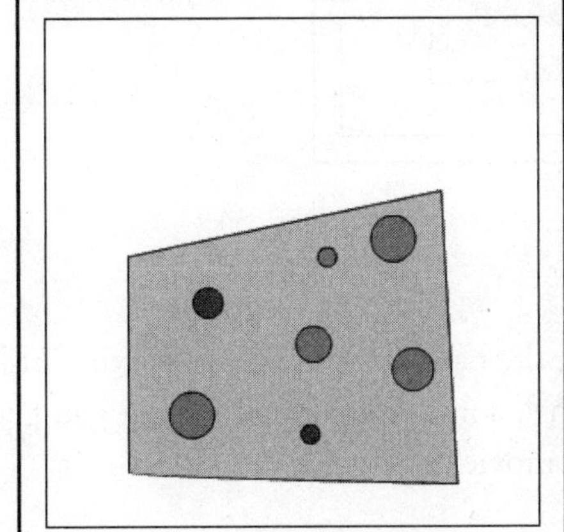

Figure 3.19

Moving the circles into the polygon

What do you notice? Perhaps you see that the two circles that are the same color as the inside of the polygon are swallowed up by it! When drawing in Flash, if two elements of the same color are connected, they're really connected and you can't pull them apart. In later sessions, you'll learn to use layers to keep shapes separate when necessary.

However, the circles of different colors can all be pulled out of the polygon. Double-click on one of the circles and move it back out. To save some wear and tear on your hand, hold down the Shift key while you double-click on the rest of them. They'll all be selected together, and you can move them out as a group.

There you go—your big block of cheese (see Figure 3.20).

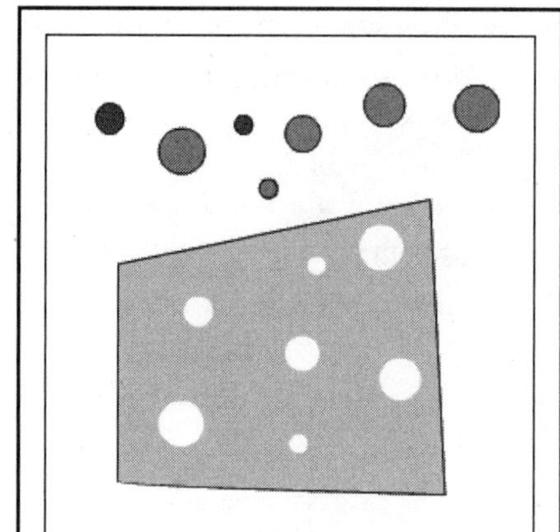

Figure 3.20

Say "Cheese!"

Take a Break

Now that you've got the base for your flower movie finished, you can take a few minutes to smell some real flowers. When you get back, you'll finish and publish the movie.

Finishing Your Flower Movie

If you can tear yourself away from the cheese lesson, open up your sample_flower.fla movie again. You'll make a few more flowers, add some grass and a pretty blue sky, and then publish the movie.

If you want to keep your flower movie separate from this new movie, just save sample_flower.fla with another name, such as sample_garden.fla, and continue on with that file.

Adding More Flowers

With a few instances of cutting and pasting, and a little rotation thrown in there for good measure, you can quickly add several more flowers to your project.

1. Using the Arrow tool, draw a box around the single flower to select all of its elements.
2. Select Modify, Group, or press Ctrl+G (Command + G on the Mac), to group the elements as one.
3. Notice the blue bounding square around the flower. This indicates that the objects are grouped. Press Ctrl+C (Command + C on the Mac) to make a copy of the flower group.
4. Press Ctrl+V (Command + V on the Mac) to paste a few copies of the flower group on the stage. Figure 3.21 shows multiple flowers on the stage.
5. Select a few of the flowers and scale them to a smaller size, then move the flowers near the bottom of the stage (see Figure 3.22).

Figure 3.21

Copies of your flowers

Figure 3.22

Some resized flowers

TIP

You can rotate your flowers so they don't all look exactly the same. From the menu bar, select Modify,Transform, Rotate 90° CW to rotate clockwise, or Modify,Transform, Rotate 90° CCW to rotate counterclockwise. Rotate is a very useful tool, not just for changing an object, but for creating other similar objects from one basic shape.

6. Select the Brush tool from the toolbox, and pick a nice green color for the fill.
7. Select the Paint Behind brush mode, a small brush size, and the tall oval brush shape.
8. Draw stems for each of your flowers, then add some grass beneath them. It's okay if you're sloppy with your grass; grass is seldom neatly groomed! Figure 3.23 shows the grass behind the flowers.

Figure 3.23

Flowers growing in the grass

Coloring the Sky

Now it gets pretty interesting; you'll use the Paint Behind brush mode to fill in a sky. Perhaps you noticed when you were drawing some grass that, no matter what you did, color never appeared on top of the flowers. Paint Behind does what it sounds like—paints behind the existing elements on the stage.

1. To paint your sky, select a nice sky blue fill color, a large brush size, and the large block brush shape.
2. Start coloring over the stage so that the blue color fills everything (see Figure 3.24).
3. When you release your mouse button, you'll see the Paint Behind mode take effect, as in Figure 3.25.

When you're through coloring and modifying your garden, save your file. In the last section of this session, which is next, you'll learn the basics of publishing your first movie!

Figure 3.24

In the process of coloring the sky

Figure 3.25

The applied paint

Publishing a Movie

Until now, you've only been viewing your project files as just that—projects. When it's time for the rest of the world to see your work, you need to publish your movie in a playback format. When you use the Publish feature in Flash, you're telling the application to take your project file (*.fla) and create a player file (*.swf).

Flash movies are designed for viewing on the World Wide Web, but you can also play movies in stand-alone format. When Flash movies are viewed on the Web, they're sitting inside an HTML document, which your browser loads, causing the movie to play. When you view a Flash movie in stand-alone format, you're bypassing the Web and your Web browser. Instead, you simply double-click the *.swf file, and it automatically launches in a Flash Player window.

For starters, you'll just publish your movie in stand-alone format and then test it.

Publishing in Stand-Alone Format

Before publishing your movie, select File, Publish Settings from the menu bar to view your settings. In the Publish Settings window, you'll see three tabs at the top. Click the Flash tab and take a gander at the settings. Following is a brief explanation of the more important settings. For now, you don't have to change a thing.

- **Load Order**. Sets the order for loading layers within a movie.
- **Protect from Import**. If you do not check this box, then anyone who views your *.swf file can convert it back to the project file. Always keep it checked, to prevent someone from stealing your original source
- **JPEG Quality**. You can adjust the compression of bitmap graphics by using the slider. A lower value results in lower image quality, but smaller files. A higher value results in better image quality, but larger files. See Appendix A for more information about this option.
- **Flash Version**. You can select which version of Flash to export to. You would assume Flash 5, since it's the newest and greatest, but if you believe your audience only has Flash 4 players, you should export as Flash 4. Be aware that not all Flash 5 features work with Flash 4.

These are only a few of the options, as you can see. You can publish your movie directly from this window by clicking the Publish button. An indicator appears, and Flash spits out a *.swf file in the same directory as your *.fla file.

NOTE To publish a file without modifying your settings, you can simply select File, Publish from the menu bar.

Navigate through your file system using Windows Explorer or a similar tool, and find the place where you saved this player file. If you look at the file size of the player file when compared to the project file, you'll see that the player file is much smaller, due to the amazing compression and optimization that is done. For example, in Figure 3.26 you can see that the project file is 52K but the player file is only 8K!

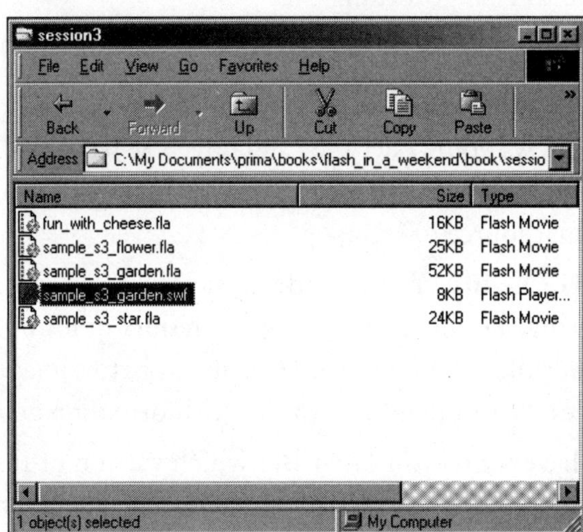

Figure 3.26

File details

To run your movie in stand-alone mode, simply double-click its file name. A Flash player window pops up, and your movie runs (see Figure 3.27). In this case, your movie is only one frame, and it doesn't do anything at all, but it's been published!

Next, you'll use the standard HTML template for publishing on the Web.

Figure 3.27

Movie published in stand-alone format

Publishing for the Web

Publishing for the Web is only one more step, and it doesn't involve the movie. To publish for the Web, you need an HTML file. That HTML file contains the information that says "Hey, open this file" to the Web browser with the Flash plug-in.

In this session, you won't make any modifications to the HTML file that Flash automatically generates. You'll just export the file and the movie and then load it through your Web browser. Things will get trickier later.

Bring the Publish Settings window back up again by selecting File, Publish Settings from the menu bar. This time, click the HTML tag at the top to see HTML settings. Familiarize yourself with the window, but don't change anything for now.

If you know HTML, you can create your own templates or code snippets for displaying the Flash movie in a Web browser.

Go ahead and press the Publish button, which generates another *.swf file as well as an HTML file. The HTML file is the same name as your project and player files, but with an *.html extension.

To open your movie locally, open your Web browser and use the File Open command under the File menu. Navigate to the location where your *.html file is, and open that file. Your Web browser loads the HTML file, which, in turn, loads the Flash movie. Figure 3.28 shows the movie playing in a Web browser.

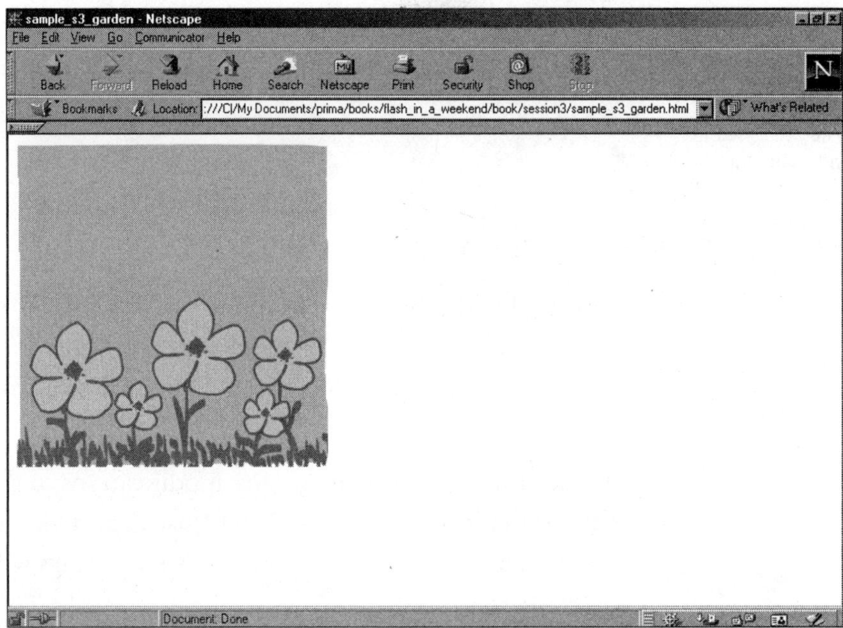

Figure 3.28

Movie loaded in a Web browser

If you have a Web site, you can place the HTML file and Flash movie on your site. For now, if you can view your movie locally, either in stand-alone format or through your Web browser, good for you!

What's Next

In the next session you'll learn more than you ever thought there was to know about color! You'll learn how to use the Fill Panel and apply gradients and how to use the Color Mixer. Most importantly, you'll learn how to maximize color use in your Flash movie.

SATURDAY EVENING

Color and Design

- Defining and Using Colors
- Using the Color Mixer
- Creating Fills with the Fill Panel

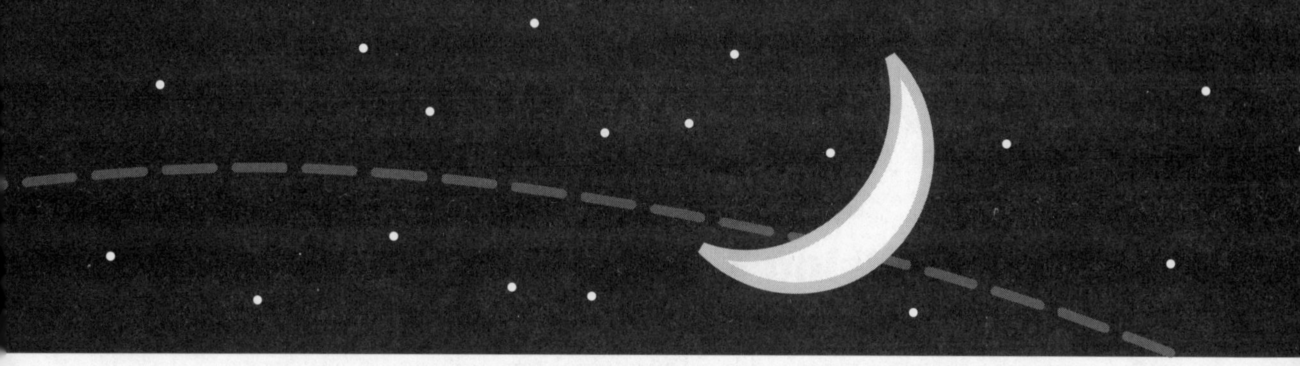

The first three sessions focused on learning the basic drawing tools and getting around the stage and toolbox. You've ploughed through certain mundane tasks to learn bits and pieces of functionality, and slowly but surely you're putting this knowledge to work and building on what you've learned.

However, an important chunk of information is still missing from your education: color. Sure, you've been coloring and filling shapes, but you haven't learned a thing about the how and why of color usage, mixing colors, or anything else besides "fill this square with red."

There's less actual drawing in this session than in the others. Instead, the goal is to fill a few gaps in basic design fundamentals. It's also a good break for your brain, as the three sessions remaining after this one will require concentration on advanced concepts, using what you've learned so far as a solid foundation.

By the end of this session, you'll know how to

- Use colors wisely.
- Change selected colors using the Color Mixer.
- Create fills using solid colors and gradients.

Defining and Using Colors

Color, as with anything related to art (and that's what you're creating!) is a subjective topic. I like a purple background; you might prefer a dark green one. How do you figure out what colors to use in your Flash movies, and when?

While art is subjective, there are still some guiding principles for using color in design, especially Web-based design. You will want to color your movies appropriately, by identifying your audience and thinking about how your colors will be interpreted. Beyond using appropriate colors, you'll soon learn that there is a subset of "safe" colors, as well—colors that are interpreted similarly on all platforms. The next few sections will deal with these topics.

Color Appropriately!

Less is more. Remember that statement, as it will come up often when determining the overall design of your movie. The key is to use colors to heighten your message or focal point without overwhelming it. If you use every color in your palette, all you will end up with is a mess of colors on your screen—no message, no focal point, just a jumble of stuff.

With most design projects, whether it's pure art or a functional animation used to sell a product or explain an idea, there will be key elements on the screen. You want those key elements to stand out, so you use contrasting colors for them. The goal is to push out to the audience the key elements of your design, while keeping the supporting elements in the background.

Besides using contrasting colors, you also want to use appropriate colors. For example, suppose you are creating a Flash movie for a toy company's Web site, to help them sell their Beanie Babies, board games, and Barbies to kids. If so, you probably wouldn't want to use dull or dark colors like brown and black. Or perhaps you are developing an introductory animation for a financial Web site. In this instance, a site done all in summery pastels may not be the best idea to capture and hold your audience's attention (let alone set the appropriate mood). If you were creating, say, an art piece featuring some pale moths and butterflies you might want to use a rich, dark background to let your audience get a good look at these small elements.

FIND IT ON THE WEB

This book only scratches the surface of color theory. If you are interested in learning more about how to use colors to do everything from lift people's spirits to elevate their blood pressure, I recommend you visit Color Matters® at http://www.colormatters.com.

Whatever the purpose of your movie, take a moment before you start creating it to think about your audience and your message, then select a group of colors to use that will deliver that message appropriately.

About the Web-Safe Color Palette

In Web-based design, you are dealing with a wide variety of users, all of whom use different monitors. These monitors come in a range of sizes, resolution capabilities, and—most importantly—color depths. As a designer, you need to be aware of these potential differences and design accordingly. For colors, that means using the Web-safe color palette.

When the Web first went graphical (yes, there was a time when it was text-based), the vast majority of users had monitors and video cards capable of displaying only 256 colors. That's it—just 256 out of the millions of possible colors. This is called 8-bit color depth. However, those basic 256 colors on a Windows system are different from the basic 256 colors on a Macintosh system. Then throw into the mix the fact that even the different Web browsers display colors differently—forty of the color values produce different results on different machines; the rest are consistent. As a result, the 216-color "Web-safe color palette" was born. A better name would be the "cross-platform, cross-browser, generic 8-bit color palette," but that's too long. Only these 216 colors are guaranteed to appear the same on both the Mac and the PC.

The Web-safe color palette became the standard for Web design, and to a great extent it still is, although over 85 percent of users have monitors capable of greater color depth. In Web design, catering to the lowest common denominator is a wise idea; in this case, the results of using more colors than your monitor can handle will often be just plain awful.

When a Web browser or other application receives a request for an unsupported color, one of two things can happen: the color is modified and becomes a color that is supported (usually the nearest color to the unsupported color), or the color will be dithered. *Dithering* is an attempt by the application to approximate the unsupported color by merging two supported colors. As you can imagine, the possibilities are great that something will go awry, or at the very least the color won't really be what you wanted.

The 216-color Web-safe palette, while limiting, is still the most practical. If you use a color outside this standard set, you are likely to see inconsistencies across systems. In Flash, the Web-safe color palette is the default palette, although you can choose to add colors and use larger and more diverse color palettes—something that's safe only if you know exactly where your work is going and what the viewers' equipment can deal with.

In the next section, you'll see how colors are defined. These are important concepts for later in this session, when you'll redefine certain aspects of those colors.

How Colors Are Defined

Most graphics-based applications, including Flash, offer several ways to define and edit colors.

- **RGB.** Colors defined by their RGB values (R = red, G = green, B = blue)
- **HSB.** Colors defined by their HSB values (H = hue, S = saturation, B = brightness)
- **Hexadecimal.** Colors noted by their base-16 value; used in HTML

The next few sections will explain these terms in greater detail.

RGB Values

Colors on a monitor are defined by how much red, green, and blue they contain. If a color has a lot of blue and red, but no green, then you're looking at a shade of purple. This is because monitors use additive colors. Additive color means that different shades of light are combined to produce a new color.

Additive color is determined by the amount of the red, green, and blue added—the more color you add, the closer to white your color will be. The less color you add, the closer your color will be to black. For example, if you have no red, no green and no blue, then you have solid black. If you have all red, all blue and all green, then you have solid white.

This is the opposite of subtractive color. You can see subtractive colors when you mix paint. This is because paint doesn't emit light, paint reflects it. Red paint only reflects red light, blue paint reflects blue light, etc. When you combine red paint and blue paint the mixture that results can reflect neither red nor blue. The more colors you add the less light the paint reflects and the darker it gets.

You may have guessed by now that your computer thinks of colors as sets of numbers. Each component of your color has a value, and it ranges from 0 (none of that color) to 255 (as much as possible of that color).

So, to review, the RGB value of black is 0-0-0. The RGB value of pure white is 255-255-255. The RGB of pale yellow is 255-255-128. You get the idea.

Later in this session, you'll learn to identify and modify RGB values using the Color Mixer.

HSB Values

Another way to define and edit color is by using HSB values.

"H" stands for *hue,* which relates to the types of colors from which a single color is derived. In other words, where the single target color falls in the spectrum of all colors. For example, does your target color fall into the red section, or is it over among the greens?

"S" stands for *saturation,* which is the intensity of the hue in your single target color. For example, if your color looks like a very strong, pure orange, then it probably has a high saturation value. As the saturation value drops, the color appears more gray.

The final piece of the puzzle is "B," which stands for *brightness.* Brightness is exactly what it sounds like—how light or dark is your color? The higher the brightness value, the lighter the color.

Just like RGB values, HSB values also use a scale from 0 to 255 in the computer world.

Hexadecimal Values

Another common method for defining and editing color values is through hexadecimal notation. You will see hexadecimal notation used in HTML to specify things like background color, font color, table border color, and so on. A hexadecimal notation of a color could look like this: 33CCFF.

If you look at these six characters, you can break them down into three sets of two: 33, CC, and FF. These correspond, from left to right, to the R (Red), G (Green), and B (Blue) values of a single color. Unlike the decimal notation (0 through 255) for R, G, and B, you use hexadecimal notation (0 through 9 followed by A through F). The table below shows how this particular hexadecimal number translates to RGB values.

Hexadecimal	RGB
33	51
CC	204
FF	255

In other words, a color with a hexadecimal notation of 33CCFF has a Red value of 51, a Green value of 204, and a Blue value of 255. Put all that together and you have a nice sky blue. Some other common examples of hexadecimal color notation are 000000 (black), FFFFFF (white), FF0000 (pure red), 00FF00 (pure green), and 0000FF (pure blue).

Take a Break

Before you begin to add your newfound color knowledge to your Flash movie, take a little while to step away from your computer. Take a look at the colors around your house and outside. What colors and color combinations do your prefer? Do you think others would like them as well? Try to keep a few good color combinations in mind when reading the next section.

Using the Color Mixer

All your newfound knowledge about color definition will come into play when you use the Color Mixer in Flash 5. The Color Mixer allows you to create and edit solid colors. If you have an object selected on the stage while you're fiddling with the Color Mixer, Flash will apply the changes to that object. You can redefine fill and stroke colors using RGB or hexadecimal notation, and you can use the Alpha value slider to determine the transparency for the color. Basically, the Color Mixer is a quick way to try out new colors for a selected object.

The Color Mixer is a panel, and as you learned in the first session, you can access panels from the menu system or through the Launcher at the bottom right of your application window. The Color Mixer icon is second from the left, as shown in Figure 4.1.

Go ahead and launch the Color Mixer Panel if it is not already launched. The next section will explain its parts.

Figure 4.1

The Launcher, indicating the Color Mixer icon

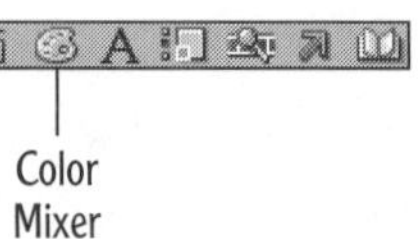

The Parts of the Color Mixer

After launching the Color Mixer, you'll see a little panel like the one in Figure 4.2 that you can keep in your workspace for easy access to its tools.

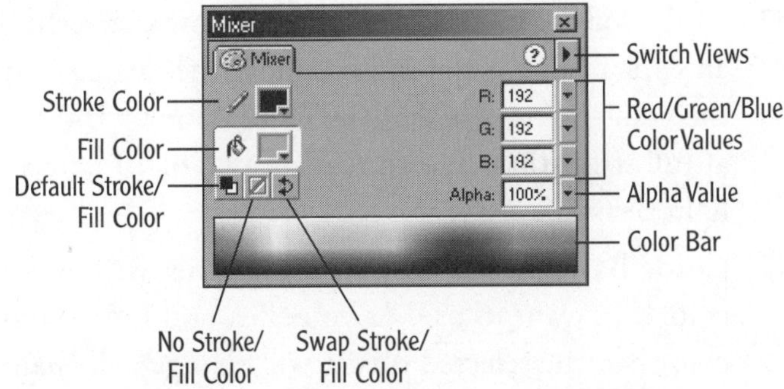

Figure 4.2

The Color Mixer Panel

The Color Mixer has the following parts:

- **Stroke Color and Fill Color.** You've used Stroke Color and Fill Color pickers before when drawing lines and filling shapes. Clicking your mouse on the color chip will display the color palette. You can pick a color from the palette or use hexadecimal notation to enter a color value. If you have selected a line and you pick a new color from the palette, the new color will be applied to whatever object is selected. The same holds true for a filled object, when you change the fill color.
- **Default stroke/fill color**. If you select this option, you return the Color Mixer swatches to white fill and black stroke.
- **No stroke/fill color**. If you select this option, you will create a transparent stroke or fill.
- **Swap stroke/fill color**. If you select this option, the current values for stroke and fill will be swapped (stroke color will become fill color, and vice versa).
- **RGB Color Values.** By entering new values in these text boxes, you can incrementally modify the values of each color, thus making a completely new color for your selected object. As you change these values, the color swatch will change accordingly, so you can see your modifications in real time.

- **Alpha Value**. Enter a percentage or use the vertical slider to specify an Alpha value. The Alpha value is the degree of transparency for the color, or its opacity. An Alpha value of 100 percent is the color at full strength, while an Alpha value of 10 percent would be very light or hazy.
- **Color Bar**. The color bar is yet another way for you to select the color you want to use. As you click and move your mouse in the color bar, the selected object will change colors and the RGB values will move around, depending on where you are. You can transform your object from red to green to funky orange just by clicking your mouse pointer in the color bar.

Now for the secret options in the Color Mixer, found by clicking on the right-arrow in the upper right corner. This allows you to switch views. While the default view gives you RGB values, you can also switch to other views. Figure 4.3 shows the HSB (hue, saturation, brightness, remember?) view.

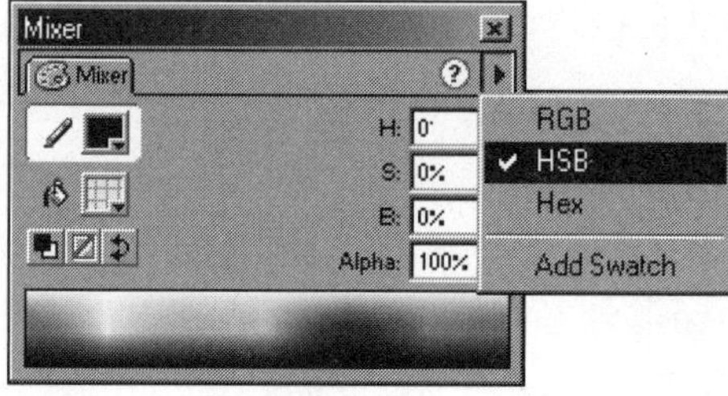

Figure 4.3

The Color Mixer Panel in HSB view

By entering new values in the HSB text boxes, you can incrementally modify the hue, saturation, and brightness of a particular selection. You can use the same right-arrow to switch to Hex view, as in Figure 4.4.

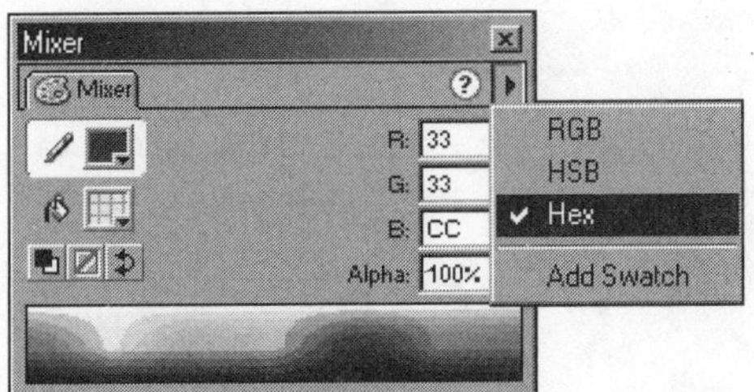

Figure 4.4

The Color Mixer Panel in Hex view

In Hex view, you get the same RGB boxes as in the RGB view. However, you can enter values in hexadecimal rather than decimal notation.

The primary use of the Color Mixer is just to settle on the best color for the selected object. If you're an artist and can tell the difference between light yellow and lighter yellow, for example, this would come in handy. The Color Mixer gives you the tools to incrementally move from step to step within the range of light yellows until you find that perfect color.

The Color Mixer and Existing Objects

Now that you know how to use the Color Mixer in theory, it's time to play with it. There's a sample file on the CD-ROM just for this purpose, but you can use your own drawing if you prefer. The next examples are based on the sample from the CD-ROM, so you'll have to make a mental leap if you're using your own drawing.

Using File, Open from the menu bar, navigate to your CD-ROM, and open the eye.fla file located in the session4 directory. The funky-looking eyeball shown in Figure 4.5 will be staring back at you from the stage. This eyeball uses lines and fills, all of which can be tweaked using the Color Mixer.

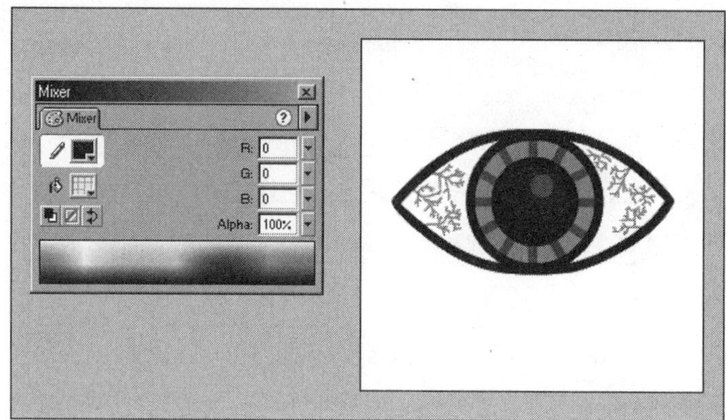

Figure 4.5

The Color Mixer and the sample eyeball

Start by changing the color of the outline of this eye, because it's the easiest to see. With the arrow tool, select the top curve, then hold down the Shift key and click on the bottom curve and the inner circle to select all three elements, as shown in Figure 4.6.

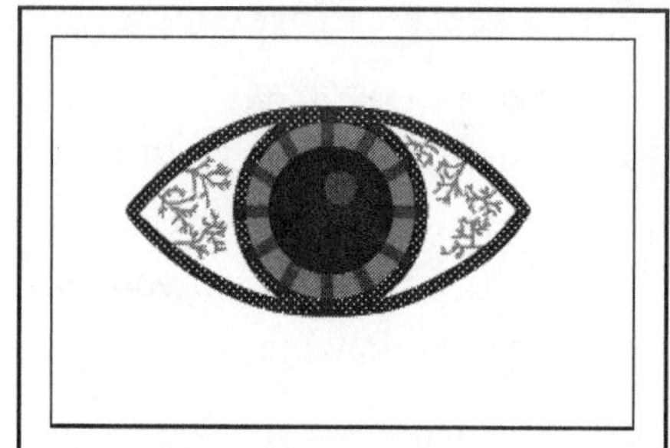

Figure 4.6

Selected lines

To instantly change the color of these selected lines, click the Stroke Color color picker in the Color Mixer. From the color palette, select a light gray. You should now see the selected lines in the eye become light gray, as in Figure 4.7.

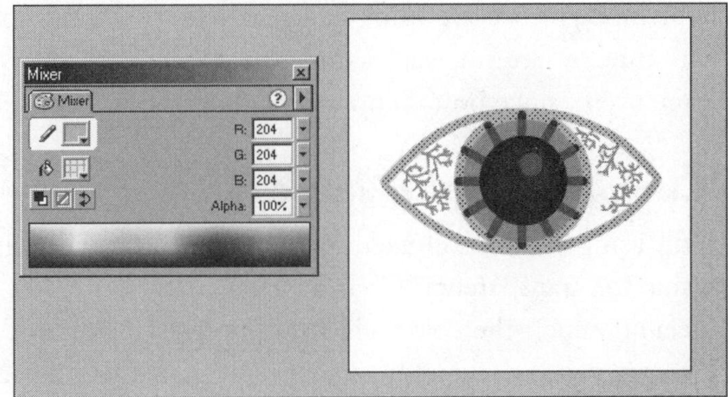

Figure 4.7

Selected lines now gray, using Color Picker

Not only are the lines gray, the RGB values are accurate, showing 204 (that's light gray) in each slot.

You can use the color bar the same way as the color palette, except you have more color selections to choose from. Keep the three lines selected, and click your mouse in the color bar. Settle on a nasty lime green and release your mouse. The lines will now be lime green, and the RGB values will have changed appropriately, as in Figure 4.8.

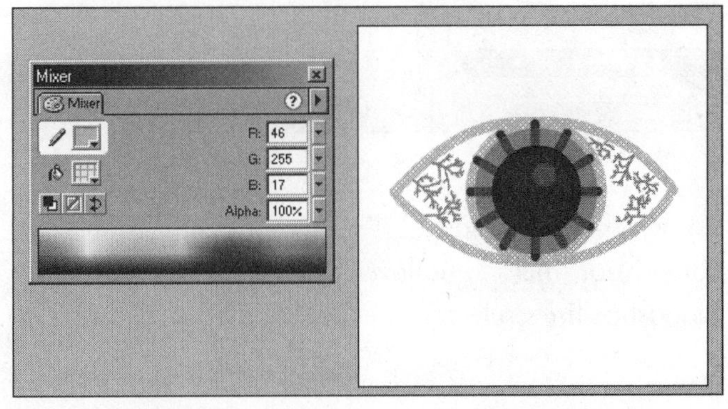

Figure 4.8

Selected lines now green, using color bar

The lime green eye outline looks terrible, so set the color back to black, this time by entering values directly into the RGB slots. Each should contain a zero, since no red, no green, and no blue equals black.

Changing Alpha Values

Still using the eyeball example, you can play with changing the Alpha value, or transparency level, of a color. If you select 100 percent (the default value), the color will be completely opaque. The lower the percentage you use, the more transparent your filled object will be, and the more you'll be able to see background elements poking through the color.

You can try this out on the bloodshot lines in the sample eye. First, you'll want to select all the little lines. Here's a trick that you'll learn more about in the next session—selecting the layer that contains the lines.

With the sample eye project open, your timeline should look something like Figure 4.9, with the layers labeled all nice and neat.

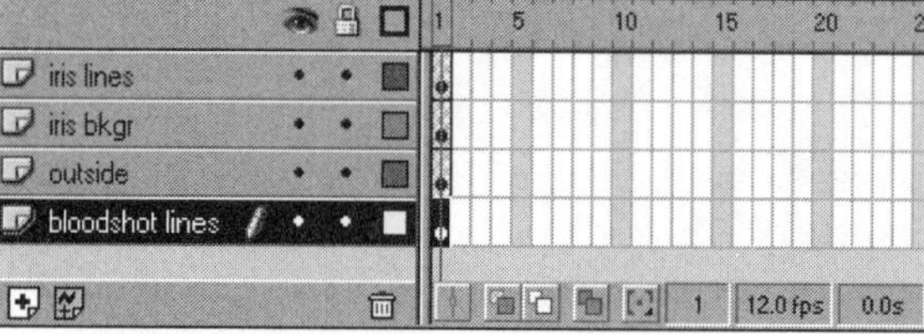

Figure 4.9

The timeline for this movie

To select the bloodshot lines, click your mouse on the layer named "bloodshot lines." The layer will be highlighted, and you will see all the bloodshot lines selected on the stage, as in Figure 4.10.

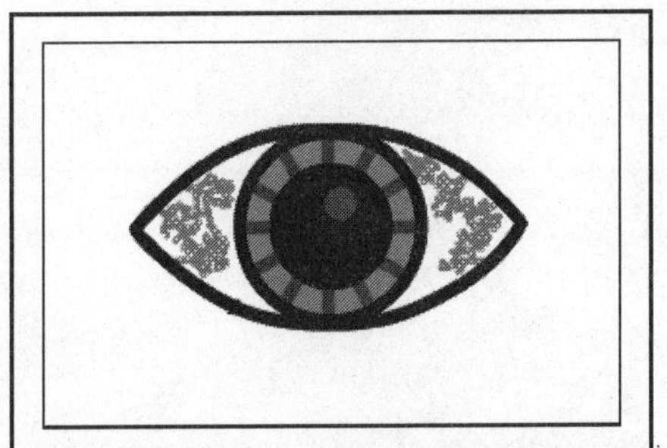

Figure 4.10

Bloodshot lines selected

Once all the lines are selected, click your mouse on the Alpha slider and move it up and down. As you do, you'll see the Stroke Color swatch change colors, indicating what the selection would look like if you stopped at that point. Move the slider to 32 percent, and the Color Mixer should look like Figure 4.11.

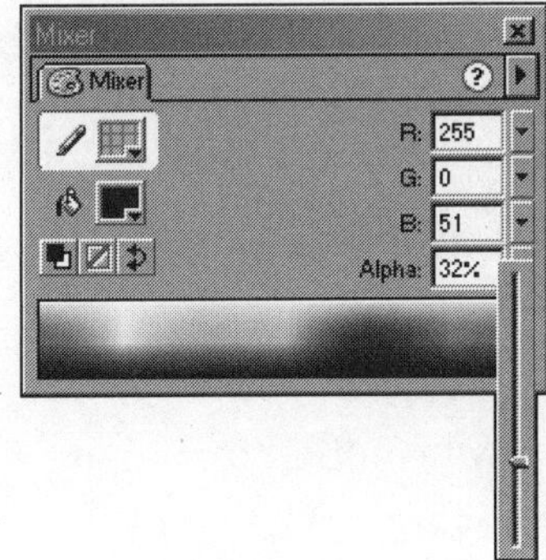

Figure 4.11

Changing the Alpha value

If you click your mouse in the movie project, your bloodshot lines will now be at 32 percent opacity. Play around with the Alpha value slider and note how it affects the transparency of the color, not the color values themselves. In other words, red is still red, it's just a different opacity.

Changing HSB Values

You can play with the hue, saturation, and brightness of a selection in much the same way as you changed the Alpha value of a selection. Try changing the hue and saturation values of the iris background in the sample eye project.

1. Select the "iris bkgr" layer in the timeline. The eyeball will look like the one in Figure 4.12
2. To get to the HSB view of the Color Mixer, click on the right-arrow in the upper right corner of the Mixer Panel.
3. Use the Hue slider to go from one end of the color spectrum to the other.

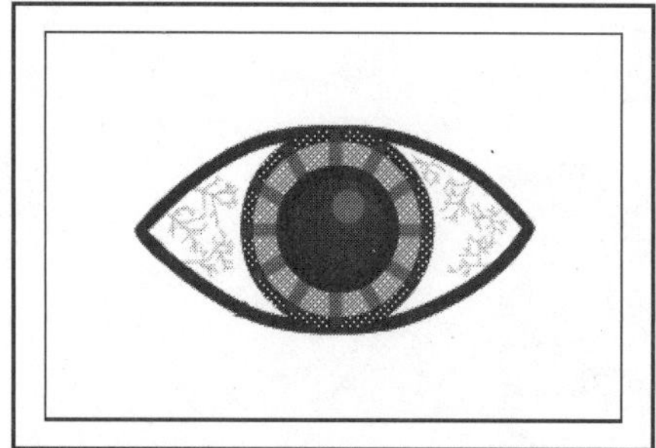

Figure 4.12

Iris background selected

Play around with the slider until you find something you like. If you settle at 56 percent for hue, your iris background will be a pukey brown color. At 124 percent the background will be a pleasant green. As you move the slider, the color swatch in the Color Mixer will change accordingly to indicate the proposed new hue.

When you settle on a color with a hue that gets the effect you want, move on to adjusting the saturation. A high saturation percentage makes the color more intense and vibrant, while a lower percentage makes the color less intense, even gray. Play with the slider until you find something you like, then click on the stage to see the color applied.

The last element in the HSB view is "B"—brightness. Brightness is really useful for creating light effects, as you can create a highlight or a shadow using just a different brightness value. In the sample eye movie, the highlight in the pupil was created using a shift in brightness.

To start changing the brightness value of the pupil highlight, do the following:

1. Select the "pupil hilight" layer from the timeline to get the effect shown in Figure 4.13.
2. In the Color Mixer, move the Brightness slider from 0 percent (black) to 100 percent (white) and watch the color shift.

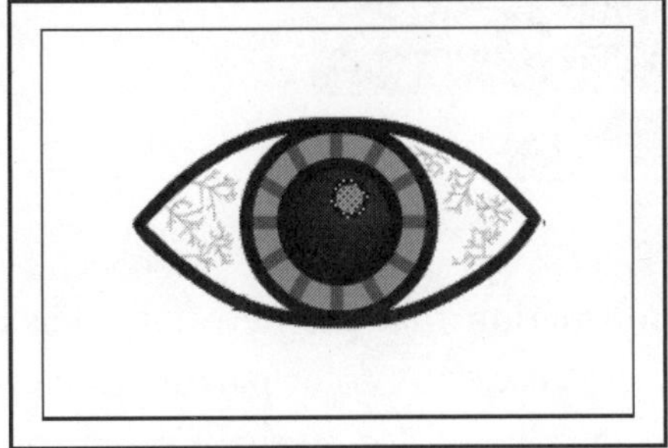

Figure 4.13

Pupil highlight selected

Play around with the slider until you find something you like. The highlight starts out very bright (100 percent), but you can make it darker, or change the hue and then change the brightness—whatever you want to do. The point is to understand how the Brightness slider affects the selection.

Adding Colors to the Color Mixer

Each time you modify the RGB value of a color, change its hue or saturation, or even change its Alpha value, you create a new and unique color. You can save these colors in the Color Mixer and access them later, rather than trying to remember what percentages you used along the way.

When you settle on a new color that you like and want to save, click on the right-arrow in the upper right corner of the Color Mixer and select "Add Swatch," as in Figure 4.14.

NOTE Adding a new swatch does not affect the Web-safe palette, it simply adds a new color to the Color Panel.

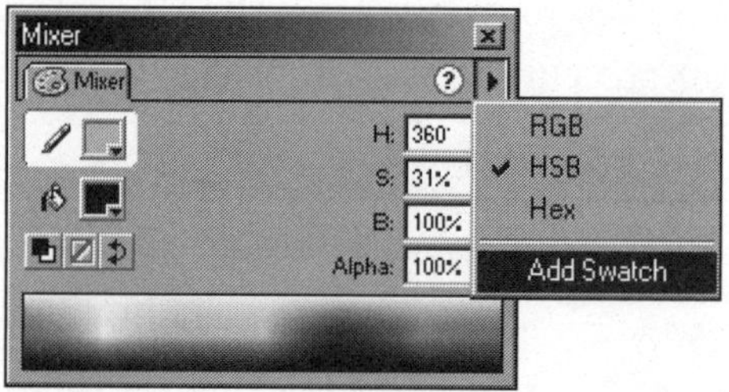

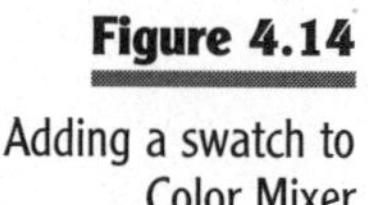

Figure 4.14

Adding a swatch to Color Mixer

You won't see a confirmation that the new color has been added to the Color Mixer, but if you access the color palette for either Stroke Color or Fill Color, you'll see your new color on the bottom row of swatches, as in Figure 4.15.

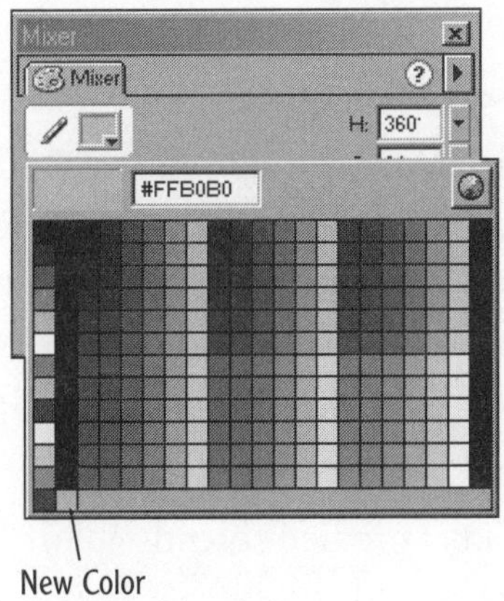

Figure 4.15

Your new color swatch is now available.

If you're using the Swatch Panel, your new swatch will appear in the same place: the bottom row of colors. This is also the same area where your custom gradients (which you'll learn to create in a moment) will appear.

Creating Fills with the Fill Panel

Another tool for messing with color is the Fill Panel (see Figure 4.16). Conveniently, you can use the Fill Panel to work with all four options you have for filling objects in Flash. Access the Fill Panel through the menu system, by selecting Window, Panels, Fill.

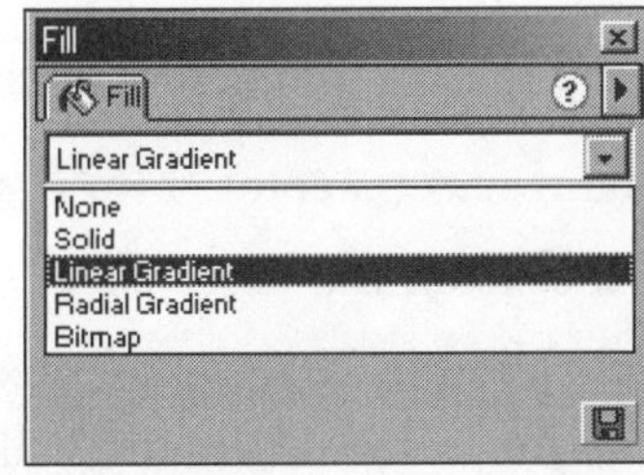

Figure 4.16

The Fill Panel

The Fill Panel is quite simple, but pick a fill type from the drop-down menu and it changes. The fill types are

- **Solid.** Just as you suspected, solid fills with a solid color. When you select this type of fill, a color chip appears and allows you to access the color palette. Pick a color from the color palette and you're ready to fill your object.
- **Linear Gradient.** A linear gradient blends colors linearly (hence the name), from one end to the other.
- **Radial Gradient.** A radial gradient blends colors from a center starting point outward toward the edges.
- **Bitmap.** A bitmap fill places a selected image into the background of the object. This is useful for creating a fill using a design you created in another drawing application, for example.

Using a generic rectangle as the base object, these next sections will let you practice creating each type of fill. For each, draw a rectangle on your own in a new movie.

Creating a Solid Fill

You've actually created a solid fill before, but not in the context of the Fill Panel. In this example, all you'll do is pick a solid color and fill your object with it.

1. Open the Fill Panel.
2. Select "Solid" from the Fill drop-down list.
3. Click on the color chip and select a color from the color palette.
4. Select the Paint Bucket tool from the toolbox.
5. Click within your object, filling it with the selected color. Your rectangle will be a generic but colorful rectangle like the one shown in Figure 4.17.

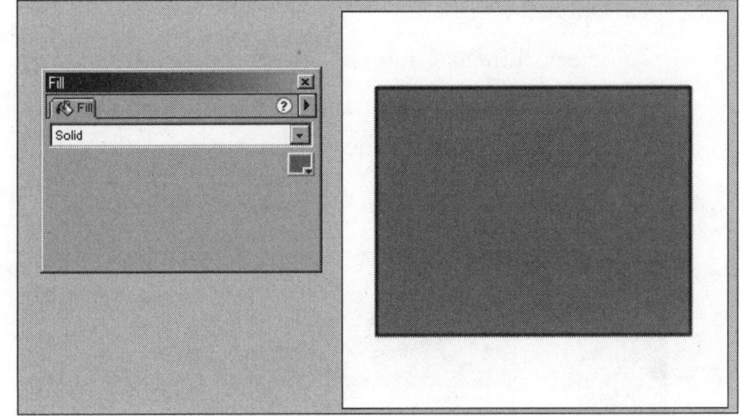

Figure 4.17

A solid filled rectangle

Admittedly, that was not too exciting. But you learned the crucial mouse clicks for creating a fill. Next you'll move to gradient fills, which are pretty cool.

Creating a Linear Gradient Fill

A linear gradient fill is a range of colors that goes from one end to another—for example, a gradient that extends from dark blue to light blue. Or you can do gradients that go from white to black to red to green, all in a straight line. Basically, you can create a gradient of any number of colors, the point being that a linear gradient extends linearly. Filling a rectangle or creating a blend of colors straight across a flat surface is the most common use of the linear gradient.

Flash provides a few canned gradients in your default color swatches, most of which are pretty ugly. But look at them nonetheless, because they are so ugly that you can't help but learn from them.

1. Open the Fill Panel.
2. Select "Linear Gradient" from the Fill drop-down list.
3. In the toolbox, select the fill chip to open the colors and gradients palette, then select the rainbow-striped chip at the bottom right. Your workspace will look something like Figure 4.18.

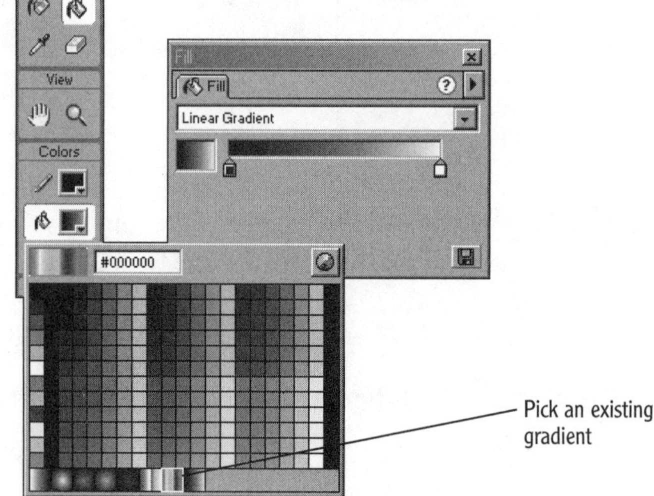

Figure 4.18

Selecting a canned linear gradient

This rainbow is a vibrant example of a linear gradient. When you select the gradient, it will populate the Fill Panel, as in Figure 4.19.

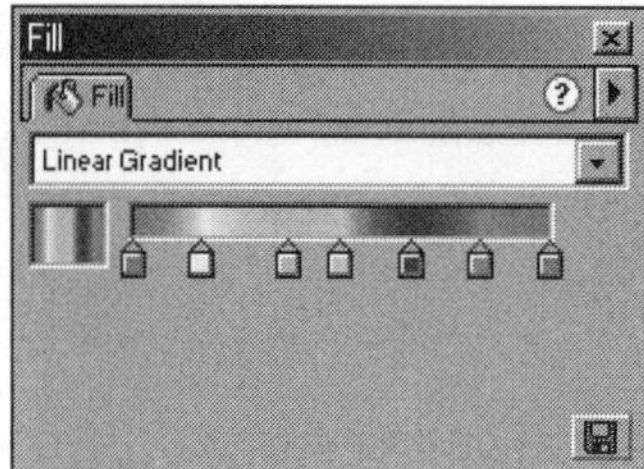

Figure 4.19

The rainbow gradient in the Fill Panel

Those little upward-pointing arrows are called Color Pointers, and they define the starting point of a color in your gradient. The rainbow gradient has seven different color points. You'll use these in a moment, but for now, select the Paint Bucket tool from your toolbox and click once inside your object. The rainbow gradient will fill your object, smoothly blending from one color to the next, as in Figure 4.20.

Figure 4.20

Rainbow-gradient-filled object

You can create your own gradient by making your own set of Color Pointers. The next exercise will let you try that, so you don't have to live with rainbow gradients any longer.

Creating a Custom Linear Gradient

To create your own gradient, simply create a set of Color Pointers—two, four, however many you want—and add the gradient to your palette for future use. Think of two colors that you really like (or any two colors that will work well in a linear gradient, such as blue and white).

1. Open the Fill Panel.
2. Select Linear Gradient from the Fill drop-down list.
3. If you see a gradient already sitting there, click your mouse on the Color Pointers and drag all but two out of the panel. They will disappear and all will be well.
4. For the two that remain, slide one to the far right and one to the far left.
5. Determine your starting color (left side), such as blue. Click the color pointer, then click the color chip on the right side of the panel to access the color palette. Find your blue and select it, as shown in Figure 4.21.

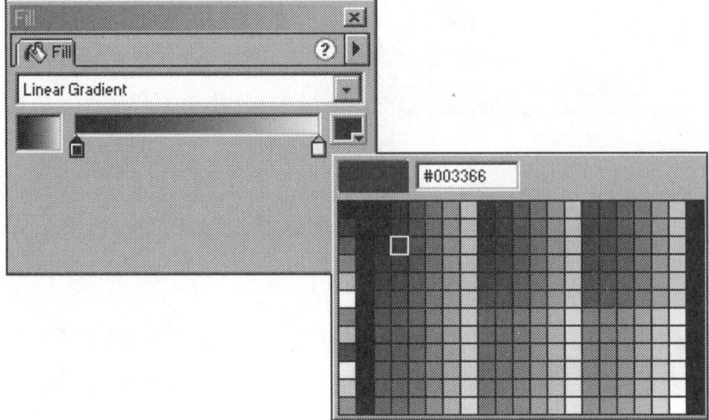

Figure 4.21

Setting the starting color

6. Repeat the process with the color pointer on the far right to select the end color, such as white. You will have a blue-to-white linear gradient in your Fill Panel.
7. Click with the Paint Bucket in your object. Your object will fill with that gradient.
8. If you like this gradient, click on the right-arrow in the upper right corner of the Fill Panel and select "Add Gradient." Your gradient will now be available in your Fill Color palette for future use.

If you want to change how soon or where one color makes the transition to the other, just drag one of the Color Pointers horizontally along the gradient window. Watch the gradient change in your shape. Putting the two Color Pointers closer together will result in a more abrupt color transition, and as you move them apart, the color shift grows more gradual. Adding additional color changes is as simple as clicking a blank area below the color bar—a new pointer will appear.

Likewise, you can change the direction of your gradient by swapping the Color Pointers. If you want to swap the color on the right with the color on the left, just drag it all the way to the other end, and do the opposite with the other pointer. The color gradient is now flip-flopped.

The next section covers radial gradients, which follow the same creation process, except in a circle instead of along a straight path.

Creating a Radial Gradient Fill

A radial gradient spreads from one color to another in an ever-expanding circle. It's either the shape that you're filling or the effect you're trying to achieve that determines whether you use linear or radial gradient. If you're filling a circle or creating a starburst effect, that's the perfect time to use a radial gradient.

As with linear gradients, Flash provides a few canned radial gradients in your default color swatches. Some of these aren't so bad, so let's take a look at them.

1. Open the Fill Panel.
2. Select "Radial Gradient" from the Fill drop-down list.
3. In the toolbox, select the fill chip to open the colors and gradients palette, then select the rainbow-striped chip at the bottom right. Your workspace should look something like Figure 4.22.

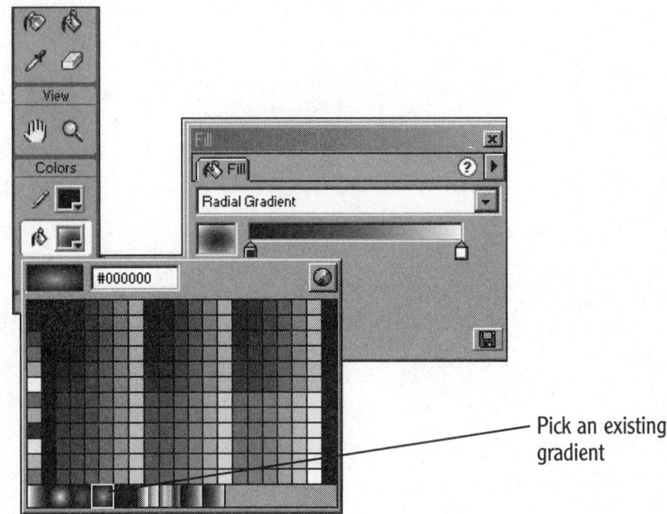

Figure 4.22

Selecting a canned radial gradient

4. Select the black and green radial gradient. The gradient will populate the Fill Panel, much the same way as the linear gradient did.
5. Use the Paint Bucket to fill your circular object. It will fit neatly, as in Figure 4.23.

Figure 4.23

Filling with a radial gradient

To make a radial gradient work well in an oval, first draw a perfect circle filled with your gradient. Then squish the circle so that it becomes an oval and the gradient will squish with it. If you just try and fill an oval with a radial gradient, it won't follow the curves of the oval properly.

Since you create radial gradients in the same way in which you created linear gradients, go ahead and play around with the Color Pointers to hit upon that magical combination of colors.

One last tip when creating radial gradient fills: the point at which you click to fill your object determines the center of your radial gradient. If you click in the center of your object, the gradient will start in the center. If you click in the upper right corner, your gradient will start there.

What's Next

In the next session you're going to learn all about organization. You discover the tools Flash has that allow you to organize your movie and the advantages of using them. Get a good night's sleep, because in the morning, the real work starts. Yes, work on a Sunday!

SUNDAY MORNING

Scenes, Layers, and Your Library

- Working with Layers
- Using Scenes
- Introducing the Library
- Using Symbols

So much for the basics! The preceding sessions introduced you to Flash 5 and explained most of the simple tools and panels. This morning, I'll show you the advanced tools you'll use to create your Flash movies, and I'll introduce and explain the importance of layers, scenes, and symbols and walk you through their use as well. By the time you move on to the next session you'll be primed and ready to create your first animation. I hope you got plenty of sleep last night, because today you're really going to blow the lid off Flash 5!

So far you've created lines, curves, text, and all kinds of other shapes and images. What you've discovered is that creating these still pictures isn't that much different from painting on a canvas, except that with Flash, the stage is your canvas and the drawing tools are your brushes. Imagine trying to create an animated cartoon using paint and canvas. You'd need an army of da Vincis! Luckily, there's a better way, and that's where scenes, layers, and the library come in.

By the end of this session, you'll know how to

- Create, remove, and rearrange layers.
- Create and delete scenes.
- Use the built-in library.
- Add and delete symbols from your library.
- Place symbols in your movie.

Working with Layers

Remember Saturday morning cartoons? You'd wake up, sometimes even earlier than on a school day, grab a bowl of sugary cereal from the kitchen, sit down in your pajamas a few feet from the TV, and watch your favorite superhero, wacky farm animal, or crime-solving dog for hours. Did you ever wonder how all those great cartoons were made?

Hand-drawn animation is hard work and takes a lot of time. The basic idea is to draw each scene over and over with tiny changes from frame to frame to show how things move against the background—like a movie, but with hand-drawn pictures instead of photographs. But even the big Hollywood studios of today couldn't afford to draw an entire still-scene for each frame of animation. Instead they paint on clear plastic sheets. Each important element gets its own page. To form a complete scene the clear pages are layered one on top of another. The bottom images show through the transparent areas of the top layers.

By using this technique the animators have made their work easier in two important ways. First, each individual part of the picture can be reused over and over again without having to be redrawn. Have you noticed that in most cartoons you see certain images—such as backgrounds or clothing—over and over? The animators are reusing these elements. Second, if an animator makes a mistake, only the layers that contain the error have to be redrawn. For example, the animator can change a reindeer's nose from pink to red without having to redo those tricky antlers.

What does this have to do with Flash? Well, Flash lets you use a similar stack of images, but rather than clear plastic sheets, you get electronic layers.

Creating and Ordering Layers

Layers are an animator's best friend. The more time you spend using Flash the more you will come to appreciate all the advantages layers offer. Each important element of your movie should have its own layer. Trust me, the first time you have to change Bigfoot into the Abominable Snowman and you realize that the forest in the background is on the same layer as the critter, you'll want to strangle yourself with your mouse cord. You should always have a unique layer for such things as the background, sounds, buttons, text, and figures.

Open a new movie by selecting File, New from the menu bar, and use the Movie Properties dialog box to create a stage that fits comfortably in your workspace. Figure 5.1 shows a new movie; take a look at the area above the stage. A default layer has been created, called "Layer 1." Notice the pencil next to the layer name. This shows that Layer 1 is active; changes made on the stage will only affect this layer.

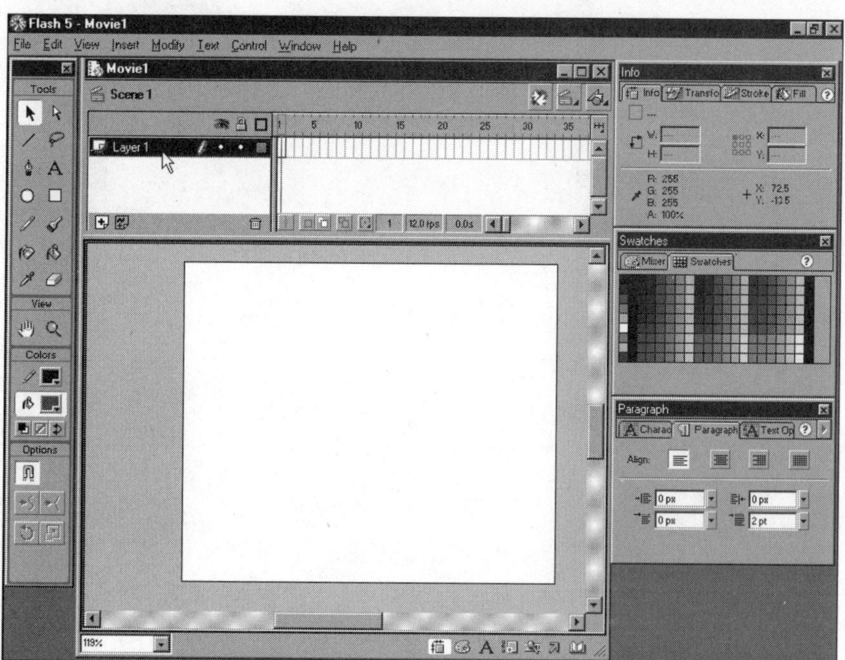

Figure 5.1

A new movie with Layer 1 active

Renaming a Layer

To rename Layer 1, follow these steps:

1. Double-click on the layer's name.
2. Type in a new name. (Use **Background** to stay with the example.)
3. Click anywhere on the stage.

The layer's name will be changed (see Figure 5.2). Make it easier on yourself by giving your layers meaningful names. Finding your snowman image is much less stressful if he's on the Snowman layer rather than buried somewhere between Layer 1 and Layer 23.

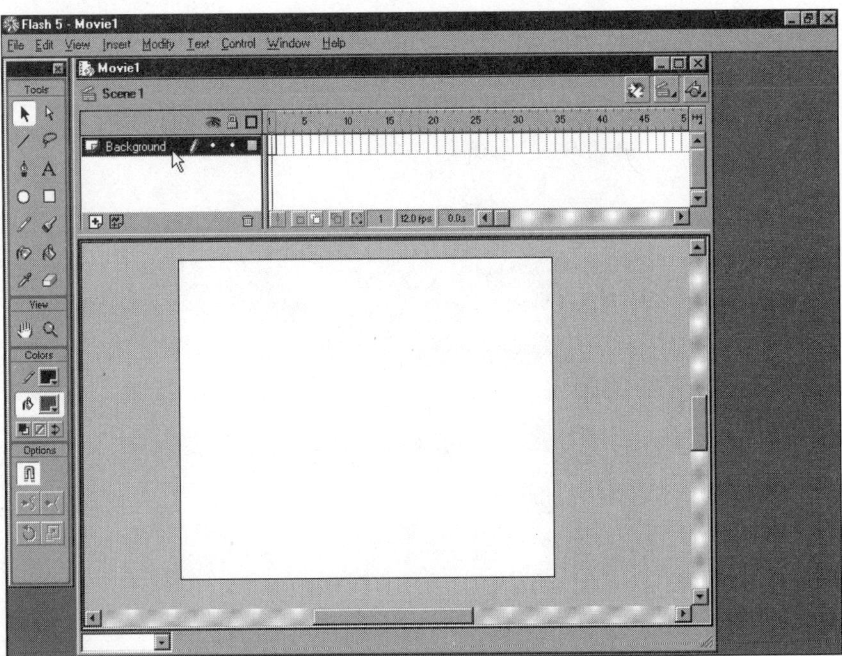

Figure 5.2

The renamed layer, "Background"

Creating a New Layer

Remember those advantages of using layers? Well, they don't kick in until you have more than one layer.

To create and name a new layer, do the following:

1. Select Insert, Layer from the menu bar, or click on the Insert Layer button (see Figure 5.3). A new layer will appear on top of the Background layer.

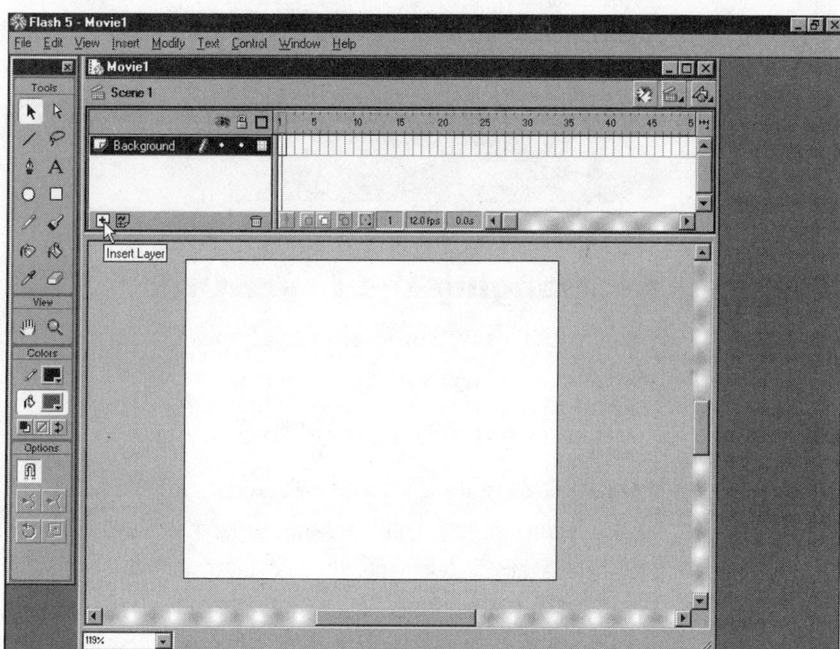

Figure 5.3

The Insert Layer button

2. Right-click (Ctrl+click on the Mac) on the layer name and select Properties. The Layer Properties dialog box will open.
3. Type a new name for the layer in the name field, as in Figure 5.4 (use **Circle** to stay with the example) and then click OK.

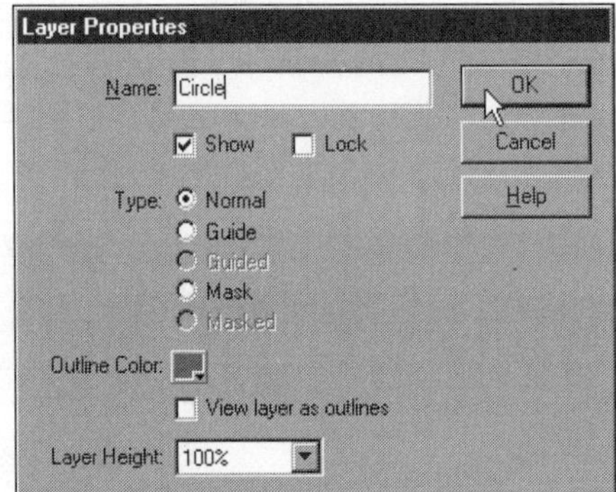

Figure 5.4

The Layer Properties dialog box

Rearranging the Layer Order

Now you'll draw some simple shapes on each of the layers and then rearrange the layer order.

1. Click on the Background layer to make it active.

NOTE As you learned in last night's session, clicking on the layer not only makes it active, it also selects all the elements on that layer. To quickly deselect everything, use the Ctrl+Shift+A (Command+Shift+A on the Mac) key combination.

2. Use the Rectangle tool to draw a large blue rectangle on the stage.
3. Click on the Circle layer to make it active.

4. Use the Oval tool to make a red circle partially on top of the rectangle. Notice the circle covers up part of the rectangle.
5. Click on the Background layer and drag it above the Circle layer. Figure 5.5 shows the Background layer above the Circle layer.

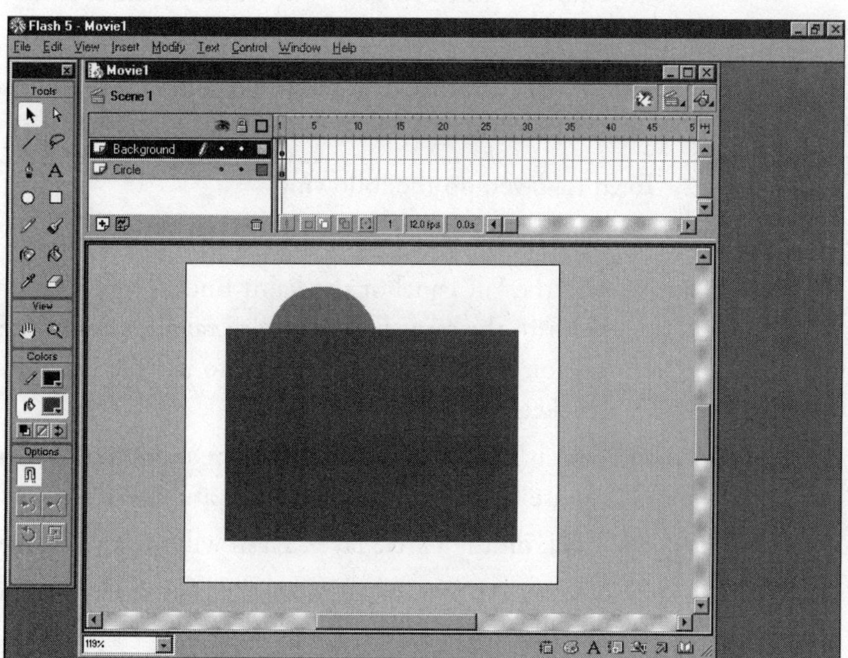

Figure 5.5

The rectangle now covers part of the circle.

By rearranging the order of the layers you can bring elements to the foreground, move them to the back, or hide them completely behind other elements.

Editing on a Layer

Editing layers is the meat and potatoes of Flash animation. Most of your time will be spent on individual layers, creating and modifying your drawings. Familiarity with layer editing is a must. Luckily, you already know how to edit a layer—you've been doing it since Friday night!

During the earlier sessions you created text, shapes, and fills on a single layer. To edit a multi-layer movie all you have to do is select the layer you want to edit, then make changes. Sound simple? It is!

To edit a layer, do the following:

1. Select the Circle layer. The red circle has been selected on the stage.
2. Use the Fill Panel or the Paint Bucket tool to change the circle's color to the same blue as the rectangle. (Refer to Saturday night's session if you've forgotten how to use the Fill Panel and the Paint Bucket tool.)
3. Select Edit, Deselect All from the menu bar to deselect the circle. Figure 5.6 shows the blue circle and the rectangle.
4. Click on the Circle layer. Flash will select the blue circle.
5. Use the Arrow tool to move the blue circle outside the rectangle, as in Figure 5.7.

Now you've seen firsthand the advantage of using layers. Remember the cheese from the third session? If the two shapes were on the same layer the circle would have merged with the rectangle and you would be back to the drawing board (or the drawing *tools*, as the case may be). With the shapes on different layers they can be preserved and edited individually. What a time-saver!

Figure 5.6

The circle and rectangle appear as a single mass.

Figure 5.7

The circle is now outside the rectangle.

Deleting a layer

Nobody gets everything perfectly right every time. You might realize that a snake is not the best mascot for a law firm or that no matter how much you love it, that groovy paisley background has got to go. Regardless of what you're working on, the ability to delete layers will come in handy.

To delete a layer, follow these steps:

1. Click the layer you want to delete.
2. Click the Delete Layer button, shown in Figure 5.8.

Or

1. Right-click (Ctrl+click on the Mac) the layer and select Delete Layer.

Figure 5.8

The Delete Layer button

CAUTION Deleted layers are gone for good. You should only delete layers you are absolutely sure you won't want in the final movie.

The next section explains how to hide a layer rather than deleting it.

Hiding and Locking Layers

Not all layers are created equal. Say you spend three hours getting that abominable snowman just perfect and ten seconds drawing a white snowbank. Which layer is more important? Will both layers be visible throughout the entire movie? Hiding and locking layers are important skills you'll need as your movie goes from a simple animation to a multi-layer Flash extravaganza.

Hiding a layer will allow you to make that snowman disappear without having to cover it up or—*gasp*—delete its layer. To hide a layer, follow these steps:

1. Select the layer you want to hide.
2. Right-click (Ctrl+click on the Mac)the layer and select Properties.
3. Uncheck Show and click OK.

Or

1. Click the dot beside the layer name and below the eye graphic.

A red x appears beside the layer name, as shown in Figure 5.9.

NOTE Elements on hidden layers cannot be edited. To edit the rectangle on the Background layer, unhide the layer, make the changes, and then hide the layer again.

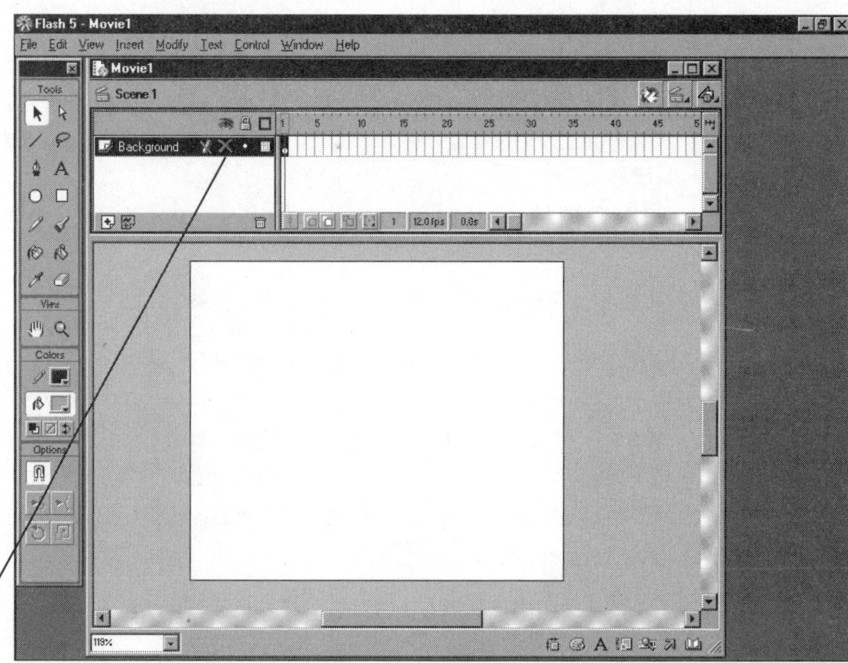

Figure 5.9

The X shows that the Background layer is hidden.

Unhiding a Layer

Unhiding a layer is just as easy:

1. Select the layer you want to unhide.
2. Right-click (Ctrl+click on the Mac) the layer and select Properties.
3. Check Show and click OK.

Or

1. Click on the red x beside the layer name. The layer name will reappear.

Locking and Unlocking a Layer

You wouldn't want to accidentally mangle your snowman after all the time you've put into him, would you? Luckily, Flash 5 lets you lock a layer to prevent just such a desecration.

To lock a layer, follow these steps:

1. Select the layer you want to lock.
2. Right-click (Ctrl+click on the Mac) the layer and select Properties.
3. Check Lock and click OK.

Or

1. Click the dot beside the layer name and below the padlock graphic.

A padlock image appears beside the layer name, as shown in Figure 5.10.

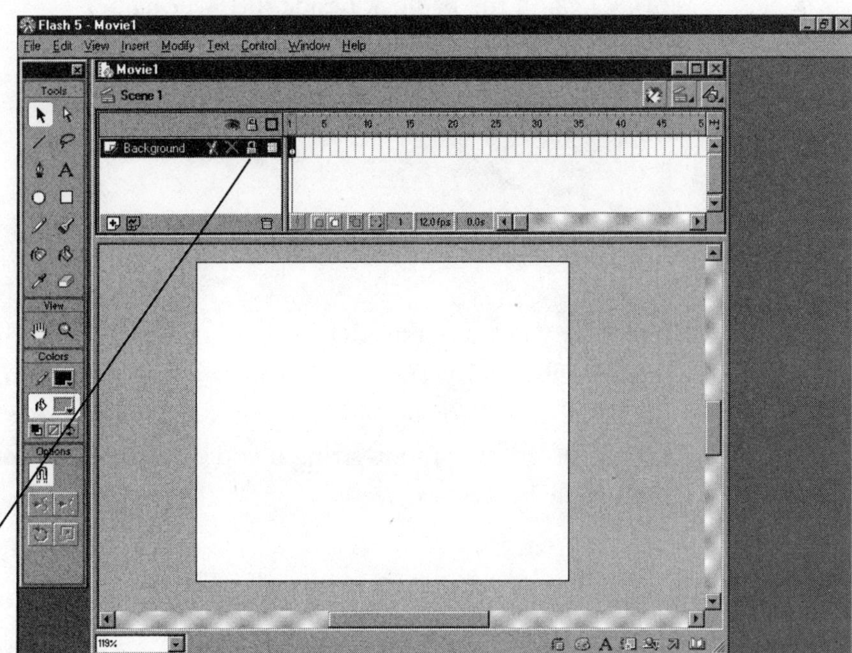

Figure 5.10

The padlock shows that the Background layer is locked and hidden.

Select the locked layer and try to make a change on the stage. Flash will let you know that the layer is locked (see Figure 5.11). To unlock a layer, follow these steps:

1. Select the layer you want to unlock.
2. Right-click (Ctrl+click on the Mac) on the layer and select Properties.
3. Uncheck Lock and click OK.

Or

1. Click on the padlock beside the layer name.

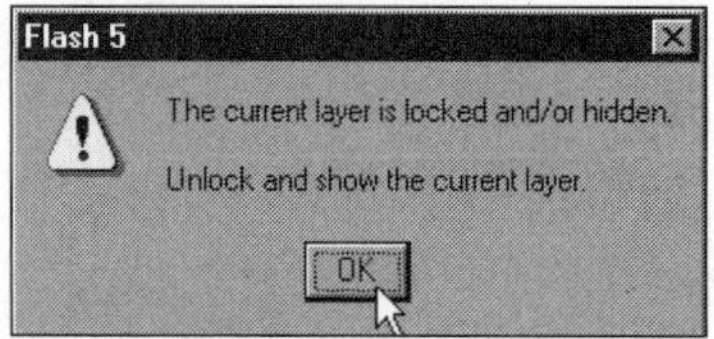

Figure 5.11

Unlock the layer before making any changes.

Now that you know the advantages of using layers and how to work with them in Flash 5, you're well on your way to creating that first Flash animation. Before moving on to the next section, save your project file (or simply discard it without saving if you don't want it). You will start a new project file in the next section.

Using Scenes

Can you imagine what your favorite movies would be like if the scenes never changed? The *Titanic* would never have hit an iceberg if it couldn't leave the dock, the Death Star would still be destroying planets if the plans never left Tatooine, and Dorothy would never have met the Wizard if she hadn't left Kansas.

Scenes in Flash are a way to change the setting and leave out the extra elements that might clutter up the new scene. Organization is the name of the game with scenes. While it's possible to create a complex animation using only one scene, after you see what scenes can do, you won't want to.

Creating Scenes

Each scene you create in Flash 5 effectively doubles your animation. Adding scenes allows you to preserve the layers and frames on which you've worked so hard, yet still have a clear slate from which to work.

Open a new movie by selecting File, New from the menu bar, and use the Movie Properties dialog box to create a stage that fits comfortably in your workspace. Figure 5.12 shows a new movie; take a look at the area above the Layers Panel. Notice that the words "Scene 1" appear below the movie title. Surprise! As with layers, you've been using scenes all along!

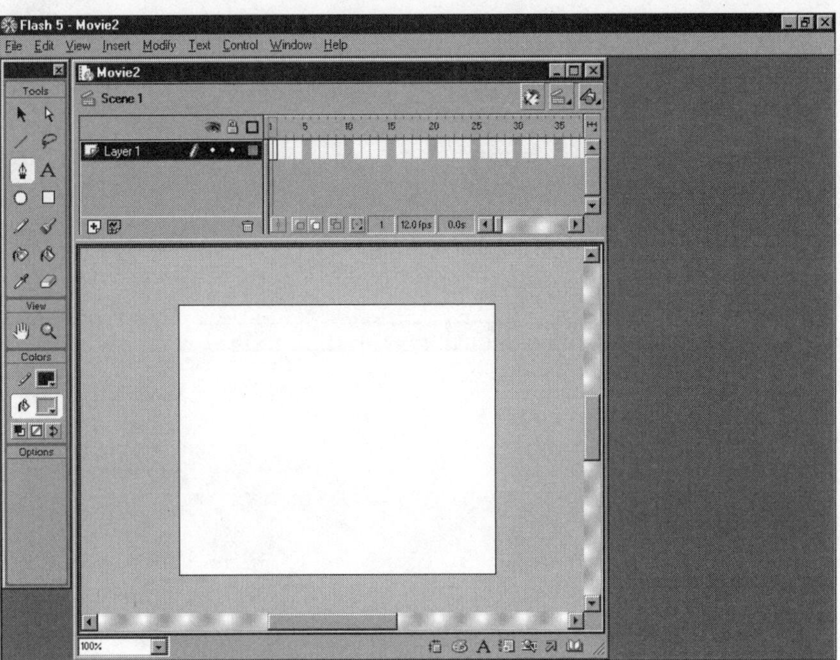

Figure 5.12

A new movie file and Scene 1

You should create a new scene for each setting in your movie. To create a new scene, do the following:

1. Select Window, Panels, Scene from the menu bar. The Scene Panel will appear on the right side of your screen, as shown in Figure 5.13.
2. Click + on the Scene Panel.

Or

1. Select Insert, Scene from the menu bar.

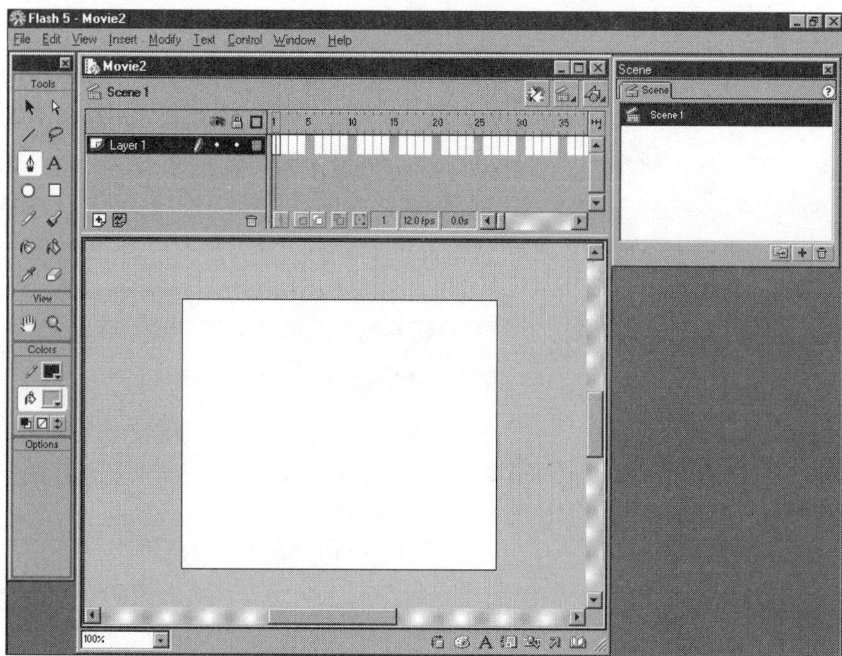

Figure 5.13

A Scene Panel

A new scene will be created and the scene name, "Scene 2," will appear. Notice that the stage and layers are all empty. Fear not! Your movie is still there—it's just on another scene.

NOTE You can use the Duplicate Scene button on the Scene Panel to copy a scene. The stage and all the layers will be copied to the new scene.

Changing Scenes

To change scenes, do the following:

1. Select Window, Panels, Scene from the menu bar.
2. In the Scene Panel, click the name of the scene you would like to edit.

Or

1. Click the Edit Scene button, as shown in Figure 5.14, and select the scene you would like to edit.

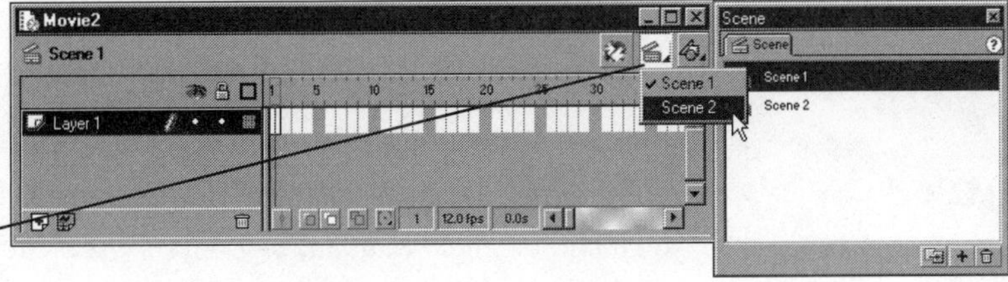

Figure 5.14

The Edit Scene button

Deleting a scene

Deleting a scene is just as easy as creating one. To delete a scene, follow these steps:

1. Select Window, Panels, Scene from the menu bar.
2. Click the Trashcan button on the Scene Panel, as shown in Figure 5.15.

Or

1. Select Insert, Remove Scene from the menu bar.

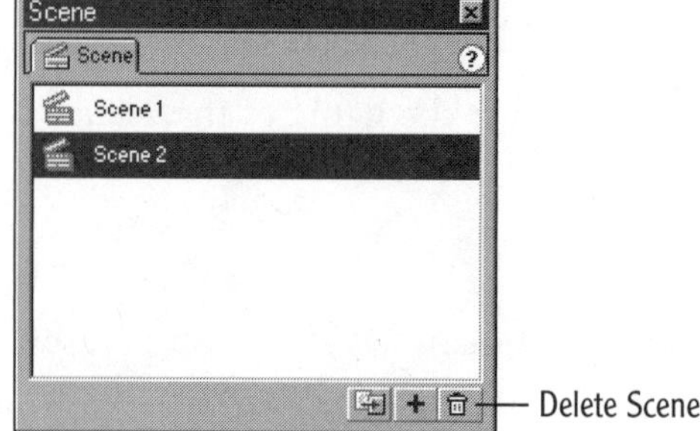

Figure 5.15

The Trashcan button

The Scene will be deleted.

Deleted scenes, like layers, are gone for good. Consider carefully before deleting a scene—and if you think you might want any of its layers elsewhere, make sure you have copies of them.

Renaming and Reordering Scenes

Of course, the makers of Flash 5 have given you the ability to rename and reorder scenes just like with layers. It's just as easy too!

To rename a scene, follow these steps:

1. Select Window, Panels, Scene from the menu bar.
2. Double-click the scene name.
3. Type in a new name and click on the stage.

Figure 5.16 shows the scene with a new name.

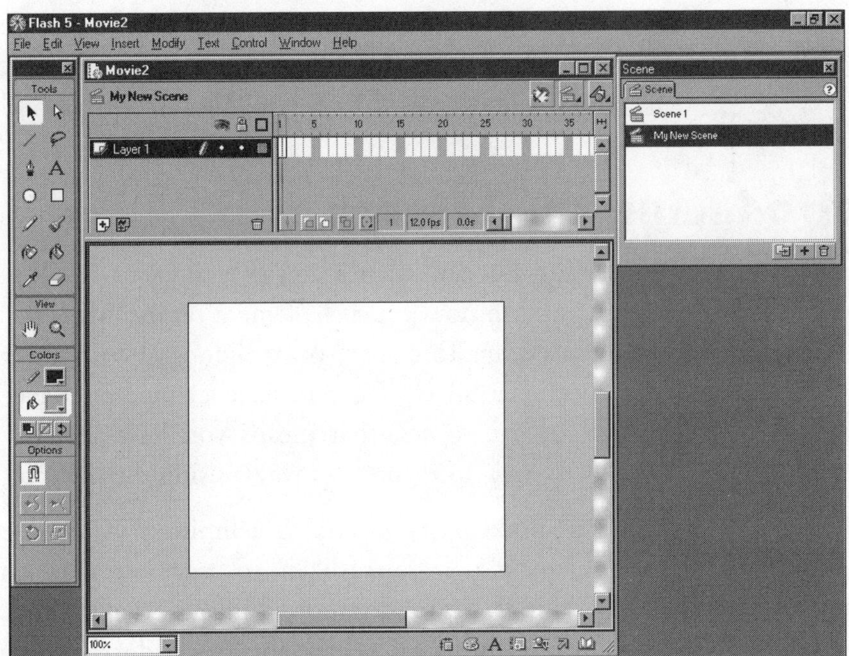

Figure 5.16

My New Scene

To reorder your scenes, follow these steps:

1. Click the scene in the Scene Panel.
2. Drag the scene to a new location.

Scenes are quite the organizer. You'll come back to them this evening. Before moving on to the next section, you can save your project file or simply discard it without saving.

Take a Break

Now that you know how to organize your Flash 5 movie using layers and scenes, it's a good time to take a quick break. Read the comics or check the score of the game, but don't linger too long. When you get back you'll be breaking new ground with symbols and the Flash library.

Introducing the Library

By using layers and scenes you've learned to organize your movie elements; you can now put each element on its own layer and create a scene for each setting. To change your Bigfoot into an abominable snowman, you know that all you have to do is change one layer in each scene. If you've got five scenes, that means you have to edit five layers, right? Wrong! There's an even easier way—using the library.

You can think of the library as a limitless warehouse of movie props. Every element that you're likely to use more than once can be placed there—sounds, buttons, imported images, movie clips, and drawings can all go into the library. The elements you add to the library are called *symbols.* Your library keeps track of where you've used your symbols, and you can edit each appearance of the symbol individually or all instances at once—even the ones that appear on locked layers in a scene.

Think of the effect this has. You can create a symbol for the abominable snowman you created and place the symbol in the library. Then, every time your movie needs a monster, you can just drag and drop from the library. When you edit your abominable snowman the library will make the changes appear movie-wide. Fantastic!

Library symbols are the building blocks of any good Flash animation. In the next two sessions you'll be using the library to create buttons, add sounds, and put together your first animated flash movie.

Common Libraries

Flash 5 comes with a number of built-in, or *common,* libraries. These common libraries are chock-full of free symbols you can use to jump-start your flash movie.

Flash 5 comes with six common libraries:

- **Buttons.** Contains a large number of pre-built buttons. You'll learn more about buttons in the next session.
- **Graphics.** Contains a few sample graphics, including the hip mouse image you'll use in a few minutes.
- **Learning Interactions.** This library contains quite a few sample interactive symbols. Each symbol includes instructions for its use.

The Learning Interactions library is a great place to start if you are interested in picking up more advanced Flash 5 techniques.

- **Movie Clips.** Contains two movie clips. Movie clips are animated symbols.
- **Smart Clips.** This library contains ready-to-go movie clips for Flash forms, such as radio buttons, check boxes, and drop-down menus.
- **Sounds.** Contains a wealth of free sound bites for your movie.

FIND IT ON THE WEB For hundreds of freeware sound files and tons of other Flash resources, check out Internet.com's Flashkit (http://www.flashkit.com/).

To open a common library, follow these steps:

1. Open a new movie by selecting File, New from the menu bar, and then use the Movie Properties dialog box to create a stage that fits comfortably in your workspace.
2. Select Window, Common Libraries, Graphics from the menu bar. The Graphics Library Panel will open, as shown in Figure 5.17.

Go ahead and close the Graphics Library by clicking the close icon at the top of the panel. You'll get back to the Graphics Library later, but right now you get to create your own library.

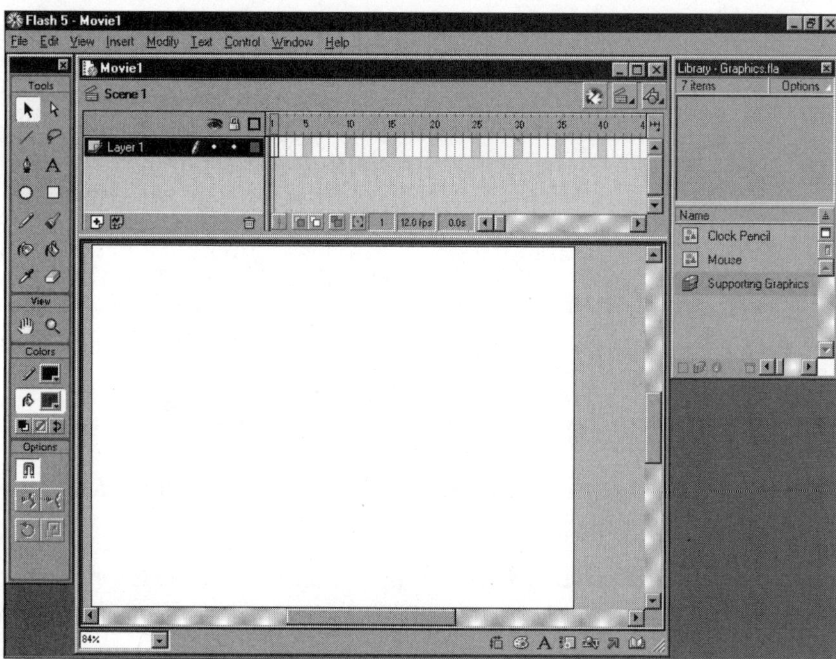

Figure 5.17

The Graphics Library Panel

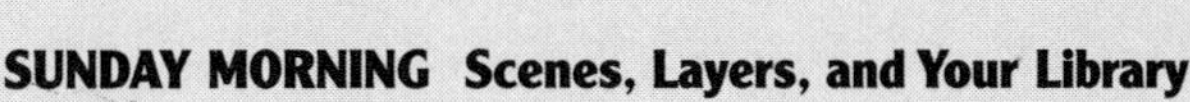

Creating and Organizing Your Own Libraries

Unfortunately, you can't add, edit, or delete symbols in common libraries; you're stuck with the symbols Macromedia included. However, you can create your own library and organize it any way you want. You can even share your libraries between movies.

Adding and Deleting Symbols

Adding symbols to your library is the first and easiest step in creating a useful library. To create a new symbol, follow these steps:

1. Open the Library Panel by selecting Window, Library from the menu bar. Alternatively, you can click the Show Library button in the Launcher bar at the bottom of the screen (Figure 5.18).

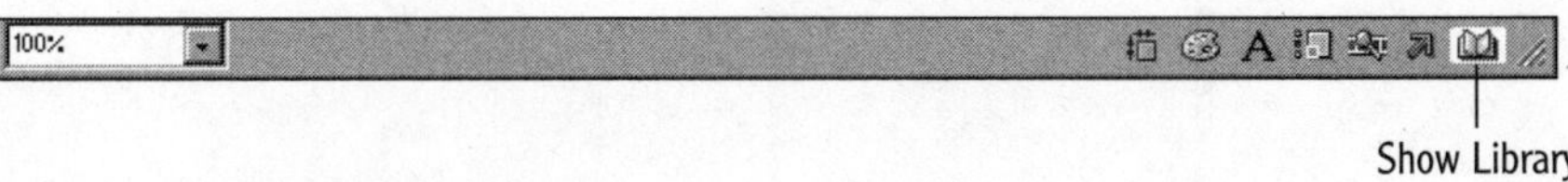

Figure 5.18

The Show Library button on the Launcher bar.

2. Click + on the Library Panel or select Insert, New Symbol from the menu bar. The Symbol Properties dialog box will open (see Figure 5.19).
3. In the Symbol Properties dialog box type a name for your new symbol.
4. For Behavior, select Graphic and click OK. (Don't worry, it won't make you blush.)

Figure 5.19

The Symbol Properties dialog box

Deleting symbols from your library is done in much the same way. To delete a symbol from your library, follow these steps:

1. Open the Library Panel if it is not already open. You can use the Ctrl+L (Command+L on the Mac) key combination.
2. Select the symbol you want to delete.
3. Click the Trashcan button at the bottom of the Library panel, as shown in Figure 5.20.
4. A dialog box will appear asking if you are sure you want to delete the symbol. Click Delete to remove the symbol or Cancel if you change your mind.

Figure 5.20

The Trashcan button

Renaming a Symbol

A large Flash animation can consist of dozens of symbols. Keeping these symbols organized will be important if you want to avoid a lot of hair-pulling confusion. Flash 5 keeps the symbols ordered alphabetically, but you can rename symbols to keep up with your changing animation.

To rename a symbol, do the following:

1. Open the Library Panel, if it is not already open.
2. Double-click the symbol you want to rename.
3. Type a new name, as in Figure 5.21.
4. Press Enter (Return on the Mac).

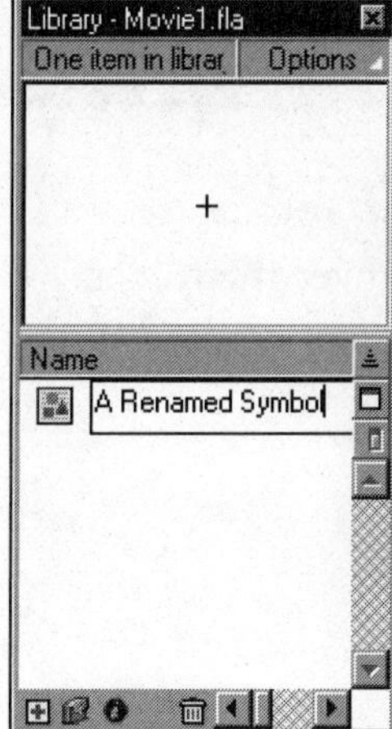

Figure 5.21

A renamed symbol called (for clarity's sake) "A Renamed Symbol"

Creating a Folder and Moving Symbols

You can also create folders in your library. Each folder can contain groups of related symbols. To create a folder in your library, do the following:

1. Open the Library Panel, if it is not already open.
2. Click the New Folder button (Figure 5.22) on the Library Panel.
3. Type a name for your folder.
4. Press Enter (Return on the Mac).

Move your symbol into the folder by following these steps:

1. Click the symbol you want to move.

NOTE You can select multiple symbols by holding down the Ctrl (Command on the Mac) key as you select each symbol.

2. Drag the symbol into the folder. You can see in Figure 5.22 how the arrow changes when you're over the folder.

You can toggle between collapsed and expanded display by double-clicking on the folder in the Library Panel.

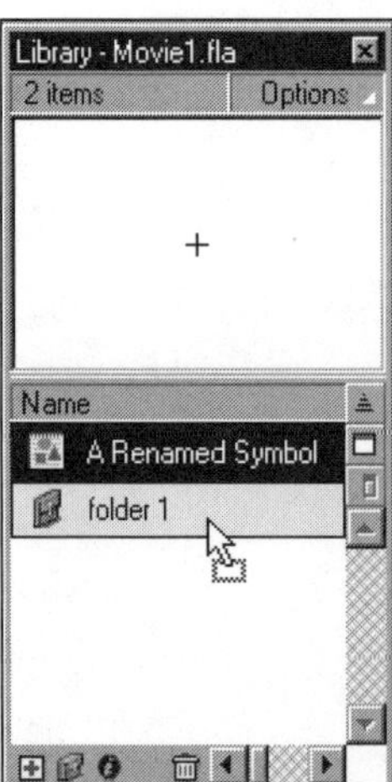

Figure 5.22

Moving a symbol into a folder

Sharing Libraries

One of the coolest benefits of the library is the ability to share the same symbols across multiple movies. By sharing your libraries you can make a change just once and be done with it. Flash 5 will modify all instances of the symbol in each movie that shares the library. In one fell swoop you can change *Bigfoot Laces Up* and *Bigfoot Marches On* into *Wanna Yeti?* and *Snowman Knows Me Like You.*

To designate a shared library, follow these steps:

1. Open the Library Panel if it is not already open.
2. Select the symbol you want to share.
3. Select Linkage from the Library Panel's Options menu (see Figure 5.23). The Symbol Linkage dialog box will open (see Figure 5.24).

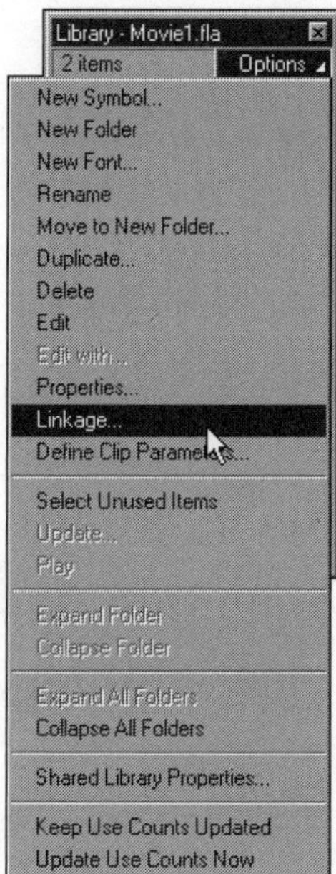

Figure 5.23

The Library Panel's Options menu with Linkage selected

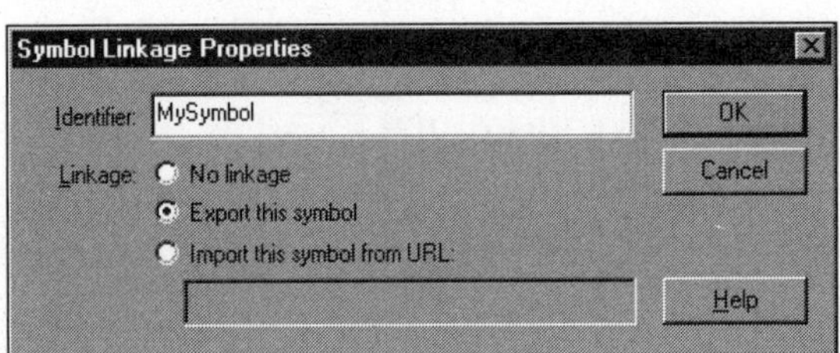

Figure 5.24

The Symbol Linkage dialog box

4. Select Export This Symbol from the Symbol Linkage dialog box.
5. Type a name for the symbol in the Identifier text box. Use letters and numbers only—no spaces or special characters such as "&" or "#."
6. Click OK. The Symbol Linkage dialog box will close.
7. Save your movie.
8. Publish your movie in standalone format. (Refer to the Saturday afternoon session if you've forgotten how).

Linked symbols will not function when you test a movie unless you have previously published the movie with the shared library.

9. Close your movie.

Linking Symbols

Now that you have designated a shared library, follow these steps to link the symbols to another movie:

1. Open a new movie.
2. Open the Library Panel.
3. Select File, Open As Shared Library from the menu bar, as shown in Figure 5.25.

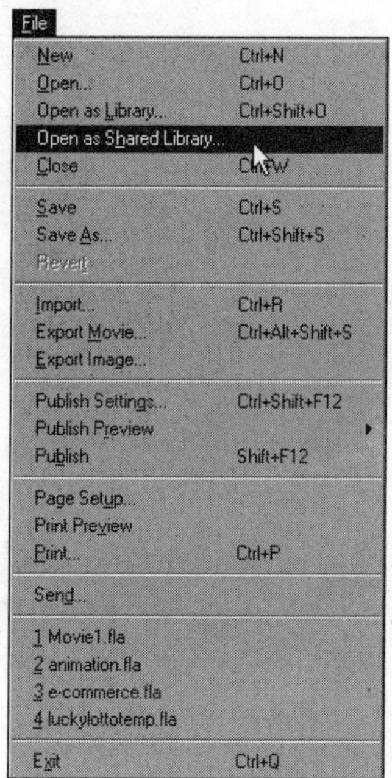

Figure 5.25

File menu with Open As Shared Library selected

4. Navigate to the movie file with the shared library and click Open.
5. Select a symbol from the shared library (see Figure 5.26).
6. Drag the symbol into the new library.

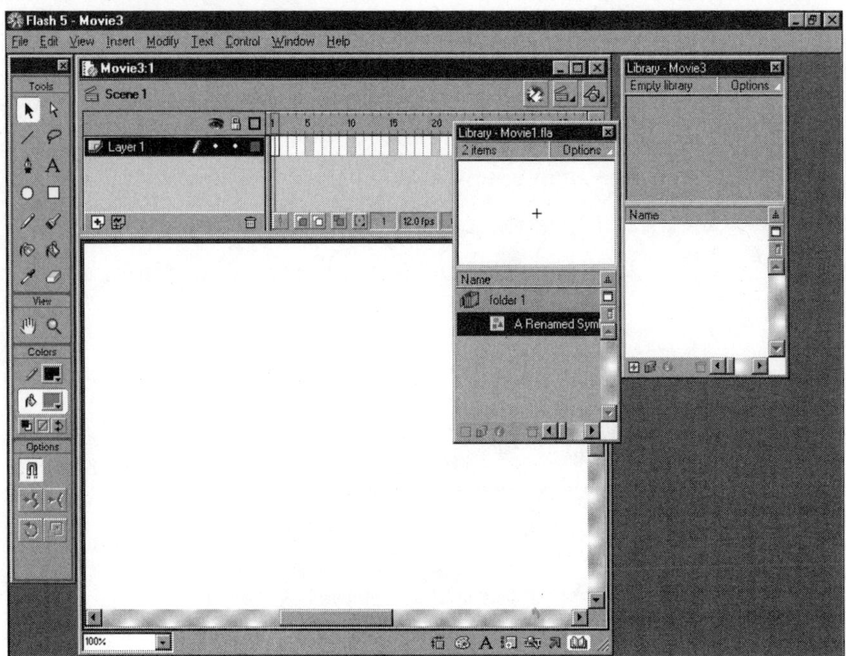

Figure 5.26

Linking a shared symbol

7. Save the new movie to the same directory as the first. The symbol will be linked.

Any changes made to the symbol in the first movie will be automatically applied in the second. Now that you know how symbols work in the library, you'll see how much better they do on the stage.

Using Symbols

So far you've created, renamed, organized, and linked symbols, but you haven't actually *used* them. Think of it this way: you've laid out the plans, bought all the nails and wood, gathered your tools, and dug the foundation, but now it's time to raise the barn!

Flash offers six basic types of symbols:

- **Movie Clips.** These are animated images that use a timeline independent of the movie. In other words, when placed on the stage they continue to wiggle around (or do whatever they do) even when the rest of the movie has stopped.
- **Buttons.** These symbols are used for interacting with the user. Buttons are capable of changing shape or color based on the mouse actions of the user. The next session gives you a chance to work with Buttons.
- **Graphics.** These symbols can be animated or still. If animated, graphics symbols use the same timeline as the rest of the movie.
- **Sounds.** Each sound file used in the movie is automatically added to the library as a sound symbol.
- **Bitmaps.** Flash 5 uses mathematical calculations, or vector graphics, to draw its images. This keeps the file size of Flash movies very low. Bitmaps, or *raster images,* are drawn in other imaging programs such as Photoshop or PaintShopPro. Raster images are defined pixel-by-pixel. This makes raster images far larger in size, but also more versatile than vector graphics. Imported raster images will appear in the library as bitmap symbols.
- **Fonts.** It is possible to add fonts as symbols and link to these fonts from other movie files. This can help avoid font installation problems when sharing files across multiple machines, but is beyond the scope of this book.

FIND IT ON **THE WEB**

If you are interested in learning more about font symbols visit Macromedia's Flash Support Center (http://www.macromedia.com/support/flash/ts/documents/sharedfonts.htm).

Placing Symbols in Your Movie

Symbols need a stage in order to perform. Happily, moving symbols onto the stage is just click-and-drag operation. To place a symbol in your movie, follow these steps:

1. Open a new movie.
2. Select Window, Common Libraries, Graphics from the menu bar. The Graphics Library will open.
3. Click the Mouse symbol and drag it onto the stage (see Figure 5.27).

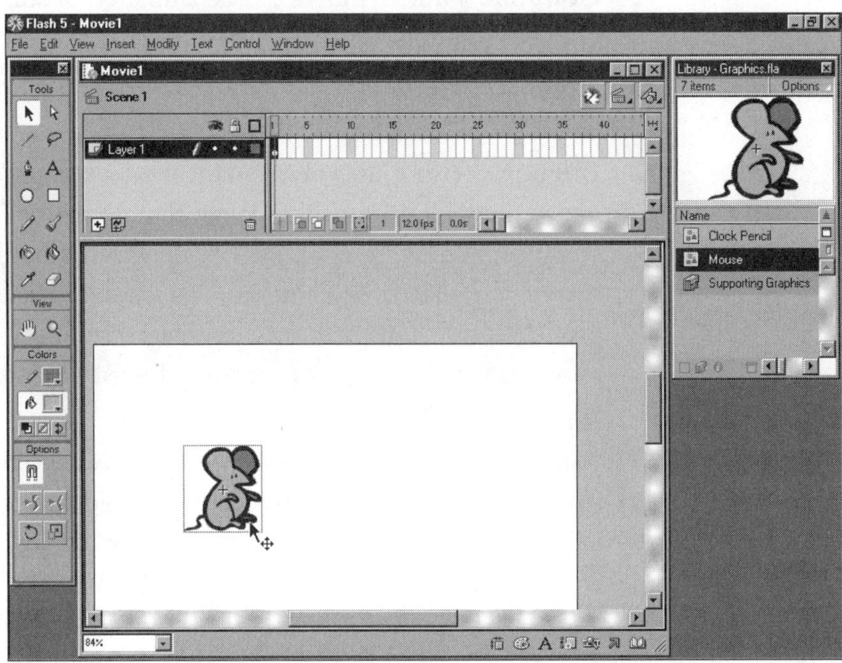

Figure 5.27

One mouse, not stirring

Editing Symbols

Here you'll find out why symbols are such a time-saver. You can edit multiple symbols at once by following these steps:

1. Drag a few more mice onto the stage.
2. Right-click (Ctrl+click on the Mac) on one mouse and select Edit. The mouse moves to the center and the rest of the stage clears, as shown in Figure 5.28. Notice the symbol image and name above the Layer Panel. This informs you that you are editing the Mouse symbol.

Figure 5.28

Editing the Mouse symbol

3. Use the Arrow tool to rotate the mouse a few degrees clockwise.
4. Click Scene 1 (above the Layers Panel) to return to the movie.

Remember that edits to the symbol appear wherever it is used, whether in scenes, on invisible and locked layers, or inside linked movies.

All the mice now lean to the right (Figure 5.29).

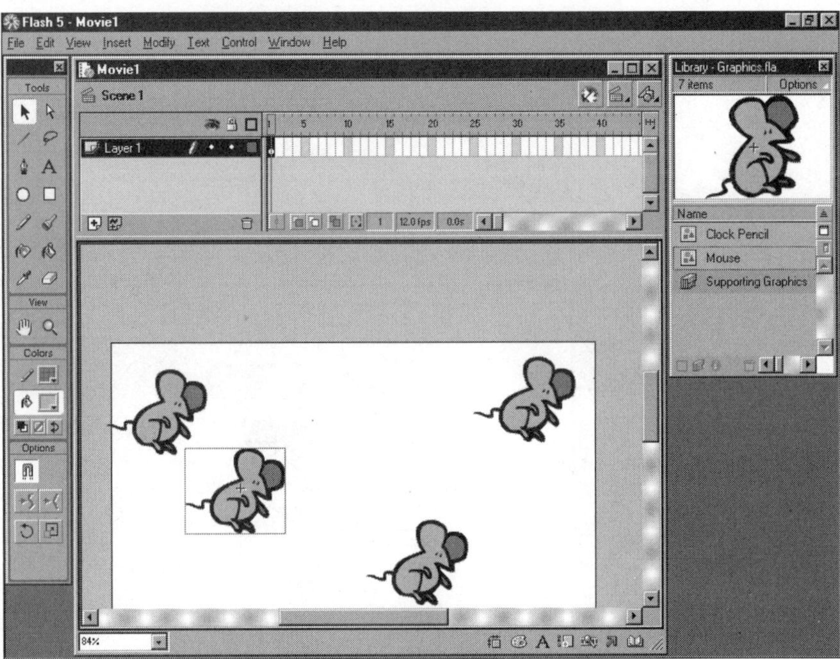

Figure 5.29

Massive Mouse tilt

You can also edit each symbol separately:

1. Click the Arrow tool.
2. Click a mouse. The blue border lets you know that the image is a symbol.
3. Rotate and scale the mouse directly on the stage.
4. Deselect the mouse. Only one mouse will change (see Figure 5.30).

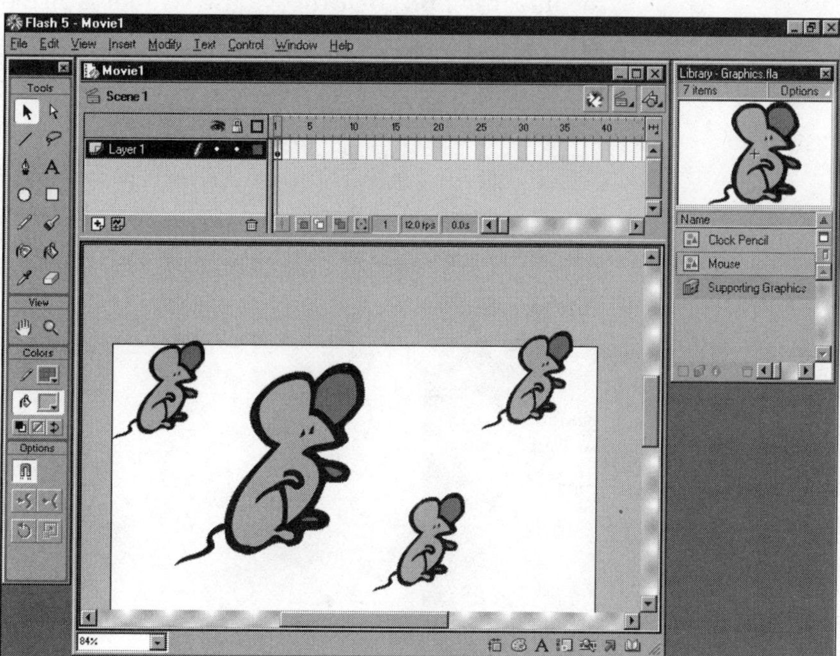

Figure 5.30

The mouse king and his subjects

Editing a Symbol in the Library

You can also edit a symbol directly in the library, without adding it to the stage. Common libraries are not editable, so you will need to have a copy of a symbol in your own library if you want to play with it. Happily, Flash takes care of that for you. To edit a symbol in the library, do the following:

1. Open the Library Panel by selecting Window, Library from the menu bar. Notice that the Mouse symbol is already in the library. All symbols that you place in a movie are automatically added to the library.
2. Click the Mouse symbol in the library.
3. Select Options, Edit from the Library Panel's menu bar (see Figure 5.31).

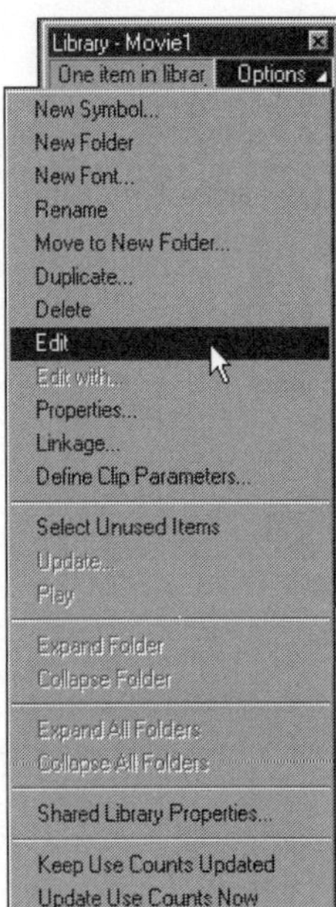

Figure 5.31

Selecting Edit from the Options menu

4. Use the Arrow tool to skew the mouse vertically.
5. Click Scene 1 (above the Layers Panel) to return to the movie.

Notice that even the large mouse that was edited individually has been skewed (see Figure 5.32).

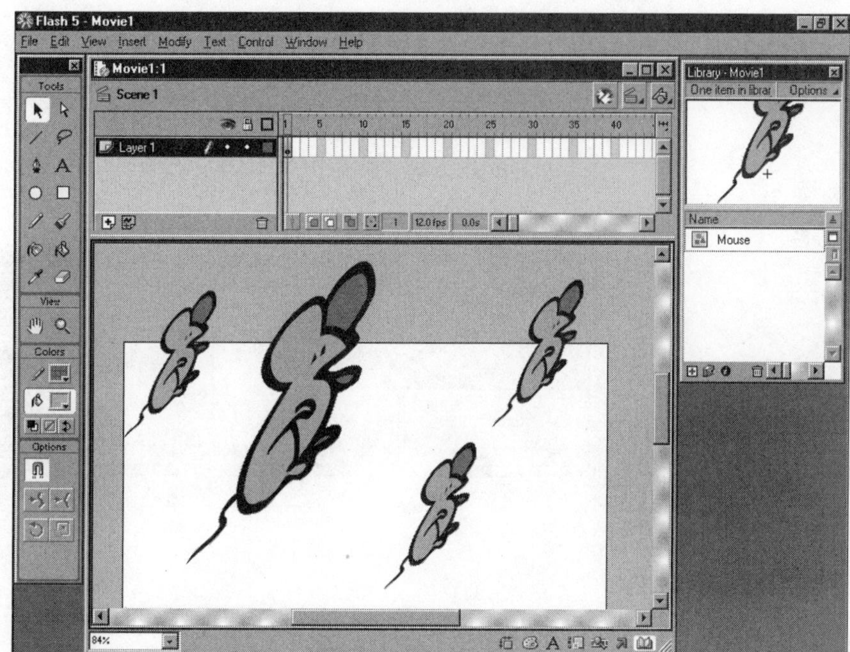

Figure 5.32

We all skew together.

Creating Symbols from Objects

You may not always know ahead of time what objects will be symbols in your movie. Sometimes you will want to convert objects you've drawn on the stage into symbols for the library.

To convert an object to a symbol, follow these steps:

1. Open a new movie and adjust the stage to fit comfortably on your screen.
2. Using the drawing tools described in previous sessions, draw an object, such as an abominable snowman (Figure 5.33).

Figure 5.33

Not Frosty, but he ain't that abominable, now is he?

3. Use the Arrow tool to select the entire object.
4. From the menu bar select Insert, Convert To Symbol, or press F8. The Symbol Properties box will open (see Figure 5.33).
5. Name your symbol and select the Graphic option under Behavior.
6. Click OK.

Figure 5.34

The Symbol Properties dialog box in use for The Abominable Snowman

Open the Library Panel and you'll notice your symbol listed. Now whenever your movie needs a monster you can use this symbol. Feel free to save your file or close without saving.

What's Next

Hold on to your keyboard—this afternoon you'll really make a Flash 5 move! The session helps you learn all about keyframes, tweening, frame rates, and timelines. Those words may all seem like gobbledygook now, but by this evening it'll all mean one thing, animation! (Well, OK, you can put down your keyboard and get some lunch first….)

SUNDAY AFTERNOON

All About Animation

- Creating Keyframes and Your Timeline
- Adjusting Frame Rates and Other Technicalities
- Tweening Color, Size, and Rotation
- Position Motion Tweening
- Shape Tweening
- Button, Button, Who's Got the Button?

So far, you've learned how to use Flash 5's tools to create and organize still graphics. Well, now it's time to get moving, literally! This afternoon I explain the basics of animation and show how to use the animation tools. You'll learn the difference between limited, or *cut-out* animation, and fluid *frame-by-frame* animation, as well as when each should be used. You'll also discover how easy it is to create awesome animated buttons.

This session will introduce quite a lot of new terms and concepts. They may seem overwhelming at first, but remember how intimidating the Flash 5 application looked when you first opened it? Now it doesn't seem all that scary, does it? By this evening you'll be creating all-star animations all on your own.

It's hard to miss animation. You've no doubt seen examples ranging from Disney's multimillion-dollar feature films to simple e-mail greeting cards. Did you know, however, that animation techniques were used in *Star Wars, The Matrix,* and many other of your favorite sci-fi movies? In fact, any film that uses computer-generated (CG) effects includes animation. Most modern CG special effects are nothing more than the merging of high-quality graphics with live footage. The special effects masters of Hollywood try to blend CG effects into a film so seamlessly that the line between animation and live action seems to disappear.

So where *is* the line? What makes animation different from live action? What ties all animation together? Some cartoons are drawn, others use clay figures, live models, or computer graphics. The key is that all animators create movies using still pictures. These individual pictures, called *frames,* appear very quickly, one after another. As the frames flash past, the eyes' in-built delay—called *persistence of vision*— creates an optical illusion that the images are actually moving.

NOTE Every movie you see in the theater is actually a kind of animation. Millions of still images are printed on a flexible film, which is still called "celluloid" even though it's been many years since real cellulose-based (and explosively flammable) celluloid was used for the purpose. The images are then projected very rapidly one by one onto the theater screen.

Learning Flash animation is all about understanding frames. Much like the pages of a flipbook, Flash frame images gradually change as the movie progresses. Each frame holds a slightly different picture from the preceding frame.

Creating Keyframes and Your Timeline

A great advantage to using Flash 5 is that the application takes a lot of the work out of animation. Rather than adjusting each frame of your movie individually, you can designate special working frames, or *keyframes,* and have Flash automatically create the animation between them. For example: to have a ball move across the screen you could place a keyframe with the ball to the left of the stage and another keyframe with the ball on the right. You can then have Flash create all the frames in between these keyframes. This process is called *tweening.*

You will tween color, shape, size, position, and opacity in a few minutes, but first you need to learn the basics of how to use keyframes.

Using Keyframes

Open a new movie by selecting File, New from the menu bar, and use the Movie Properties dialog box to create a stage that fits comfortably in your workspace. Notice the area above the stage and to the right of the Layers Panel? This is the timeline (see Figure 6.1). Each frame and keyframe in your movie is numbered and given a symbolic box, like a frame on a strip of film. The red line indicates the current position in the timeline, and the stage displays the frame for that position.

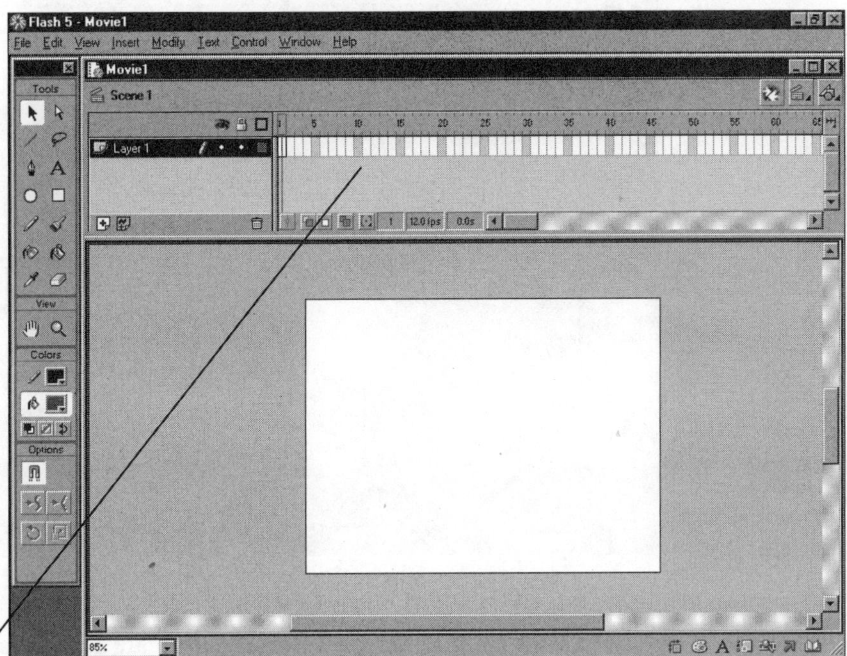

Figure 6.1

The timeline

To create a new keyframe in the timeline, do the following:

1. Double-click on Layer 1 and rename it "Animation."
2. Click the first rectangle in the timeline on the Animation layer (Figure 6.2). Frame 1 will be highlighted.
3. Select Insert, Keyframe from the menu bar or press F6.

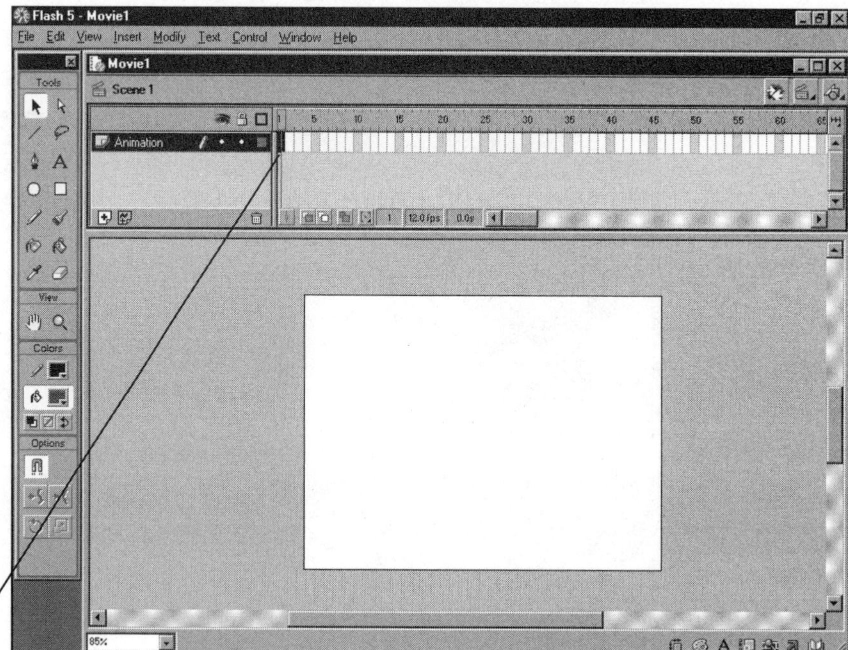

Figure 6.2

Frame 1 of the Animation layer

A border appears around frame 1 to indicate that it is now a keyframe. The timeline advances one frame.

To see how keyframes affect animation, follow these steps:

1. Click on frame 1 in the timeline.
2. Use the Oval and Pencil tools to draw a smiley face on the stage.
3. Right-click (Ctrl+click on the Mac) on frame 5 and select Insert Keyframe, as shown in Figure 6.3.

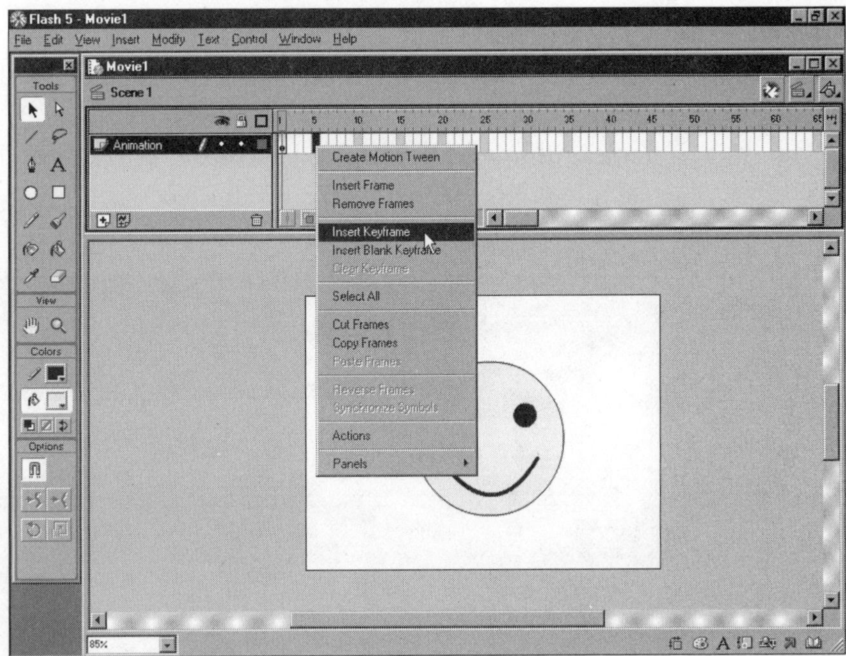

Figure 6.3

Inserting a keyframe at frame 5

NOTE Standard keyframes automatically add the contents of the stage from the frame before. To add a keyframe with a blank stage, select Insert Blank Keyframe.

4. Use the Oval tool to add a nose to your smiley face at frame 5.
5. Click on the timeline above frame 1 to move the animation to the beginning of the movie.
6. Press Enter (Return on the Mac) to advance the timeline.

As the movie progresses through the timeline you can see that the nose appears only when the movie reaches frame 5.

Changing the Stage at Keyframes

Flash 5 allows you to make edits or changes to the stage only on keyframes. Go ahead and try to select just frame 3. Figure 6.4 shows frames 1 through 4 are selected instead. If you made a change on the stage like this all four frames would be affected.

Figure 6.4

Frames 1 through 4 selected

When you need to make a change in your movie at frame 3 you can insert a new keyframe. To insert a keyframe between frames 1 and 5, follow these steps:

1. Click on the timeline above frame 3 to move the animation to that frame (see Figure 6.5). The red bar moves to frame 3.
2. Select Insert, Keyframe from the menu bar, or press F6.

Figure 6.5

The timeline at frame 3

A new keyframe has been created at frame 3. You can now make changes on the stage that will appear when the movie reaches that frame.

Clearing a Keyframe

If you change your mind and would like the movie to move directly from frame 1 to 5 you can clear the keyframe on frame 3.

To clear a keyframe, follow these steps:

1. Select the keyframe you wish to clear.
2. Select Insert, Clear Keyframe from the menu bar or press Shift+F6.

Before moving on to the next section, you should save your project file or quit without saving. You start a new project in the next section.

Adjusting Frame Rates and Other Technicalities

Some movies are fast-paced thrillers; others are slow, plodding narratives. Most are somewhere in between. The speed of the animation is determined by the frame rate.

The frame rate is measured in how many frames per second (fps) are shown on the stage. A movie will show a dozen frames every second at 12 fps and two dozen at 24 fps. Of course, you could create a 10 fps movie with 10 frames showing a piano falling off a building and the animation would appear to play at the same speed as a 20 fps movie where the piano takes 20 frames to hit the ground.

Changing the Animation Speed

You can adjust the animation speed by changing the frame rate of your Flash 5 movie. To change the frame rate, follow these steps:

1. Open a new movie.
2. Select Modify, Movie from the menu bar. The Movie Properties dialog box will open.
3. Adjust the movie dimensions as you've done in the past, but don't click OK yet. As you can see the default frame rate is 12 frames per second (fps).
4. Change the frame rate to 24, as in Figure 6.6. This will make the movie play twice as fast.
5. Click OK.

NOTE 12 fps should work just fine for most movies. Be careful about how you adjust the frame rate—too fast and viewers may miss parts of your animation, too slow and the movie will seem herky-jerky.

Figure 6.6

Setting the speed to 24 fps

Stop and take a closer look at the timeline in Figure 6.7. As you can see, the new frame rate is displayed at the bottom of the timeline. Next to the frame rate is the current frame number and the elapsed time in seconds for the movie. The scrollbar on the timeline can help you navigate through your frames.

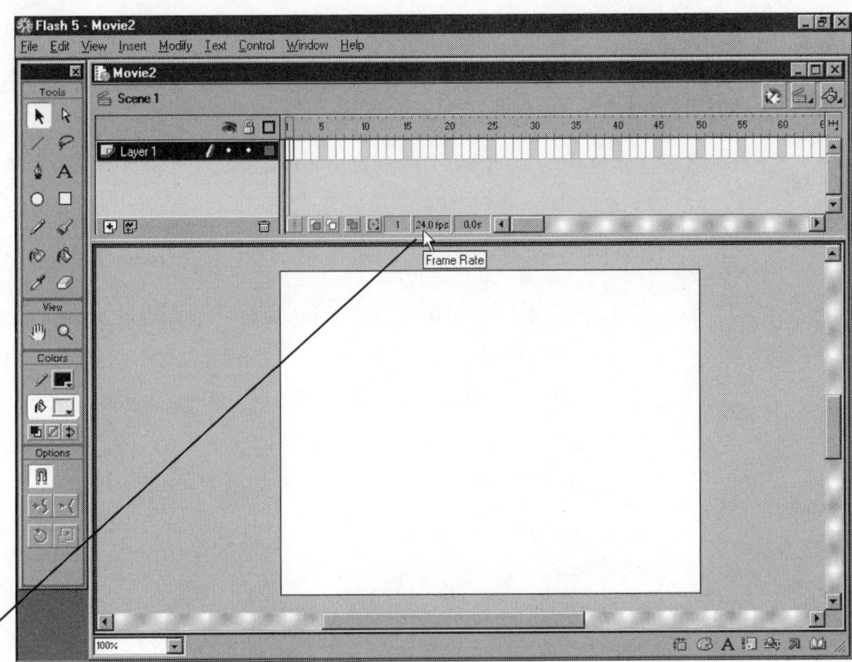

Figure 6.7

The frame rate on the timeline

Creating Transitions and a Storyboard

Simple movies such as your smiley face can be created on the fly, without prior planning. Before you start building a complex Flash 5 animation, however, you need to come up with a design plan or *storyboard.* The storyboard can be a text outline, a comic-book-style graphic layout, or just a few sketches on a piece of paper. All the major points of the animation should be described in the storyboard. These points will become your keyframes.

When beginning your animation process be sure to give yourself enough room between keyframes to accomplish the transition animation. Consider how long each transition should take. At 12 fps a second passes in the final movie every 12 frames. If an animation effect should take only half a second, place the keyframes six frames apart. A good rule of thumb is that simple animations should take 5 to 10 frames, complex animations 15 to 20, and multistage animations 10 frames per segment.

If you need to increase the spacing between two keyframes without affecting the rest of the movie, you can add frames to the timeline. The added frames push the rest of the frames down the timeline without disrupting the spacing elsewhere.

To add a frame to the timeline, do the following:

1. Open a new movie by selecting File, New from the menu bar, and use the Movie Properties dialog box to create a stage that fits comfortably in your workspace.
2. Create Keyframes at frames 1, 10, and 20. This creates two animation transitions that are each ten frames long.
3. Click on the timeline above frame 5 to move the animation to that frame.
4. Select Insert, Frame from the menu bar (see Figure 6.8) or press F5.

The keyframes at 10 and 20 have moved to 11 and 21, respectively. Now the first transition is 11 frames, but the second is still 10.

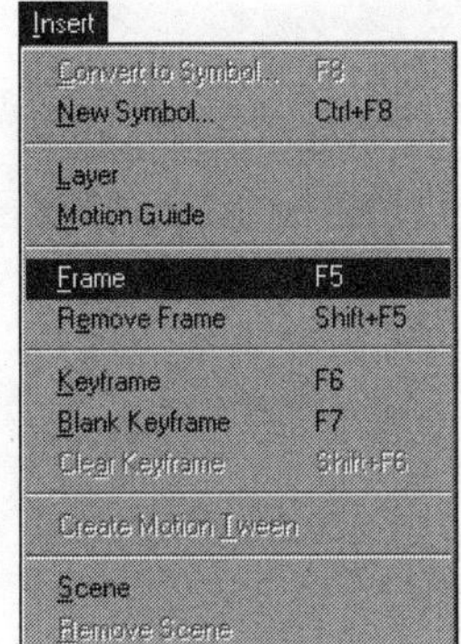

Figure 6.8

Inserting a frame

Removing Frames

Removing a frame is just as easy. To remove a frame, follow these steps:

1. Click frame 1.
2. Hold down the Shift key and click on frame 21 to select all of the frames (see Figure 6.9). Holding the Shift key allows you to select multiple frames at once.
3. Select Insert, Remove Frames from the menu bar, or press Shift+F5.

All the frames have been removed. Of course you can delete frames one by one if you wish.

Changing the Frame View

As you add more frames to your movie you may want to change the frame view to make it easier to navigate the timeline. To change the frame view, follow these steps:

1. Click the Frame View button on the timeline.
2. Select Medium, as shown in Figure 6.10.

Each frame has expanded. Doesn't feel quite so cramped anymore, does it? The timeline has a number of frame views; try them out until you find one that feels comfortable.

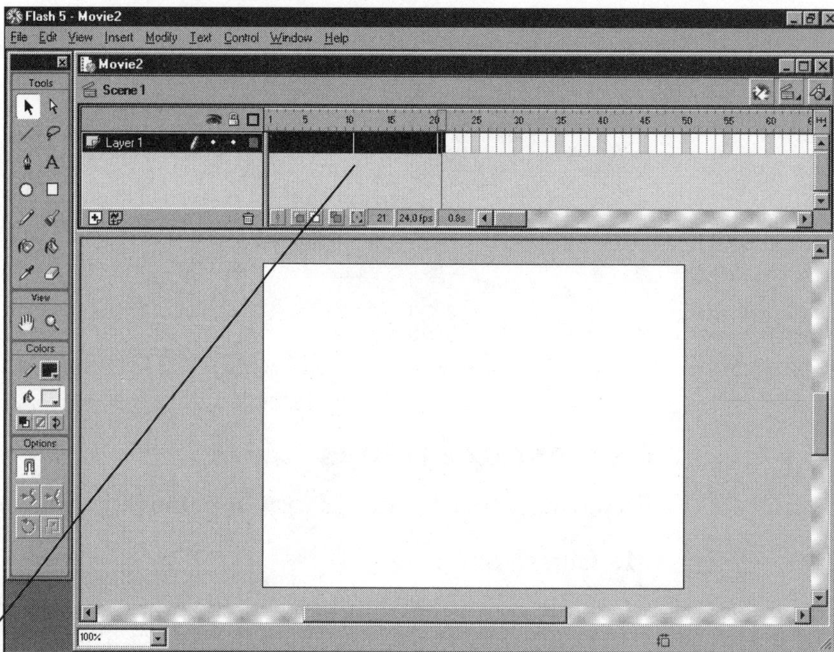

Figure 6.9

Removing a frame

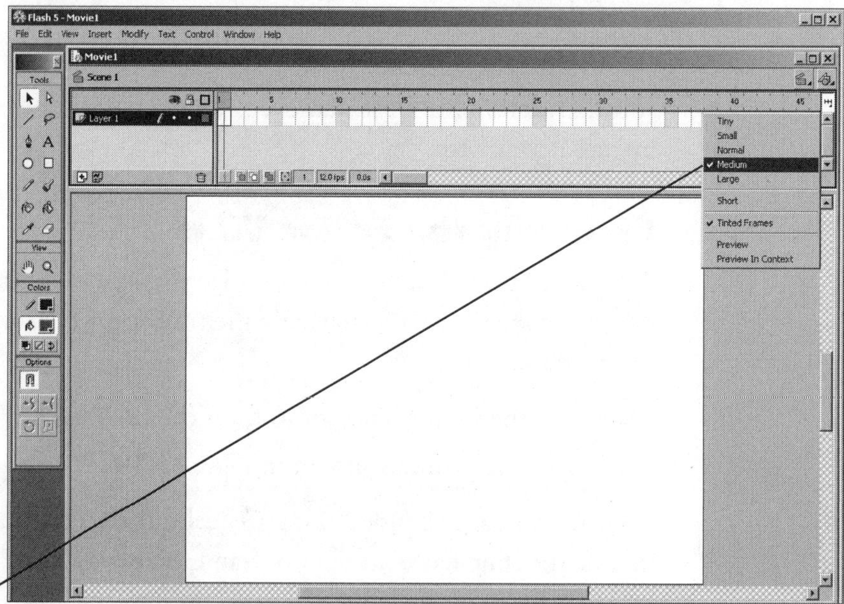

Figure 6.10

Expanding frames

Tweening Color, Size, and Rotation

It's time to see Flash 5 at its best. The program is like a big cartoon factory that squashes, rips, folds, mashes, and mangles one product into another. All you have to do is tell the factory what you want and give it a product to change and a few seconds later that old beat-up Volkswagen Bug becomes a shiny new Boeing 747 jetliner. Flash 5 calls this process tweening.

There are two types of tweening: shape and motion. Shape tweening changes one object into another. You'll find out more about shape animation later this afternoon. Motion tweening adjusts the object's properties. Most often this involves changes in color, opacity, size, rotation, or position.

To see motion tweening in action, do the following:

1. Locate the crazytext.fla file in the session6 folder on the CD-ROM that accompanies this book.
2. Drag the file from the CD-ROM to the desktop to make a copy of the file on your hard drive.
3. Double-click to open the file in Flash 5. As you can see, the file consists of 60 frames of animation on a single "crazy text1" layer.
4. Select Control, Test Movie from the menu bar, as shown in Figure 6.11. The application opens a Flash Player window that shows how the finished movie will look when animated.

Tweening Color

You'll be surprised just how easy creating tweening effects can be. You can close the crazytext.fla file or keep it open as an example. The following instructions will take you through the process of duplicating the tweening effects in crazytext.fla.

Open a new movie and use the Movie Properties dialog box to adjust the stage to fit comfortably on your screen. Keep the frame rate at the default 12 fps.

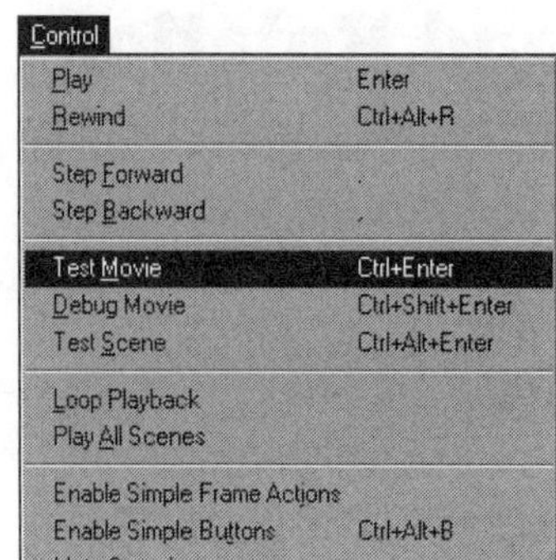

Figure 6.11

Testing a movie in Flash 5

To tween color, follow these steps:

1. Click the text tool and type a word or short phrase on the stage. Use a bright color and a large font. Figure 6.12 shows I've chosen to use 70 point Jokerman.

Flash 5 automatically creates a keyframe at the current timeline position when you add text or draw on a blank frame.

2. Use the Arrow tool to center the text on the stage.
3. With the text highlighted, select Modify, Break Apart from the menu bar. This will create a shape out of the text and allow you to add a gradient.
4. Click the Paint Bucket tool and the rainbow gradient in the Swatches Panel to add a rainbow gradient to your text.
5. Create a graphic symbol from the text by selecting Insert, Convert To Symbol from the menu bar. Motion tweening only works on symbols. If you select an object and create a motion tween, Flash 5 will automatically create a symbol of the object for you.
6. Insert a keyframe at frame 15.

Figure 6.12

Going Bananas

7. Click on frame 1 to reposition the timeline to that frame.
8. Select Insert, Create Motion Tween from the menu bar. Figure 6.13 shows an arrow in the timeline indicating a motion tween between frames 1 and 15.
9. Open the Effect Panel by selecting Window, Panels, Effect from the menu bar.

The Effect Panel is a great place to make color changes to specific instances of symbols in your movie. You can use the Panel to adjust tint, brightness, color, or opacity.

10. In the Effect Panel select Tint and choose a dull color. Figure 6.14 shows I've chosen a pale blue (or it would if this book were in color).

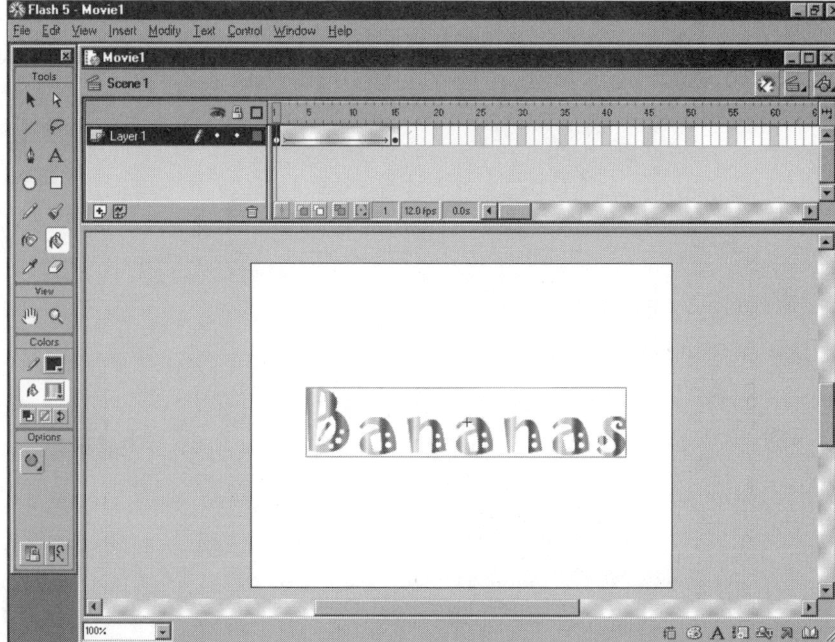

Figure 6.13

Banana tween

Figure 6.14

Blue bananas (trust me!)

11. Test the movie by selecting Control, Test Movie from the menu bar or by pressing Ctrl+Enter (Command+Return on the Mac).

Oh, by the way, you've just created your first Flash 5 animation!

Now that you've seen how easy it is to create color motion tweens, give tweening size and rotation a try.

Tweening Size and Rotation

To tween the size of your text, follow these steps:

1. Add a keyframe at frame 25.
2. Use the Arrow tool and the Scale Option to stretch the text vertically.
3. Select frame 15 in the timeline.
4. Select Insert, Create Motion Tween from the menu bar.
5. Test your movie by selecting Control, Test Movie (see Figure 6.15).

Figure 6.15

Tall bananas

To tween rotation, follow these steps:

1. Add a keyframe at frame 35.
2. Use the Arrow tool and the Rotate Option to rotate the text clockwise.
3. Select frame 25 in the timeline.
4. Select Insert, Create Motion Tween from the menu bar.
5. Test your movie by selecting Control, Test Movie.

Go ahead and try to duplicate some of the other tweening effects from the crazytext.fla file. All the tweens in the file are made in this same way. To tween rotation simply rotate the text rather than scaling it. As you can see from crazytext.fla, more than one property can be tweened at the same time. Objects can change color, size, rotation, and opacity all at the same time.

A quick way to fade out an object is to tween it toward zero opacity. Opacity is controlled by the Alpha option on the Effect Panel.

Save your file or discard without saving. In the next section you'll create a new movie file.

Position Motion Tweening

Now that you know how to change the color or size of an object, it's time to find out how to make it move across the stage. Simple position tweening is much the same as tweening color or size.

Open a new movie and use the Movie Properties dialog box to adjust the stage to fit comfortably on your screen. Keep the frame rate at the default 12 fps. Use the drawing tools to create a ball, floor, and shadow symbol, each on separate layers. These can be as simple or as complex as you desire.

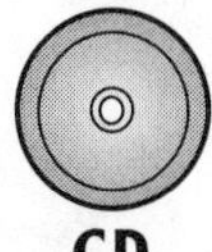

In the session6 folder on the CD-ROM you will find the bounce_ball.fla file. This file has a number of pre-built symbols you can use in this lesson if you don't feel like drawing your own. Be sure to move the file onto your hard drive and unlock the layers before following the steps in the next exercise.

To move an object across the stage, do the following:

1. Select frame 1 of the ball layer.
2. Position the ball on the left side of the stage (as in Figure 6.16) using the Arrow tool.
3. Create a keyframe at frame 5.
4. Hold down the Shift key and move the ball to the right of the stage. Holding down Shift keeps the object at a 90-degree angle to the original position.

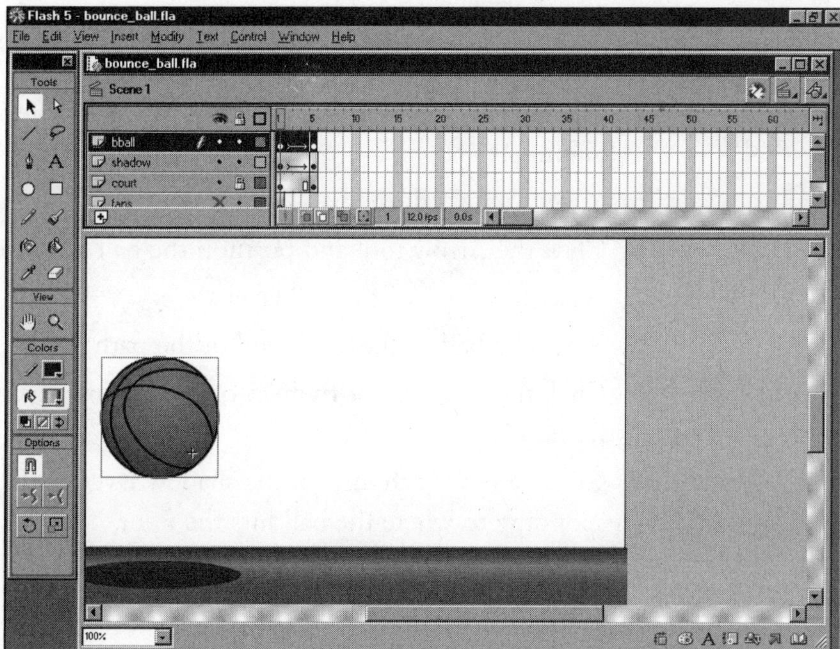

Figure 6.16

The ball, stage left

5. Select frame 1 of the ball layer.
6. Select Insert, Create Motion Tween from the menu bar.
7. Repeat this procedure using the shadow.
8. Create a keyframe at frame 5 of the floor layer.
9. Test the movie.

This is a quick and easy way to animate an object on the stage, but it has its limitations. Using this method Flash 5 will only tween in straight lines, but what if you want the object to follow a curved path?

Creating a Guide Layer

To make an object follow a curved path you will need to define a path for the object using a *guide layer.* To create a guide layer, follow these steps:

1. Clear the keyframe at frame 5 of the ball layer and create new keyframe at 15.
2. Select the first frame of the ball layer.
3. Select Insert, Motion Guide from the menu bar.
4. Use the Pencil or Pen tool to draw a path for the ball to follow (see Figure 6.17).
5. Select frame 1 of the ball layer.
6. Click the Arrow tool and position the ball at one end of the path.
7. Select frame 15 of the ball layer.
8. Move the ball to the other end of the path.
9. Click the keyframe at frame 5 of the shadow layer and drag it to frame 15.
10. Create a new keyframe on the shadow layer in the frame corresponding to where the ball hits the floor.
11. Use the Arrow tool to shrink the shadow and position it under the ball.
12. Test the movie. If you've timed it right the shadow will follow the ball as it bounces across the stage (see Figure 6.18).

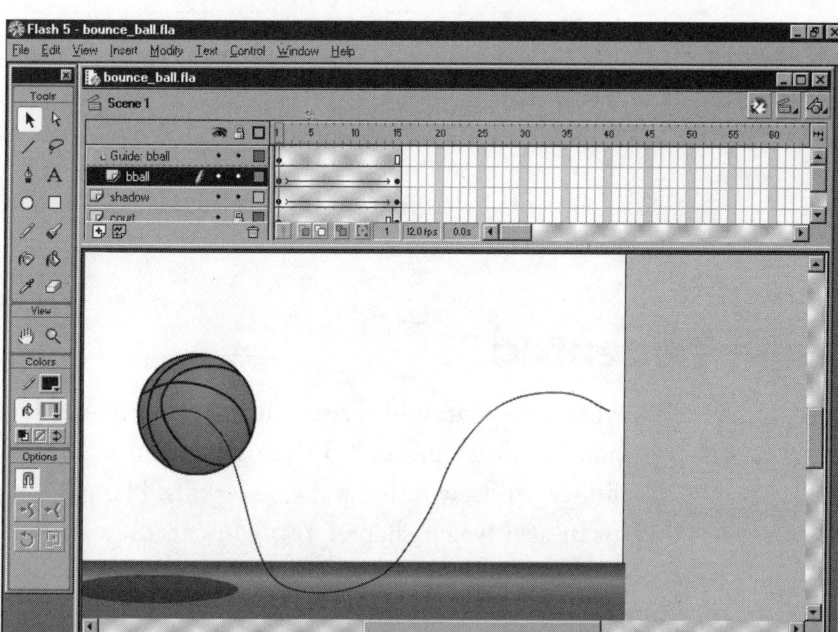

Figure 6.17

Bouncing ball path

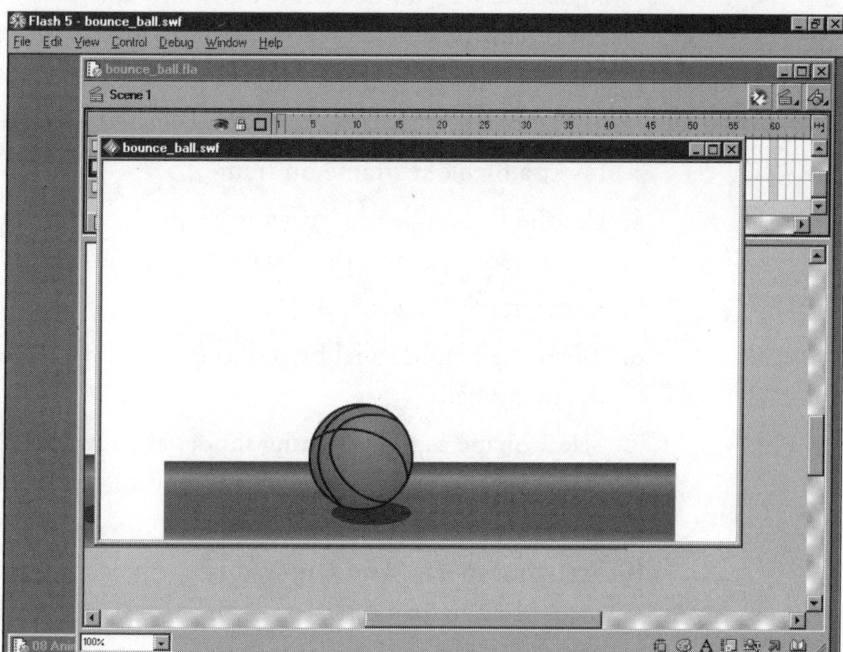

Figure 6.18

The ball hits the court

NOTE You can make changes to the guide layer at any time by selecting it in the Layer Panel and editing it on the stage.

Save your file or discard without saving. In the next section you'll create another new movie file.

Shape Tweening

Moving objects around the screen and animating color and shape changes is quick and easy in Flash 5. If you're like me, your mind is overflowing with ideas on how to use these new skills. Hang on, it gets even better—you can also tween shapes! Yes, you can draw two completely different objects and Flash can create a morphing animation between them. To create a shape tween, follow these steps:

1. Open a new movie and use the Movie Properties dialog box to adjust the stage to fit comfortably on your screen. Keep the frame rate at the default 12 fps.
2. Use the Pen tool to draw a four-pointed star on the stage, like the one in Figure 6.19. Use the Arrow tool to center the star on the stage.
3. Insert a blank keyframe on frame 15.
4. Use the Rectangle tool to draw a square on the stage. Use the Arrow tool to center the square on the stage.
5. Select frame 1.
6. Open the Frame Panel by selecting Window, Panels, Frame from the menu bar.
7. Select Shape as the tweening mode, as shown in Figure 6.20. An arrow appears in the timeline to indicate a shape tween between frames 1 and 15.
8. Test your movie. The star gradually changes into a square. If you made the square a different color from the star, the color tweens as well as the shape.

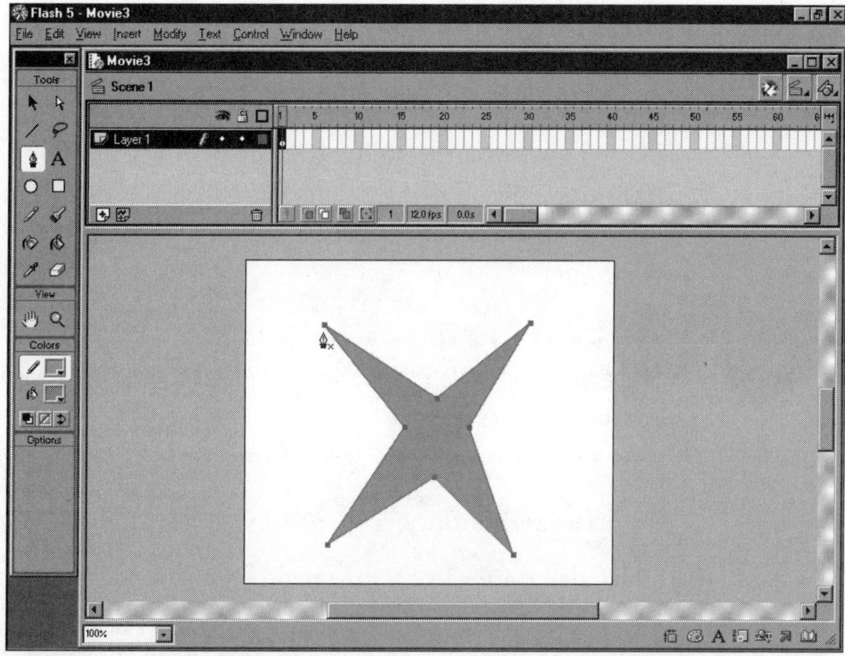

Figure 6.19

A quick star

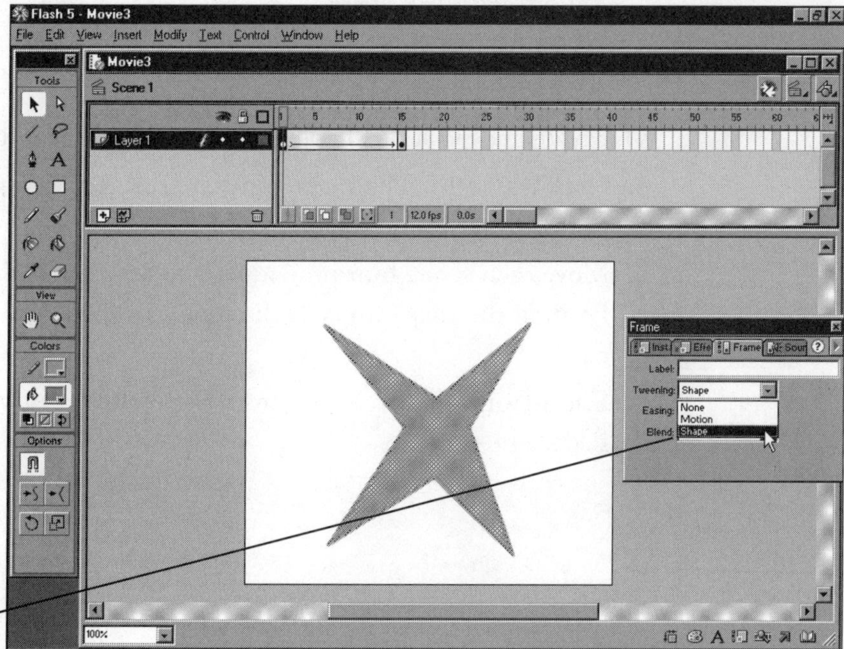

Figure 6.20

Selecting shape tweening

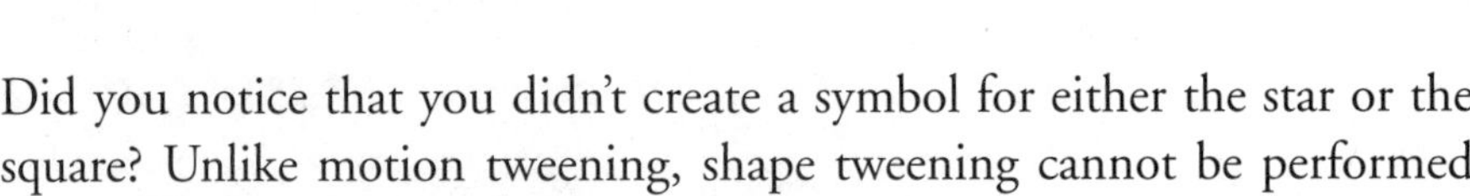

Did you notice that you didn't create a symbol for either the star or the square? Unlike motion tweening, shape tweening cannot be performed on symbols or grouped objects.

Flash 5 gives you the ability to control how the shape tween animates the transition. By inserting shape hints into the movie you can change the way the shape is tweened. The best way to explain how this is done is to try it out.

NOTE Shape hints don't affect the beginning or final frames of the animation, just the transition frames between.

To insert and position a shape hint, follow these steps:

1. Click frame 1 of your movie.
2. Select Modify, Transform, Add Shape Hint from the menu bar. A red circle appears in the stage. Each shape hint is lettered so that you can tell them apart.
3. Use the Arrow tool to move the shape hint to one of the points of the star (Figure 6.21).
4. Create and position shape hints for each point of the star.
5. Click frame 15. The shape hints are stacked on top of one another in the center of the stage.
6. Move each shape hint individually to a different side of the square. Position the shape hints in the center of the sides, not at the corners.
7. Select Control, Test Movie from the menu bar to test your modified shape tween.

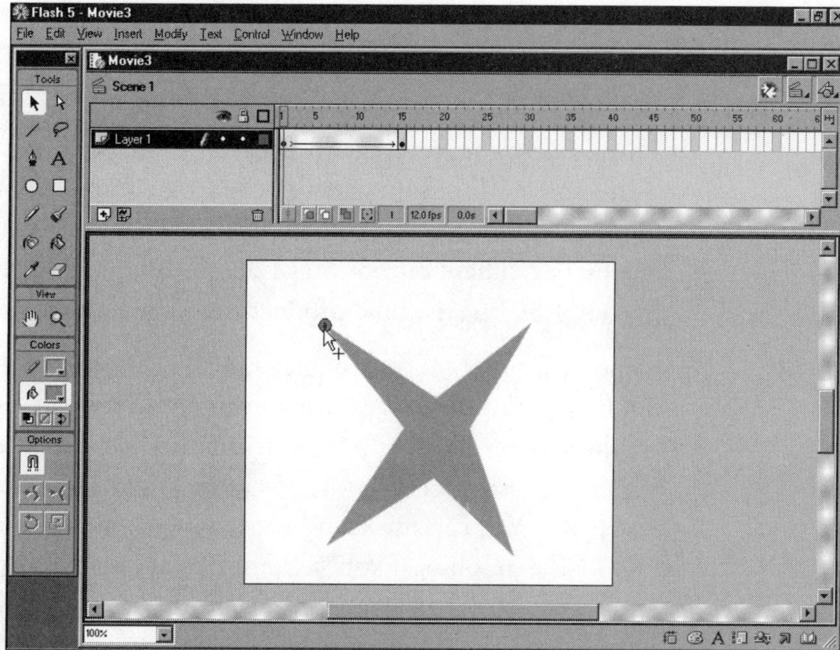

Figure 6.21

The first shape hint

Now you've got a cool rotating effect! Each shape hint tells Flash 5 where that point of the graphic should be in the final frame. The application then calculates a path for the entire shape based on the best path to these points.

Save your file or discard without saving. In the next section you'll create a new movie file.

Fluid Animation

Tweening is fun, fast, and easy, but sometimes a movie calls for more precise control than you can get with tweening. If you find yourself spending a lot of time trying to get a tween effect just perfect, you should consider just creating each frame individually. You can create a new keyframe for each frame of the animation and make the changes on the

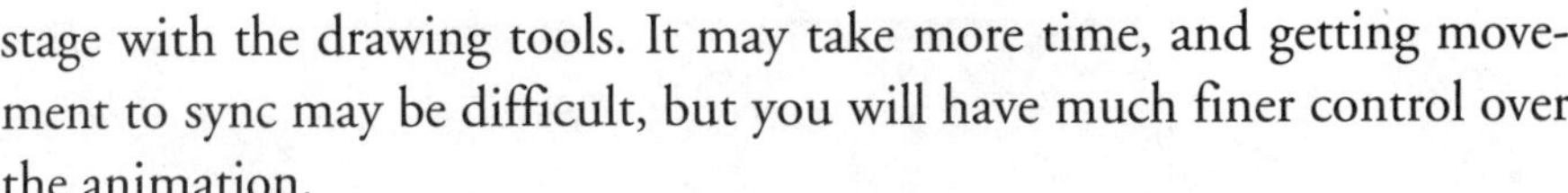

stage with the drawing tools. It may take more time, and getting movement to sync may be difficult, but you will have much finer control over the animation.

This frame-by-frame method is called *fluid animation.* It is the type of animation used for films such as *Cinderella* and *Snow White.* Every single frame of the movie is painstakingly drawn by hand and photographed one by one. These cartoons take dozens of animators hundreds of hours to complete, but the final product can be breathtaking.

Sometimes pinpoint control may not be your concern, but you still might not have the option of tweening. Although Flash can produce some great graphics, other drawing programs can produce effects that can't be easily duplicated using Flash 5. These images are most often bitmapped, or raster files. You can use such images in your movie, but you will have to import the graphics. Flash 5 cannot create motion or shape tweens for raster images. When you need to create a Flash movie using imported graphics you should create a fluid animation.

To create a fluid animation, follow these steps:

1. Open a new movie and use the Movie Properties dialog box to adjust the stage to fit comfortably on your screen. Keep the frame rate at the default 12 fps.

ON THE

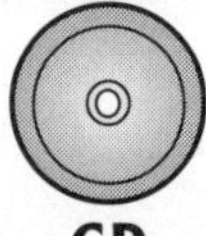

CD

In the session6 folder on the CD-ROM you will find the running_dog.fla file. This file has two pre-built movie clip symbols that use fluid animation. You can use these symbols as a guide for the following instructions. Be sure to move the file onto your hard drive and unlock the layers before editing the file.

2. Select File, Import from the menu bar.
3. Navigate to the first image of your animation (in this case, the dog from running_dog.fla) and click Open. The image appears on the stage (see Figure 6.22).

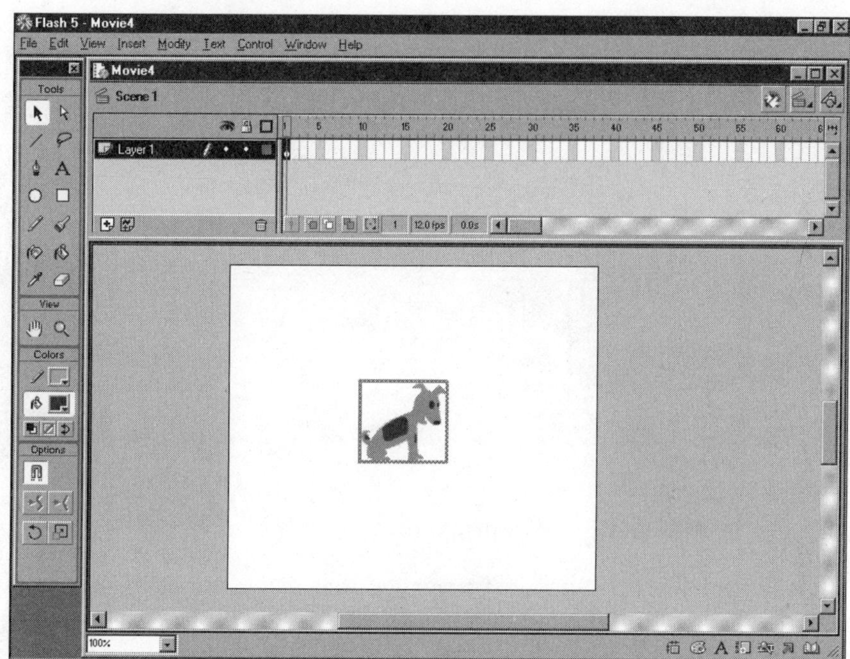

Figure 6.22

A lonely dog on the stage

4. Center the graphic on the stage.
5. Insert a blank keyframe at frame 2.
6. Import your second image and center it on the stage.
7. Repeat this process, creating one keyframe for each image.
8. Select Control, Test Movie from the menu bar to test your fluid animation (Figure 6.23).

Figure 6.23

The running dog animation

To import multiple raster graphics at the same time, follow these steps:

1. Rename your image files using the same title followed by a number indicating the order. For instance, the files might be named dog1.gif, dog2.gif, dog3.gif, and so on until you run out of dogs.
2. Place the image files in the same folder.
3. Select File, Import from the menu bar.
4. Navigate to the first image file and click Open. A dialog box (see Figure 6.24) opens asking if you would like to import all the graphics in the sequence.

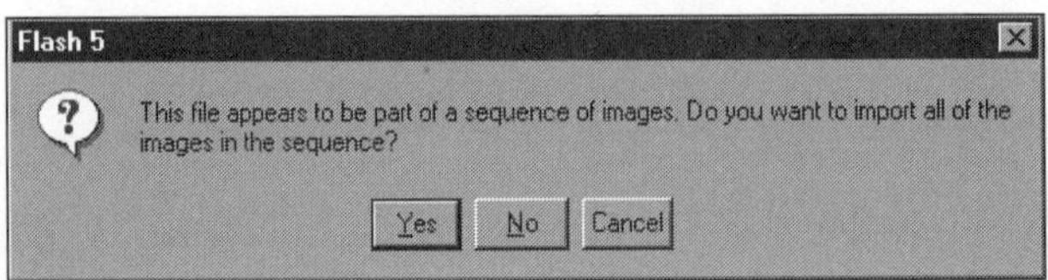

Figure 6.24

Flash has detected a sequence of images.

5. Click Yes.

Flash automatically creates a new keyframe for each image in the sequence. All the work is done for you!

Take a Break

You've learned a lot this afternoon and there's still quite a bit to go. Take a few minutes to cool off. When you get back I'll show you how simple it is to create interactive animated buttons.

Button, Button, Who's Got the Button?

Congratulations, you've got animation! You've learned how to use motion and shape tweening and frame-by-frame techniques to create animated movies. There's only one thing more your Flash 5 movies want, and that's control. Viewers of your movies will appreciate being able to start or stop the animation and perform other interactive functions. For this you need buttons.

A button is a special kind of animated symbol. Instead of frames, a button has a timeline of *states.* Each state determines how the button appears on the stage based on the viewer's actions. Following are the four button states:

- **Up**. Whenever the user's mouse pointer is not over the button the Up state is activated.
- **Over**. When the user places the mouse pointer on the button the Over state is shown.
- **Down**. The Down state is activated when the user clicks on the button.
- **Hit**. This state is not actually visible in the movie. The graphic in the Hit state defines the active area of the button. In other words, the hit state defines where the mouse pointer needs to be in order to activate the Over and Down states.

Use the Button Library

As you saw this morning, Flash 5 comes with a number of built-in libraries. One of these is the Button Library. Besides giving you a lot of easily accessible drag-and-drop buttons, this is a great place to see examples of how buttons work.

Open a new movie and use the Movie Properties dialog box to adjust the stage to fit comfortably on your screen. Keep the frame rate at the default 12 fps. Frame rate doesn't affect buttons because they don't use frames.

To add a button from the Button Library, do the following:

1. Select Window, Common Libraries, Buttons, to open the Button Library Panel.
2. Select Pill Button.
3. Drag the button to the stage. Figure 6.25 shows the button on the stage.

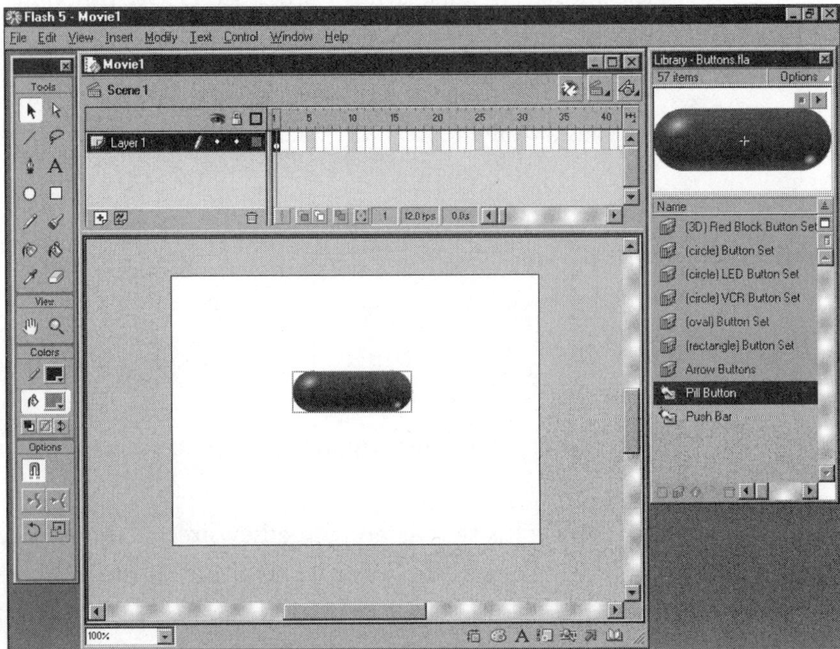

Figure 6.25

The Pill button on the stage

4. Press Ctrl+Enter (Command+Return on the Mac) to test the movie. See what happens when you move your mouse pointer over the button or click it.

Editing a Button

As it looks now the button wouldn't be too helpful for the viewer. You need to add some descriptive text to the button. To edit the button, follow these steps:

1. Right-click (Ctrl+click on the Mac) the button on the stage and select Edit. Figure 6.26 shows how button states replace the frames in the timeline.

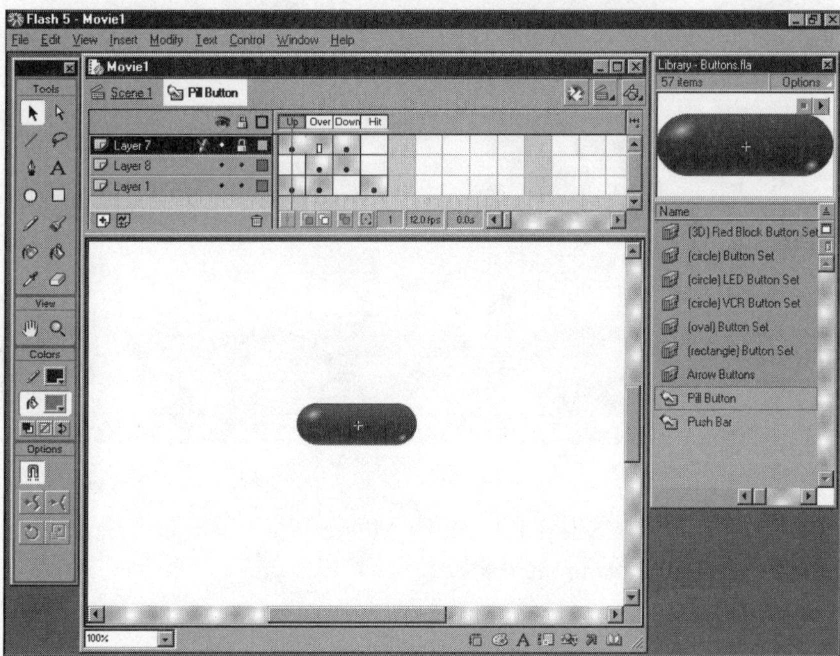

Figure 6.26

Editing a button

2. Select Insert, Layer from the menu bar.
3. Rename the layer "Text" and drag it to the top of the Layers Panel if it is not there already.
4. Use the Text tool and the Character Panel to add the word "Play" to the button. Use a large font type and a bright color. Figure 6.27 shows that I've chosen 29 point Impact type in a pale yellow.

Figure 6.27

Now it's a "Play" button.

5. Select Edit, Edit Movie from the menu bar to return to editing the movie.
6. Select Control, Test Movie from the menu bar to test the button.

Build Your Own Button

Using the built-in button library is quick and easy, but most of the time you'll want to create your own buttons from scratch. The available buttons in the Button Library are pretty standard—just simple shapes and text—but your buttons can be any size or shape.

To create a button, follow these steps:

1. Open a new movie and use the Movie Properties dialog box to adjust the stage to fit comfortably on your screen.
2. Select Insert, New Symbol from the menu bar.

NOTE You can also convert existing graphics into buttons using the Convert To Symbol command you learned in this morning's session. The converted graphic becomes the Up state of the new button.

3. Select Button as the behavior and give your button a name, then click OK.
4. Draw a circle on the stage and use the Fill Panel and the Linear Gradient option to give it a 3D texture (Figure 6.28).
5. Double-click Layer 1 and rename it **Circle**.
6. Select Insert, Layer from the menu bar. Rename the new layer **Center**.
7. Select the Up state of the Center layer.
8. Draw a white circle inside the other on the stage. Leave about an eighth of an inch around the edges (see Figure 6.29).
9. Create a new layer above Center and name it **Face**.
10. Select the Up state of the Face layer and use the Oval and Pen tools to create a smiling face on the stage.

NOTE The Pen tool is great for drawing cartoon smiles. Try it out!

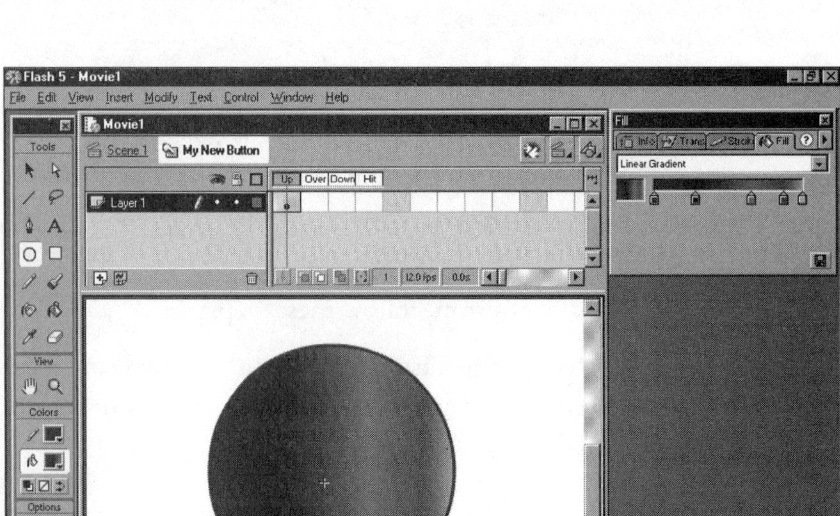

Figure 6.28

My New Button

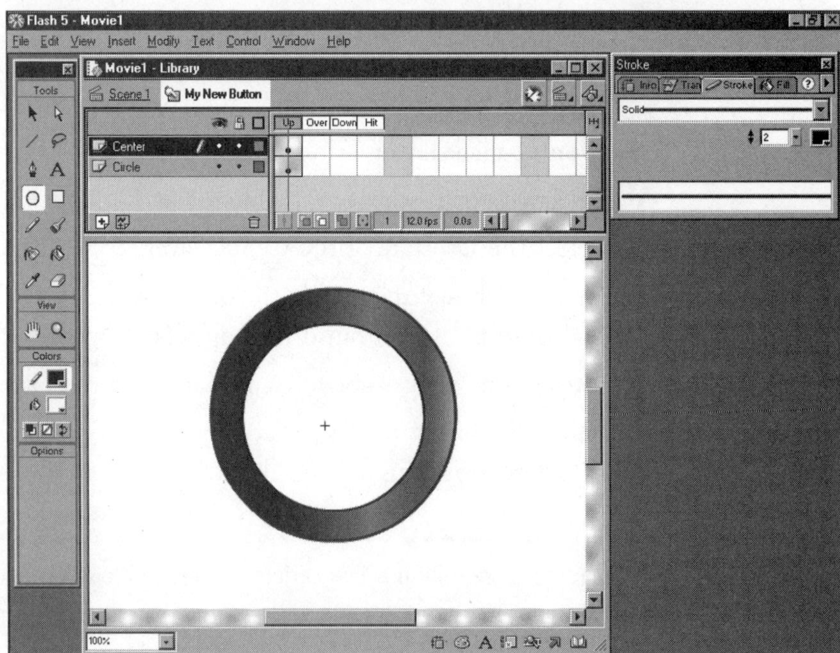

Figure 6.29

The base of the button

Making You Button Interactive

Your button is looking good, but it needs some interactivity. For that you will have to add the other three states. To make your button interactive, follow these steps:

1. Right-click (Ctrl+click on the Mac) the Down state on the Circle layer and select Insert Keyframe. This will allow the Circle layer to appear in all states.
2. Right-click (Ctrl+click on the Mac) the Over state on the Center layer and select Insert Keyframe.
3. Use the Fill Panel to change the color of the white circle to yellow or green (see Figure 6.30).
4. Right-click (Ctrl+click on the Mac) the Over state on the Face layer and select Insert Keyframe.
5. Use the Arrow tool to drag the edges of the mouth into a frown.

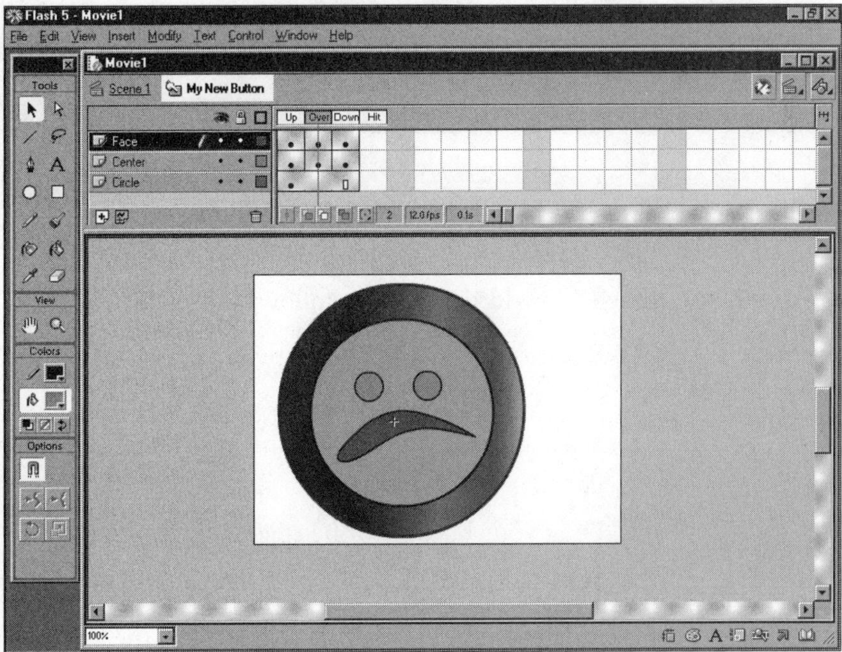

Figure 6.30

The Over state

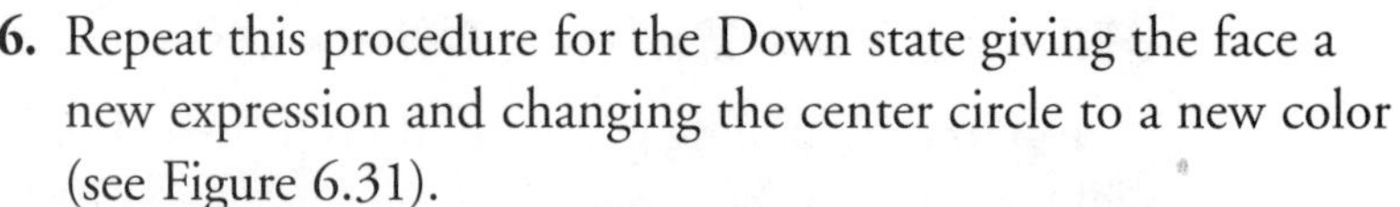

6. Repeat this procedure for the Down state giving the face a new expression and changing the center circle to a new color (see Figure 6.31).

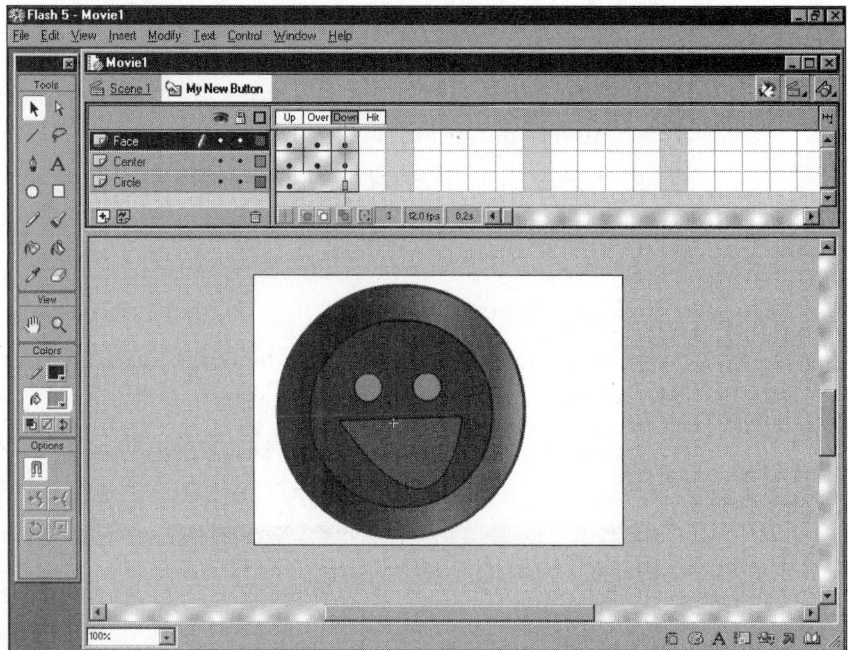

Figure 6.31

The Down state

Adding the Button to Your Movie

Flash automatically adds the button to your Library, but it isn't in the movie. To add the button, follow these steps:

1. Return to the movie stage by selecting Edit, Edit Movie from the menu bar.
2. Select Window, Library from the menu bar to open the Library Panel.
3. Drag your button to the stage.
4. Select Control, Test Movie from the menu bar to test the button.

Flash 5 automatically uses the Up state as the boundary for the button if you do not specify a Hit state. This means that the Over state will be acti-

vated when the mouse moves over any visible part of the button. If you want to specify an active, area you can add a Hit state.

To add a Hit state to your button, do the following:

1. Double-click the button on the stage. You can now edit the button.
2. Insert a keyframe on the Hit stage of the Center layer. Flash 5 copies the Down state of the layer onto the Hit state. Now only the area defined by the center circle will be active.
3. Select Edit, Edit Movie from the menu bar to return to editing the movie.
4. Select Control, Test Movie from the menu bar to test the button.

As you can see in Figure 6.32, the button only changes when your mouse pointer moves into the center circle. You can easily change this active area by editing the Hit state. Any area of the Hit state that contains an object will be active in the final button. Try making just the eyes active. Hint: you will have to clear the keyframe you just created on the Hit stage.

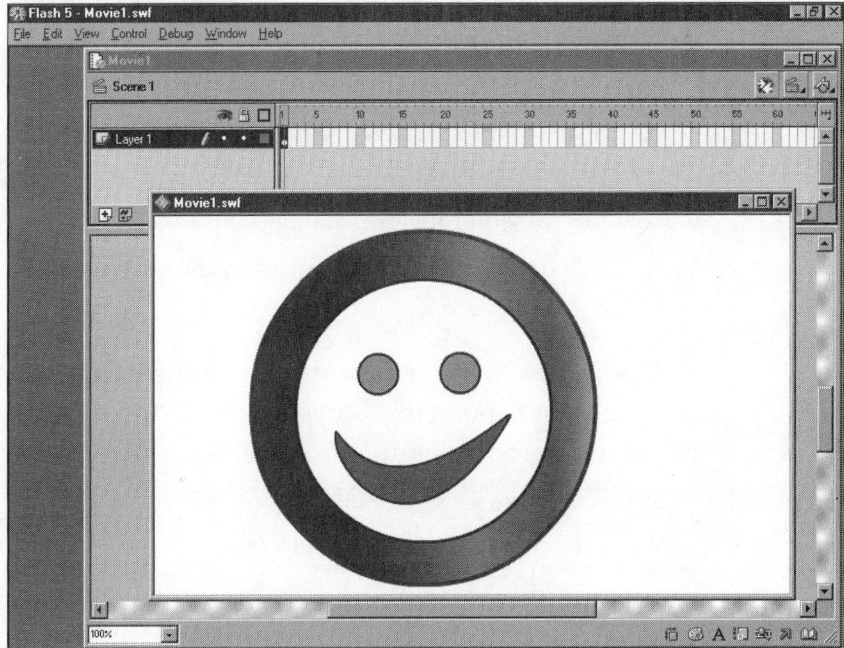

Figure 6.32

The Hit state has been defined.

Adding Simple Actions to Your Button

We use buttons every day, when using elevators to keyboards to doorbells. Imagine pressing the Up button for a dead elevator: the button recesses into the wall and lights up, but the elevator never shows. That's what the viewers of your movie will experience with your buttons as they are now. They may look good and they animate in response to the mouse, but they don't actually cause anything to happen.

To make your movies truly interactive you have to link your buttons to Flash 5 commands. These commands are called *actions* and are produced in a language called *ActionScript.* Flash 5 has an extensive ActionScript library with a large number of built-in actions ranging from simple play and stop actions to complex modification of variables and changing dynamic text fields. A full description of ActionScript is beyond the scope of this book, but if you are interested in learning more, *Flash 5 Design: From Concept to Creation* (Prima Tech) will introduce you to a number of Flash 5's more complex functions—including ActionScript.

Adding actions to buttons in Flash 5 may seem a little intimidating. It's really quite simple. There may be a lot of options available, but you only need to use a few. Here's a description of the basic actions covered here:

- **Stop**. Halts the advancement of the movie timeline.
- **Play**. Starts the timeline progression at the frame rate defined in the Movie Properties dialog box.
- **Go To**. Moves the animation to the specified frame.
- **Get URL**. Opens a specific Web site in a browser window.

Open a new movie and use the Movie Properties dialog box to adjust the stage to fit comfortably on your screen. Add a button to the stage. You can use one of the buttons from the Button Library or you could use one you created in the last section.

To add an action to a button, follow these steps:

1. Use the Arrow tool to select the button on the stage.
2. Select Window, Actions from the menu bar. The Actions Panel appears.
3. Click + and select Basic Actions, Stop from the menu, as shown in Figure 6.33.

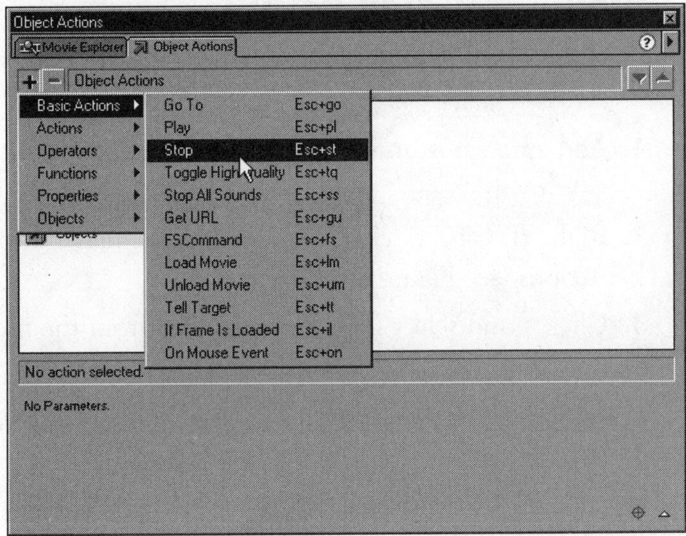

Figure 6.33

Selecting Stop from the Actions Panel

Now you need to test your action:

1. Close the Actions Panel by selecting Window, Actions from the menu bar.
2. Insert a keyframe at frame 12.

CAUTION

Buttons can have different actions on different frames. When you inserted the keyframe at frame 12 the action was copied with it, but the actions are not linked. If you need to change what the button does, you will have to change the actiontwice, once in frame 1 and once in frame 12.

3. Draw a triangle with the Pen tool by making three points on the stage, and then clicking on the starting point.
4. Insert a keyframe at frame 24.
5. Select Control, Test Movie from the menu bar. Watch the animation for a few seconds. The triangle appears and disappears. Now, click on the button. The animation stops!

Adding the Play Action

Starting the animation again will require a new button and the Play action. To add the Play action to your movie, follow these steps:

1. Add a new button in frame 1 from the Button Library or create your own.
2. Right-click (Ctrl+click on the Mac) the new button and select Actions (see Figure 6.34).
3. Click + and select Basic Actions, Play from the menu.
4. Click x to close the Actions Panel.
5. Right-click (Ctrl+click on the Mac) the play button and select Copy.
6. Click frame 12.

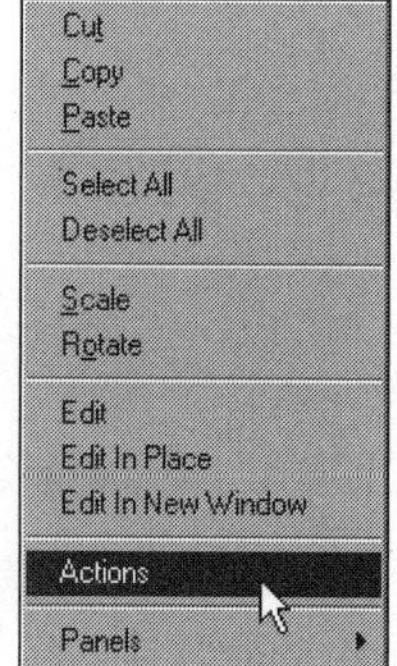

Figure 6.34

Opening the Actions Panel

7. Right-click (Ctrl+click on the Mac) the stage and select Paste. The play button is added to frame 12 (see Figure 6.35).

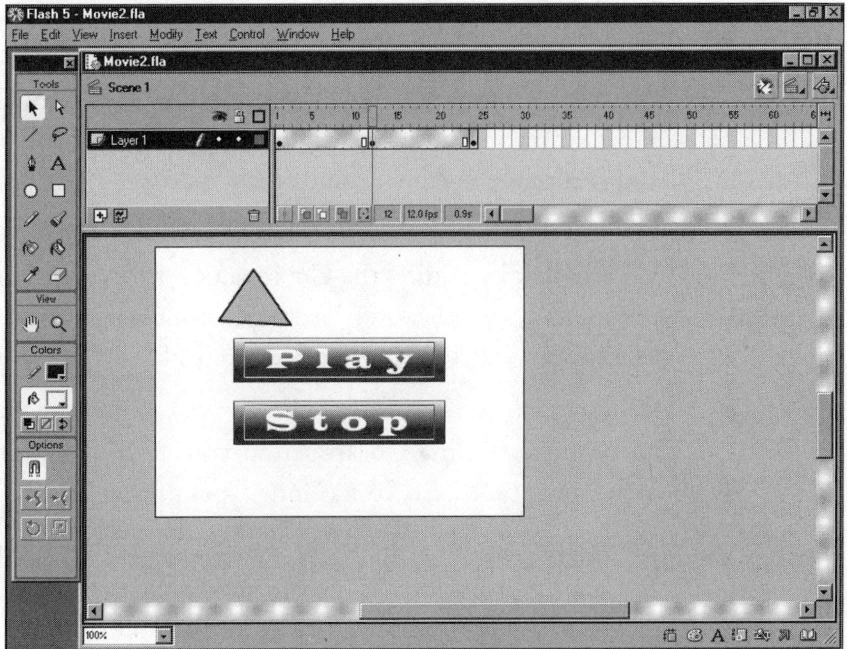

Figure 6.35

The play button at frame 12

8. Click frame 24.
9. Right-click (Ctrl+click on the Mac) the stage and select Paste.
10. Select Control, Test Movie from the menu bar. You can now stop and start the movie by using the buttons.

Take a moment to save your movie file. You use it again in the next section.

Using the Go To Action

Have you ever used an 8-track player? Before the luxury of CDs, minidiscs, or even cassettes, music collectors had only two choices: vinyl records or 8-track tapes. The 8-tracks were a vast improvement over vinyl; they were more portable, the players were smaller, and the sound quality was better. The problem was that 8-track players couldn't rewind or fast forward. If you wanted to listen to a specific song you had to sit and wait, and eventually the tape would reach your song. The only controls 8-track users had were Stop and Play. Sounds like your movie, doesn't it?

Let's fix that by adding the Go To action to your buttons. This will allow the user to skip forward, back up, or change scenes. Using the Go To action is similar to using the Stop and Play actions with just a few extra steps.

To properly use the Go To action you need to be familiar with all the available options. Go To has four types of options:

- **Scene**. Specifies the scene to which the move should move. If you have multiple scenes in your movie file each scene will appear in the Scene drop-down menu. The default selection is the current scene.
- **Type**. Determines how the movie will know the frame to which it will move. The default selection is frame number. Other options include the next frame or previous frame.
- **Frame**. Identifies the target frame. This will most often be the number of the frame. The default is 1.
- **Go To And Play**. Tells the Flash player what to do once it reaches the new frame. The box is checked by default; the movie will continue playing from the target frame. Unchecking the box will cause the player to move to the target frame and stop playing.

Using these options in combination you can cause the movie to move to any frame on any scene and stop or play as desired. You can see that without making any changes to your Go To action the movie will move to the first frame of the current scene and play from that point.

But you need to see it in action to appreciate it. Add a new button on the stage for your Go To action. You can create your own or use one out of the Button Library. To add a Go To action, follow these steps:

1. Right-click (Ctrl+click on the Mac) the Go To button and select Actions. The Actions Panel will open.
2. Click + and select Basic Actions, Go To from the menu.

Take a moment to look at the lower section of the Actions Panel (Figure 6.36). Notice how you can adjust the target Scene and frame. When you're familiar with how to adjust the Go To action, return the options to their default positions.

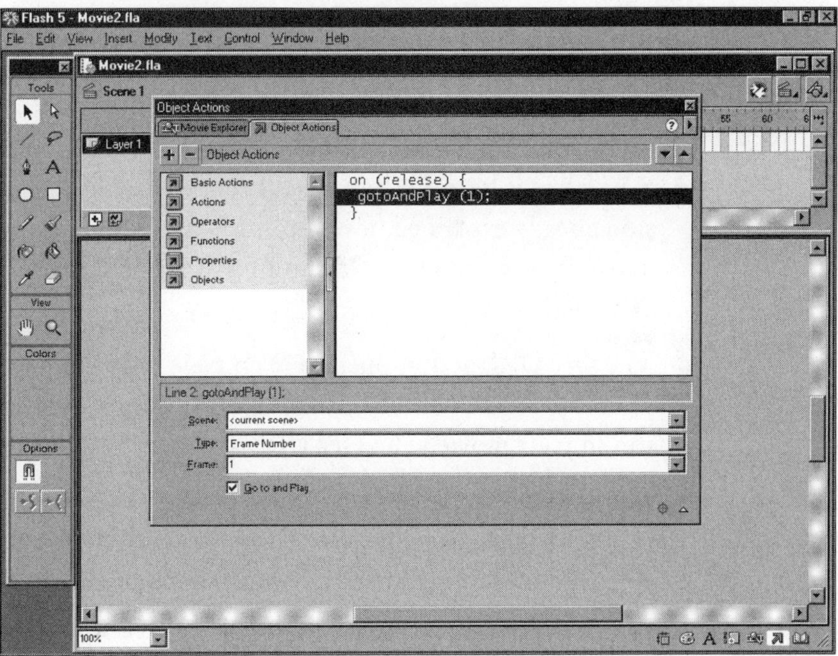

Figure 6.36

The Actions Panel

Testing Your Button

To test out your button, follow these steps:

1. Close the Actions Panel by selecting Windows, Actions from the menu bar.
2. Use the same Copy and Paste method you used on the Play button to copy the Go To button to frames 12 and 24.
3. Select Control, Test Movie from the menu bar. Click the Stop button, then the Go To button. The movie moves to the beginning and plays. Piece of cake!

Take a few minutes to experiment by changing the options for the Go To action. After you are confident you know how to make your movie move to any frame you desire, save and close your file. You'll start a new movie in the next section.

Linking to Web Pages

Designing Web pages using Flash technology is becoming more and more popular. Flash 5 offers a number of advantages over other Web production methods—smaller graphics, smoother animation, trouble-free sound, and no browser compatibility concerns. Creating an entire Flash 5 Web site is beyond the scope of this book, but Saturday afternoon's session already explained how you can publish a Flash movie as a Web page. There is even a way to add Internet functionality to your movie: the Get URL action.

The Get URL action opens a Web page when it is activated. Viewers of your movie will have the ability to visit Web pages by clicking on a button in your movie. The Get URL action has a number of options:

- **URL**. This is the location of the Web page that the action will open, such as http://www.prima-tech.com. You can use relative or absolute links just as you would with an anchor tag in HTML.
- **Window**. Specifies where the Web page will appear. To open the page in the same window choose "_self." You can open a new

window by selecting "_blank." If the movie is on a Web page that uses frames, the name of the target frame can be entered here.

- **Variables**. Developers of dynamic Web sites can use this option to submit Flash variables using the Get or Post methods.

Open a new movie and use the Movie Properties dialog box to adjust the stage to fit comfortably on your screen. Add a button to the stage. You can use one of the buttons from the Button Library or you could use one of the ones you created earlier.

To link to a Web page, follow these steps:

1. Right-click (Ctrl+click on the Mac) the button and select Actions. The Actions Panel will open.
2. Click + and select Basic Actions, Get URL from the menu.
3. Type the location of the Web page in the URL field and select "_self" as the window type as shown in Figure 6.37. Enter the entire URL, including the "http://" prefix.
4. Close the Actions Panel.

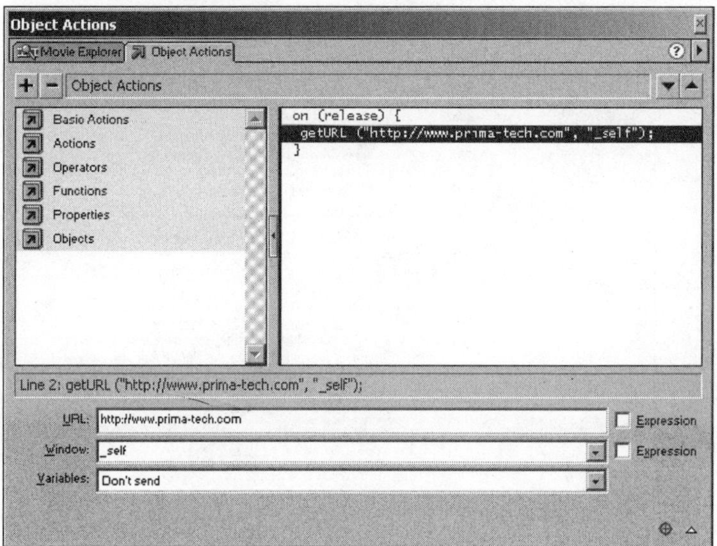

Figure 6.37

The Get URL action options

To test the Get URL action you need to publish the movie as a Web page. To test the button, follow these steps:

1. Save the file by selecting File, Save from the menu bar.
2. Select File, Publish Settings from the menu bar.
3. Click the Formats tab.
4. Select HTML and click Publish. Flash 5 creates an .swf and .html file in the same folder as the movie file.
5. Click OK.
6. Double-click the HTML file on your hard drive.
7. Click the button in your browser. Flash loads the Web page into your browser (Figure 6.38).

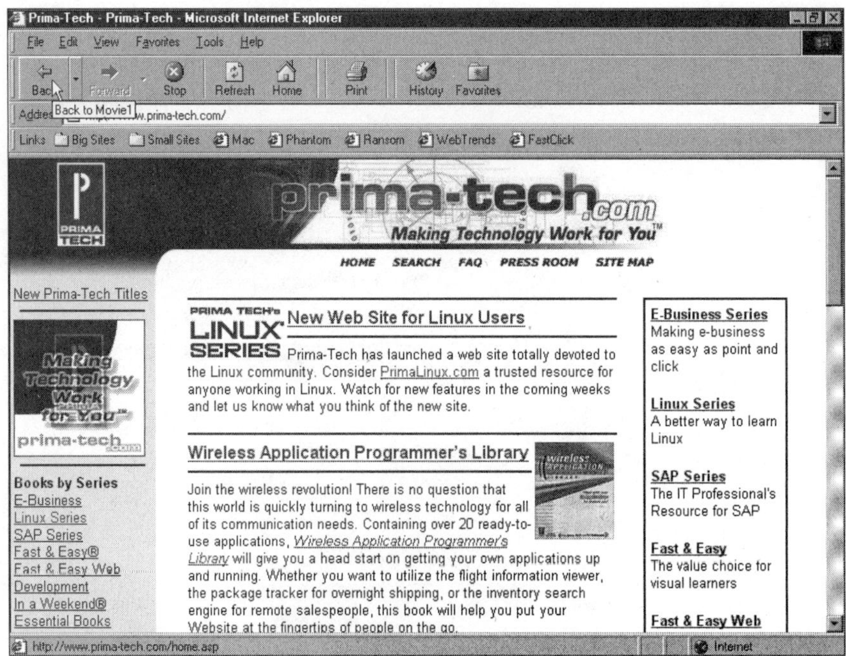

Figure 6.38

A linked Web page

Experiment with different Window options for the Get URL action. After you feel sure you know how to load Web pages from a Flash 5 movie, save and close your file.

What's Next

You've learned all the basics of Flash 5 animation. You can draw shapes, add text, buttons, and symbols, and animate your graphics. It's about time to put it all together.

You've spent all weekend learning the tools for creating Flash 5 movies. This evening you have a chance to create a final project that will require all your new skills to complete. Along the way I'll show you a few shortcuts and tricks you can use to make your movies even better.

SUNDAY EVENING

Creating Your Final Project

- Working with the Movie Clips
- The Control Panel
- Putting It All Together

It's time to put all your new skills to the test. For the final project you'll be using most of the Flash 5 tools you've seen this weekend to develop a user interface that allows the viewer to play a number of different kinds of movie clips. This session is step-heavy, without a lot of chit-chat—I hope you're ready to work!

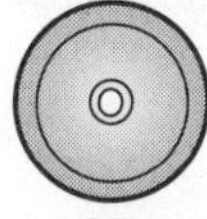
ON THE CD

You can see an example of the finished project on the CD-ROM included with this book. To see the movie, double-click the final_project.exe file (final_project.hqx on the Mac) in the Session7 folder. In the same folder is final_project.fla. You can open this file in Flash 5 and use it as a reference as you create your own final project.

Working with the Movie Clips

Your final project involves four animated movie clips. Each movie clip displays a different type of animation, including color and size motion tweening, position motion tweening, shape tweening, and fluid animation.

Open a new movie and use the Movie Properties dialog box to set the stage width to 550 and the height to 200 (see Figure 7.1). Leave the frame rate at 12 fps.

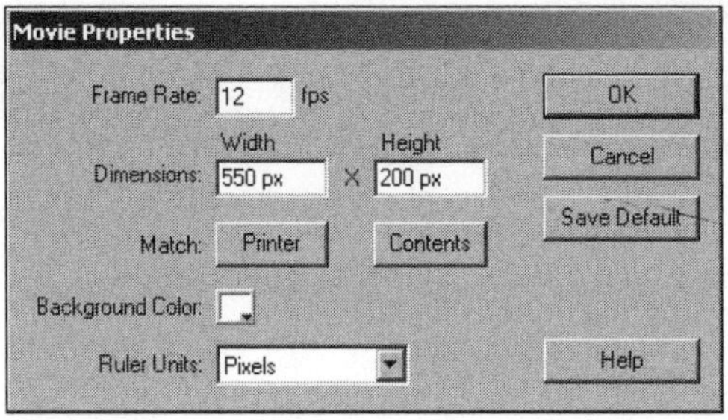

Figure 7.1

Setting the stage for your movie

Creating Welcome Text Animation

The first animation is the simplest: a welcome message that scrolls up the screen. The text should fade in at the bottom in small type then fade out and expand as it moves to the top of the page.

To add the text to your movie, follow these steps:

1. Rename layer 1 **Welcome**.
2. Click on the Text tool.
3. Type **Welcome to my Animation Control Panel** or some other welcome message on the stage (see Figure 7.2).
4. Open the Character Panel by selecting Window, Panels, Character from the menu bar.
5. Select the text with the Text Arrow tool and change the font, size, and color in the Character Panel. Pick a small font and choose a bright yellow or green color.
6. Click on the Arrow tool and drag the text to the bottom of the stage (see Figure 7.3). You can use the Paragraph Panel to center the text.

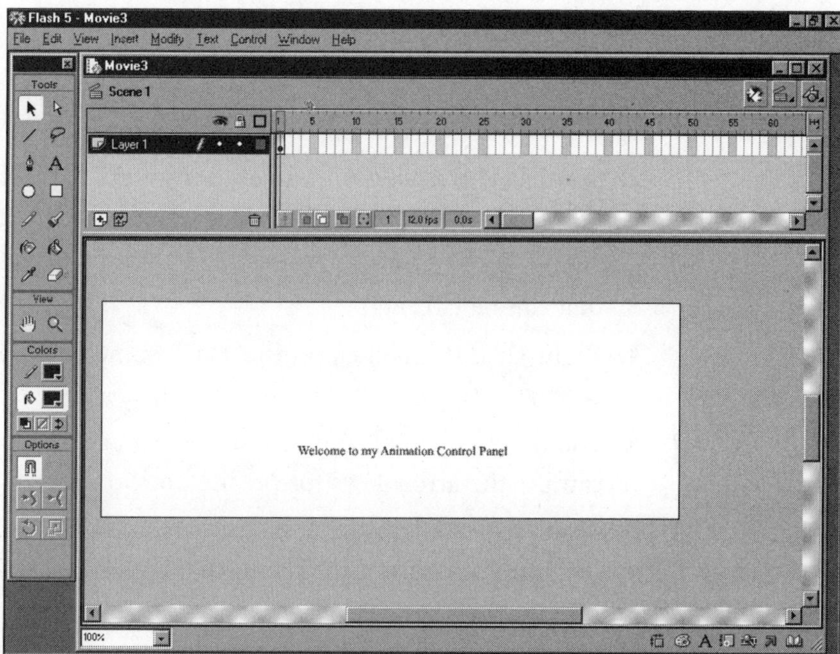

Figure 7.2

The welcome text

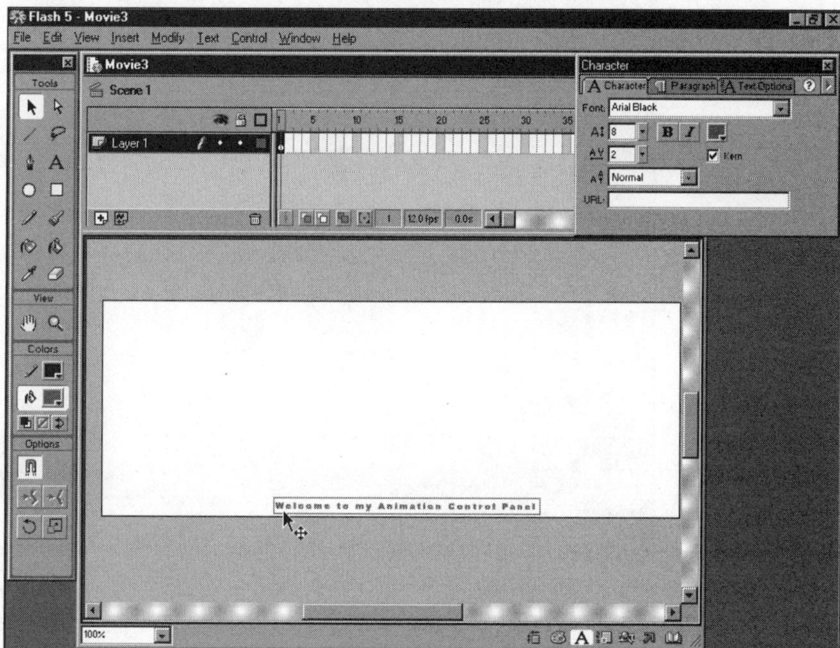

Figure 7.3

The first text position

Tweening Your Text

To tween the text, follow these steps:

1. Click on frame 1 of the Welcome layer.
2. Select Insert, Convert to Symbol from the menu bar. The Symbol Properties dialog box will open.
3. Name the symbol and click OK. The text will turn into a symbol that can be tweened.
4. Right-click (Ctrl+click on the Mac) frame 30 and select Insert Keyframe from the menu that appears.
5. Use the Arrow tool to position the text at the top of the stage. You can use the arrow keys for precise positioning.
6. Right-click (Ctrl+click on the Mac) frame 1 and select Create Motion Tween from the menu that appears, as shown in Figure 7.4.

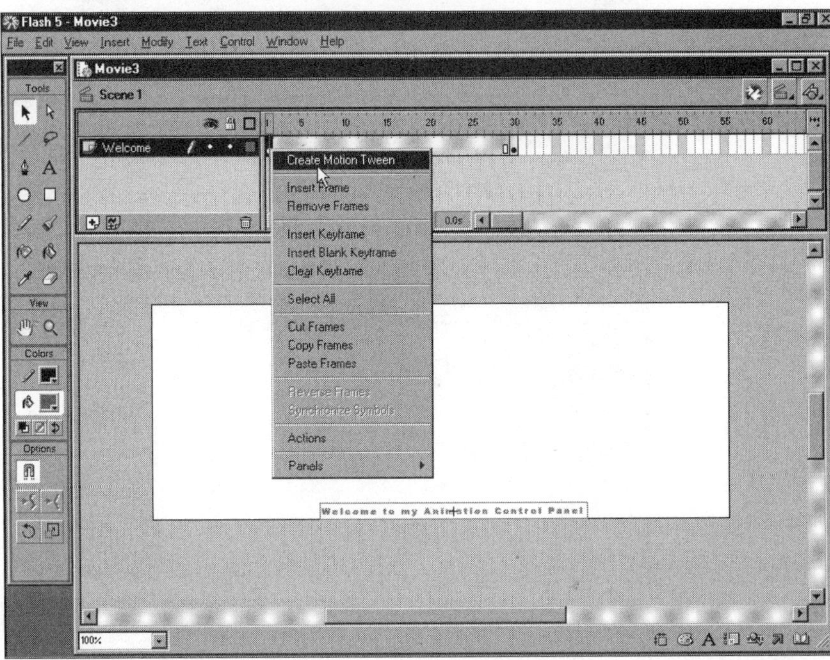

Figure 7.4

Creating the tween

Adjusting Text and Adding Effects

Adjust the text size and color by following these steps:

1. Click frame 30.
2. Open the Effect Panel by selecting Window, Panels, Effect.
3. Choose Tint as the effect type.
4. Pick a dark blue or purple as the Tint Color (see Figure 7.5).

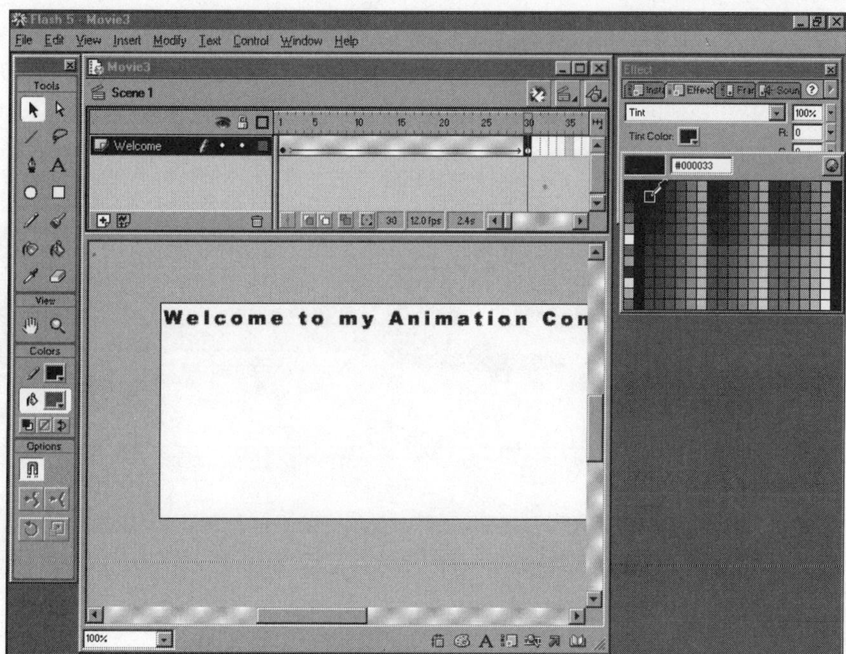

Figure 7.5

Changing the text color

5. Click the Arrow tool and select the Scale option from the Tools Panel.
6. Hold the Shift key and drag the corner of the bounding box until the text fills the top of the stage.

To add the fade effect, follow these steps:

1. Insert keyframes at frames 5 and 25.
2. Select frame 1 in the timeline.
3. Open the Effect Panel, if it is not already open.
4. Choose Alpha as the effect type and type **0** as the percent (see Figure 7.6).
5. Repeat step 4 on frame 30.

You can improve the effect of the animation by adding more text. Each line should have its own layer and should appear just below the previous one, as shown in Figure 7.7.

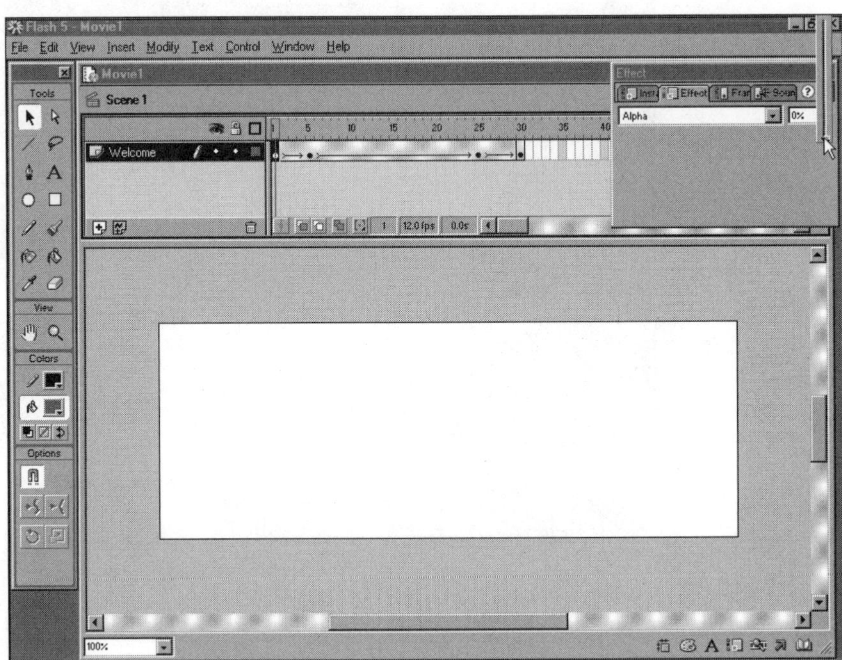

Figure 7.6

Choosing zero opacity

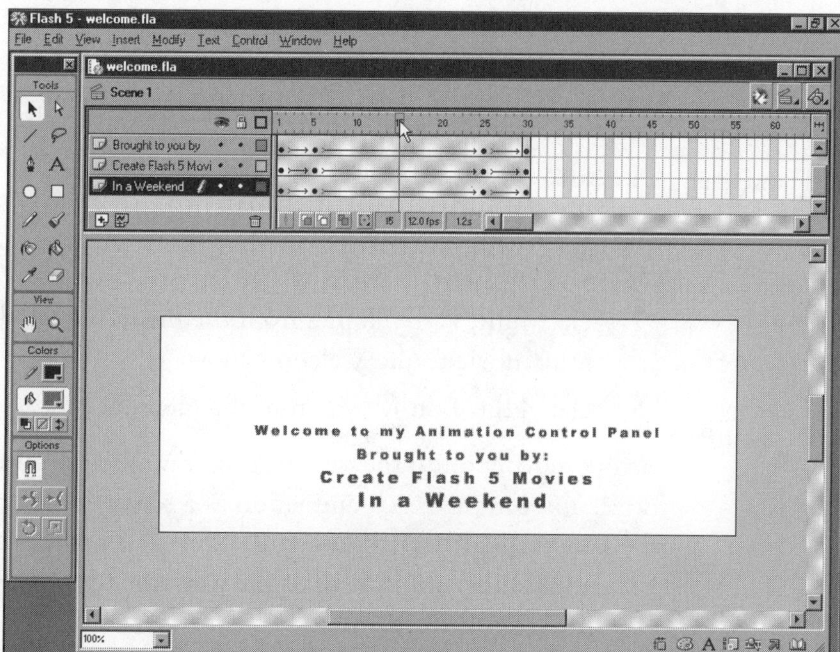

Figure 7.7

A completed animation

Converting Text to a Movie Clip

The animation sequence is done; it's time to convert it to a movie clip. To convert the Welcome text animation into a movie clip follow these steps:

1. Open the Library Panel, if it is not already open.
2. Choose Edit, Select All from the menu bar.
3. Copy all of the frames by selecting Edit, Copy Frames from the menu bar.
4. Select Insert, New Symbol from the menu bar.
5. Name the symbol **Welcome** and click OK (see Figure 7.8).

Symbol Properties
Name: Animation: Welcome
Behavior: Movie Clip / Button / Graphic
OK Cancel Help

Figure 7.8

Creating the first animation movie clip

6. Click on frame 1 of the movie clip.
7. Select Edit, Paste Frames from the menu bar. Flash copies the entire movie to the Welcome movie clip.
8. Select Edit, Edit Movie from the menu bar.

Before moving on to the next section, save your project file to your hard drive. You can save each animation as a separate file or create all four on the same stage. If you choose to use the same file for the next animation, you should hide and lock all of the welcome text layers.

Creating a Biplane Animation

The next animation is a position motion tween of two planes chasing each other across the stage. You can draw your own planes from scratch, or you can use the Biplane symbol from the Movie Clips Common Library.

If you are creating separate files for each animation you should open a new movie. Use the Movie Properties dialog box to adjust the stage width to 550 and the height to 200.

Adding and Modifying the Biplane Clip

To add the Biplane movie clip to your movie, do the following:

1. Create a new layer and name it **Orange Plane**.
2. Select Window, Common Libraries, Movie Clips from the menu bar.
3. Drag the Biplane symbol onto the stage.
4. Close the Movie Clips Common Library.

Now you will have to make a few modifications to the clip.

1. Double-click the Biplane to begin editing the symbol.
2. Click the Lock/Unlock All Layers button above the Layers Panel to select the Unlock option. Now you can edit the layers.
3. Choose Edit, Select All from the menu bar.
4. Select Window, Panels, Transform to open the Transform Panel (see Figure 7.9).

Figure 7.9

Opening the Transform Panel

5. Select Constrain in the Transform Panel and set the width to 25% (see Figure 7.10).
6. Press Enter (Return on the Mac) to apply the change.
7. Click on the Timeline at frame 1 to deselect all frames.

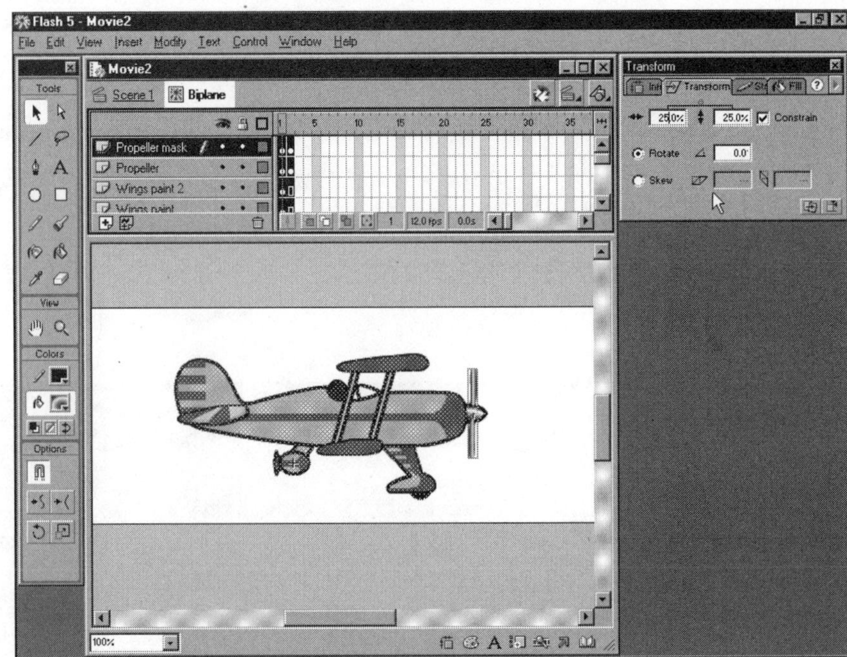

Figure 7.10

Shrinking the biplane

8. Right-click (Ctrl+click on the Mac) on frame 1 of the Propeller mask layer and select Copy Frames.
9. Right-click (Ctrl+click on the Mac) on frame 2 of the Propeller mask layer and select Paste Frames.
10. Repeat steps 8 and 9 for the Propeller layer.

The original Biplane symbol has an animated propeller. Once the symbol shrinks to one-quarter size, the animation can't be seen. Copying the first frames of the Propeller layers onto the second frames erases the unnecessary animation.

11. Select Edit, Edit Movie from the menu bar to return to your movie.

Making and Coloring the Chase Plane

You've got one plane, now you'll need a second. To create the chase plane, follow these steps:

1. Press Ctrl+L (Command+L on the Mac) to open the Library Panel. Your Biplane symbol is listed at the top.
2. Right-click (Ctrl+click on the Mac) the Biplane movie clip and select Duplicate, as shown in Figure 7.11.
3. Name the new symbol **Chase Biplane**.
4. Click OK.

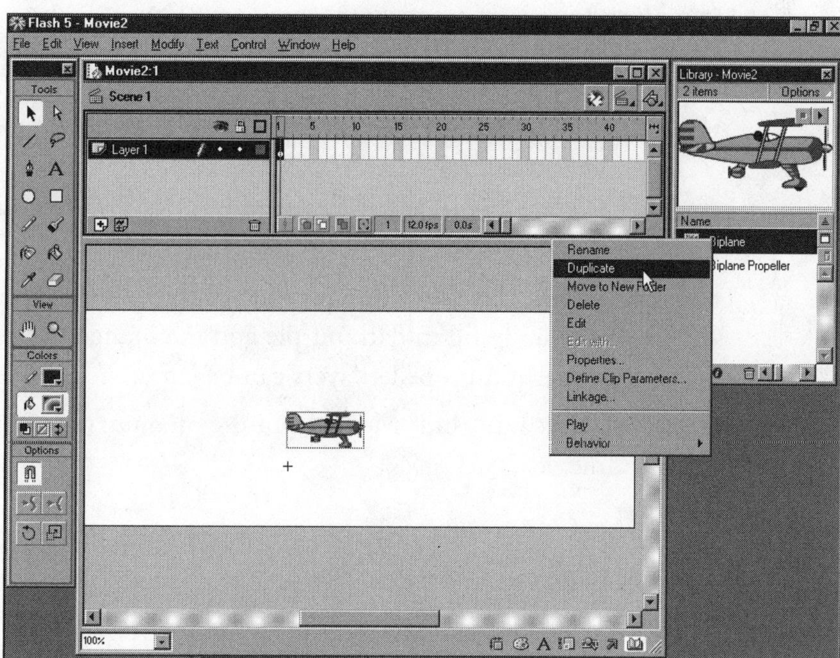

Figure 7.11

Copying the Biplane symbol

Now it's time to color the new biplane. To do so, follow these steps:

1. Double-click the Chase Biplane symbol in the Library Panel.

Be sure to double-click on the movie clip icon and not on the text of the symbol name.

2. Select frame 1 of the Wings paint 2 layer.
3. Hold the Shift key down and click on frame 2. Both frames are highlighted in the timeline, and the objects in the stage are selected.

Using the Shift key to select and change multiple frames at once is a great timesaver.

4. Open the Fill Panel by selecting Window, Panels, Fill from the menu bar.
5. Change the fill color (see Figure 7.12). For my animation, I've chosen a dark purple.
6. Repeat this procedure for each of the colored layers. Change the burgundy fill to dark purple and the orange to bright red. The wheel and propeller layers can be left alone.
7. Select Edit, Edit Movie from the menu bar to return to your movie.

Figure 7.12

Painting the wings purple

Animating the Planes

Now you're ready to animate! The red plane will start out above and behind the orange plane. As they move across the stage, the orange plane will perform a loop and end up chasing the red plane. To create the animation, follow these steps:

1. Select the Orange Plane layer and select Insert, Motion Guide from the menu bar.
2. Use the Pen tool to draw a looping path for the plane to follow, as shown in Figure 7.13.
3. Insert a keyframe at frame 30 of both the Guide layer and the Orange Plane layer.
4. Select frame 1 of the Orange Plane layer.
5. Position the plane at the start of the motion guide.
6. Select Insert, Create Motion Tween from the menu bar.

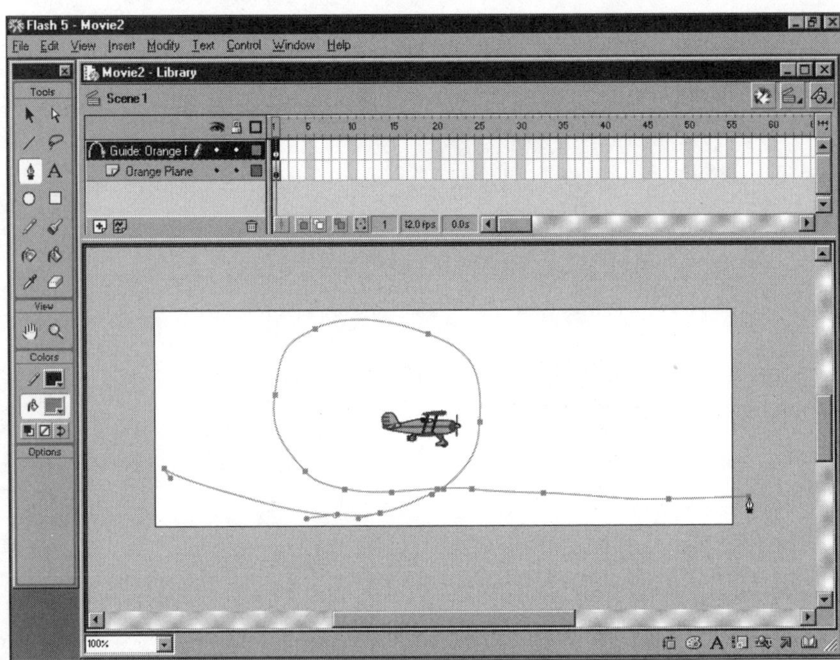

Figure 7.13

The looping path

7. Select frame 30.
8. Position the plane at the end of the motion guide.
9. Press Enter (Return on the Mac) to test the animation (see Figure 7.14).
10. Create a new layer and call it Red Plane.
11. Drag the layer above the Guide layer.
12. Open the Library Panel, if it is not already open.
13. Drag the Chase Plane symbol onto the stage and position it just behind and above the orange plane at frame 1.
14. Select Insert, Create Motion Tween from the menu bar.
15. Create a keyframe at frame 30 of the Red Plane layer.
16. Move the red plane off the stage to the bottom right, as shown in Figure 7.15.
17. Press Enter (Return on the Mac) to test the animation.

Figure 7.14

The orange plane in a loop

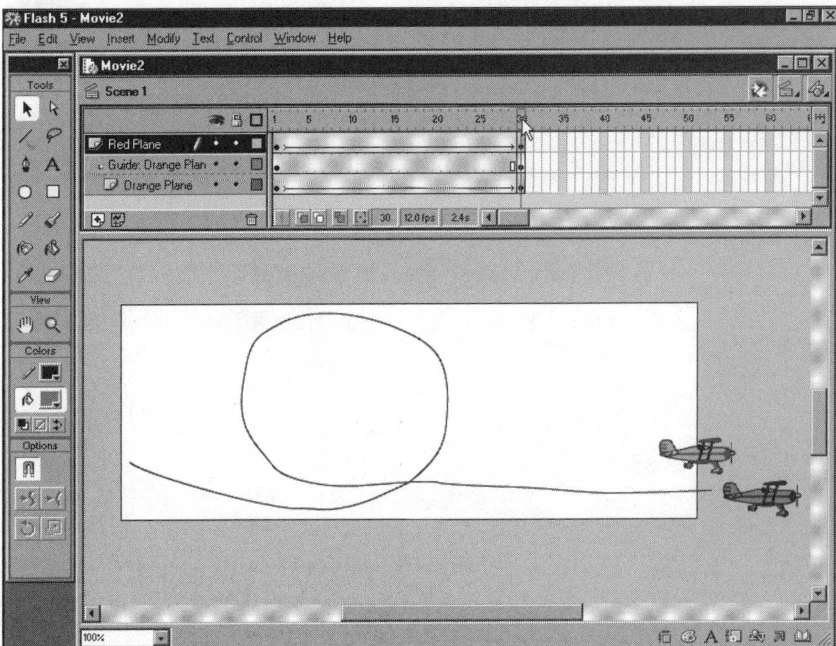

Figure 7.15

The chaser is now being chased

For a more realistic animation, create a number of keyframes between frame 1 and frame 30. At each point where a plane changes direction, create a keyframe and use the Arrow tool to adjust the rotation of the plane to match the path (see Figure 7.16).

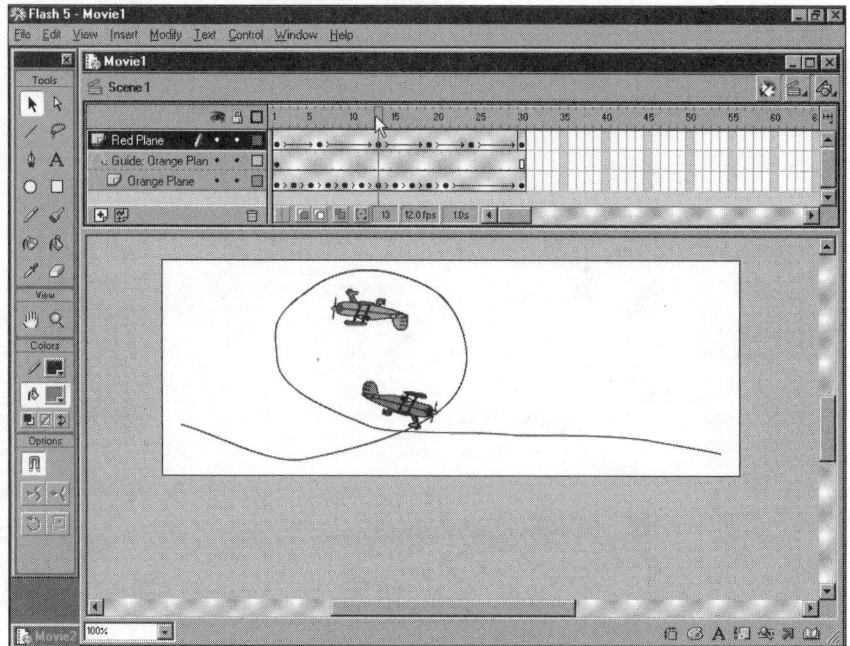

Figure 7.16

A better loop

Converting to a Movie

To convert the plane animation into a movie clip, follow these steps:

1. Open the Library Panel, if it is not already open.
2. Choose Edit, Select All from the menu bar.

3. Copy all the frames by selecting Edit, Copy Frames from the menu bar.
4. Select Insert, New Symbol from the menu bar. The Symbol Properties dialog box will open (see Figure 7.17).

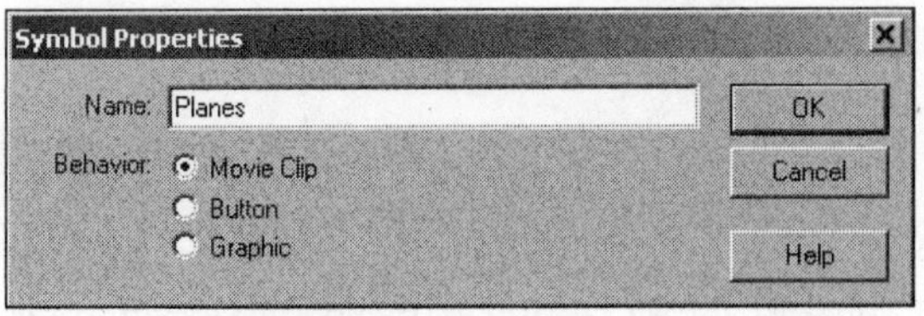

Figure 7.17

Creating the second animation movie clip

5. Name the symbol **Planes** and click on OK.
6. Click frame 1 of the movie clip.
7. Select Edit, Paste Frames from the menu bar. Flash copies the entire movie to the Planes Movie Clip.
8. Select Edit, Edit Movie from the menu bar to return to your movie.

Before moving on to the next section, save your project file to your hard drive. If you choose to use this same file for the next animation, you should hide and lock all the Biplane layers.

Creating Morph Animation

Your third movie clip will be a shape tween. You'll draw a number of 3D shapes and use Flash 5's shape tweening ability to create a morphing effect.

Open a new movie if you are creating separate files for each animation. Use the Movie Properties dialog box to adjust the stage width to 550 and the height to 200.

Adding a Sphere

The first shape is a simple sphere. To add a sphere to your movie, follow these steps:

1. Create a new layer and name it **Morph**. All the shapes will be drawn on this layer.
2. Click the Oval tool in the Tools Panel.
3. Hold the Shift key down and use the Oval tool to draw a circle.
4. Use the Arrow tool to center the circle on the stage.
5. Open the Fill Panel by selecting Windows, Panels, Fill from the menu bar.
6. Choose Radial Gradient as the Fill Type.
7. Create a simple blue-to-black gradient (see Figure 7.18).
8. Select the Paint Bucket tool and click inside the circle, then click a spot just off center to the top left of the circle.

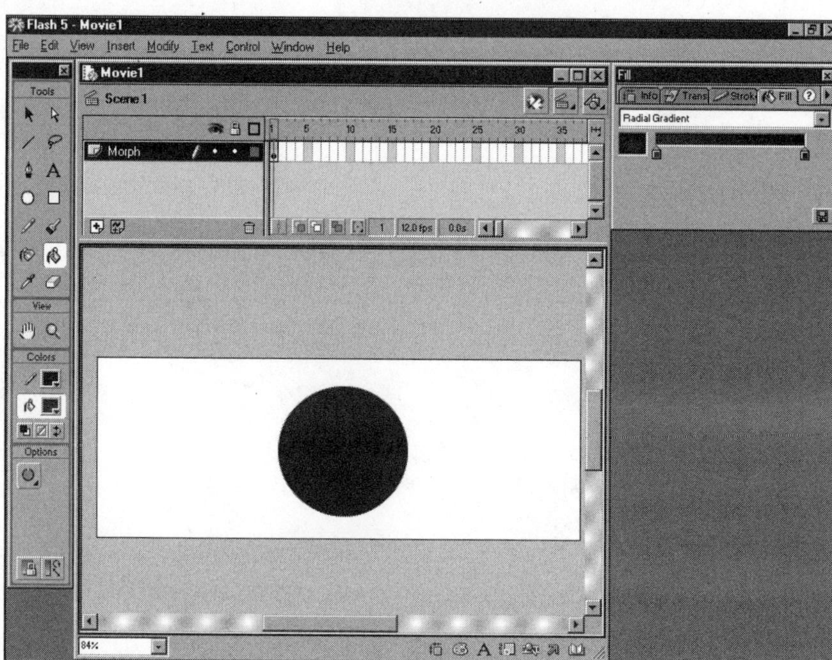

Figure 7.18

An easy 3D gradient

Creating a Cube

The next shape is a cube. To create a cube, do the following:

1. Create a blank keyframe at frame 6.
2. Click the Rectangle tool in the Tools Panel.
3. Hold the Shift key down and use the Rectangle tool to draw a square.
4. Use the Arrow tool to select the square.
5. Select Window, Panels, Transform from the menu bar.
6. Select Skew as the transform type and set the vertical skew to 30 degrees.
7. Press Enter (Return on the Mac) to apply the skew. This is the first side of your cube (see Figure 7.19).

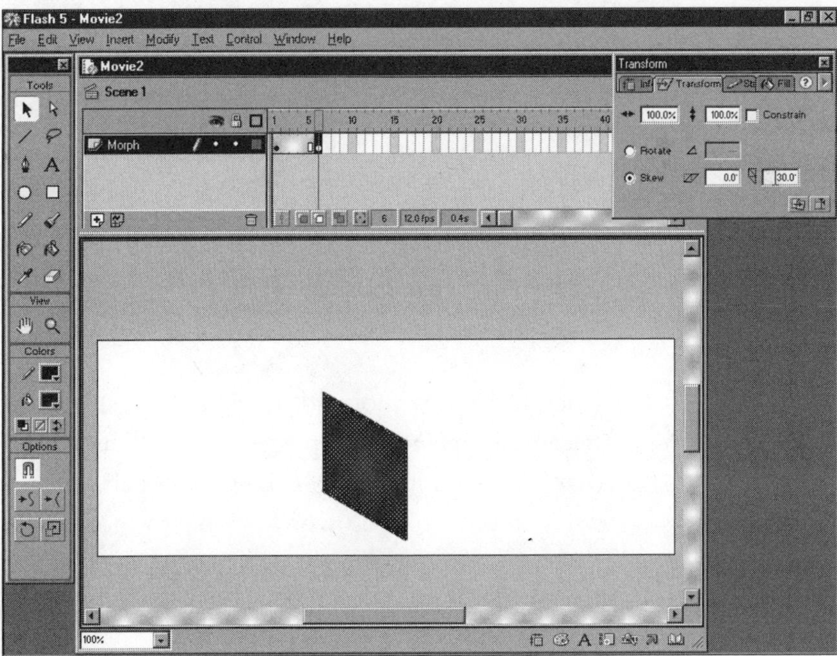

Figure 7.19

The first side of the cube

8. From the menu bar select Edit, Copy.
9. Right-click (Ctrl+click on the Mac) on the stage and select Paste. This adds the second side of your cube to the stage.
10. Select Modify, Transform, Flip Horizontal from the menu bar (see Figure 7.20).

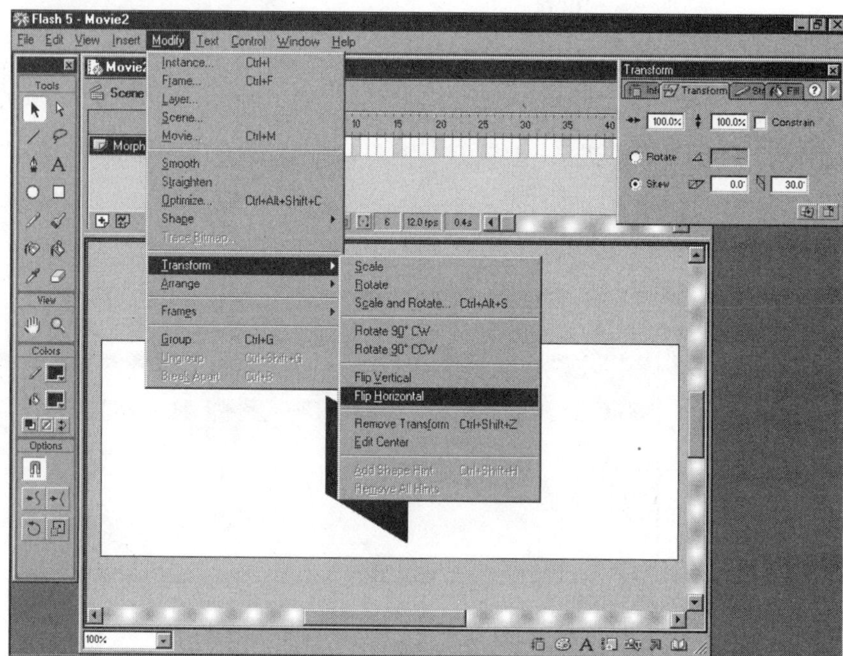

Figure 7.20

Flipping the second side

11. Click the Arrow tool and move the two sides next to one another. Because we want to keep these sides editable separately, be careful that they do not touch. If the sides touch, Flash will combine the two graphics and you won't be able to move them separately.

For precise positioning of objects, use the arrow keys on your keyboard with the Arrow tool selected.

12. Right-click (Ctrl+click on the Mac) on the stage and select Paste. This adds the third side of your cube to the stage. Make sure this new side is selected.
13. In the Transform Panel select Rotate and type **120** in the angle field.
14. Press Enter (Return on the Mac) to apply the rotation.
15. Use the Arrow tool to move the third side just above the other two. Be sure none of the sides touch (see Figure 7.21).

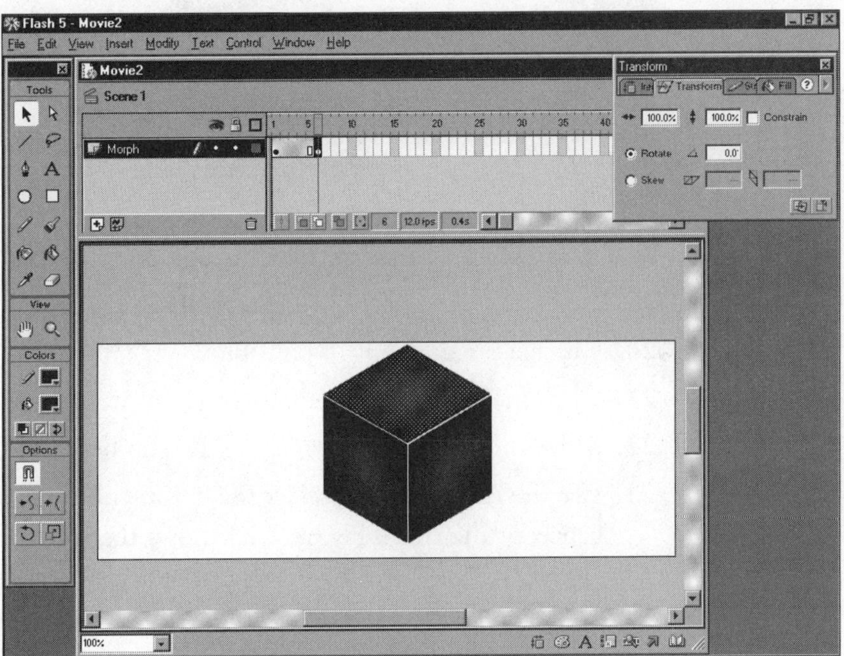

Figure 7.21

The basic cube

16. Open the Fill Panel.
17. Create a red, light blue, dark blue radial gradient.
18. Select the Paint Bucket tool.
19. Click on the left corner of the top side and the top corner of the left side (see Figure 7.22).

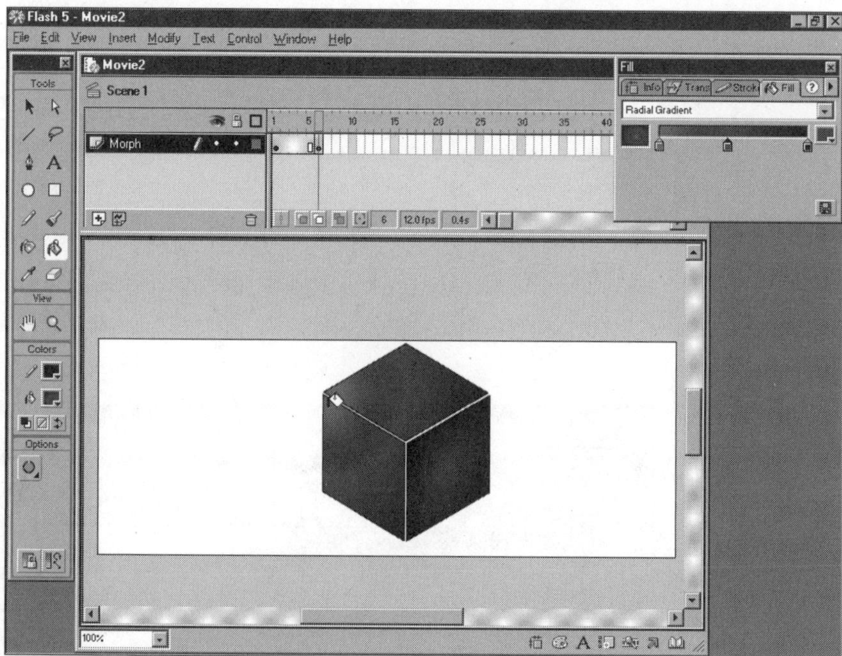

Figure 7.22

A gradient cube

20. Change the gradient to light blue, dark blue.
21. Click the left corner of the right side.
22. Move the three sides to remove the gap between them.
23. Use the Arrow tool to select the entire cube and position it in the center of the stage. Figure 7.23 shows the finished cube.

Creating the Shape Tween

Now you can create the shape tween. To morph between the sphere and the cube, follow these steps:

1. Select frame 1.
2. Press Ctrl+F (Command+F on the Mac) to open the Frame Panel.
3. Add a shape tween (see Figure 7.24).
4. Press Enter (Return on the Mac).

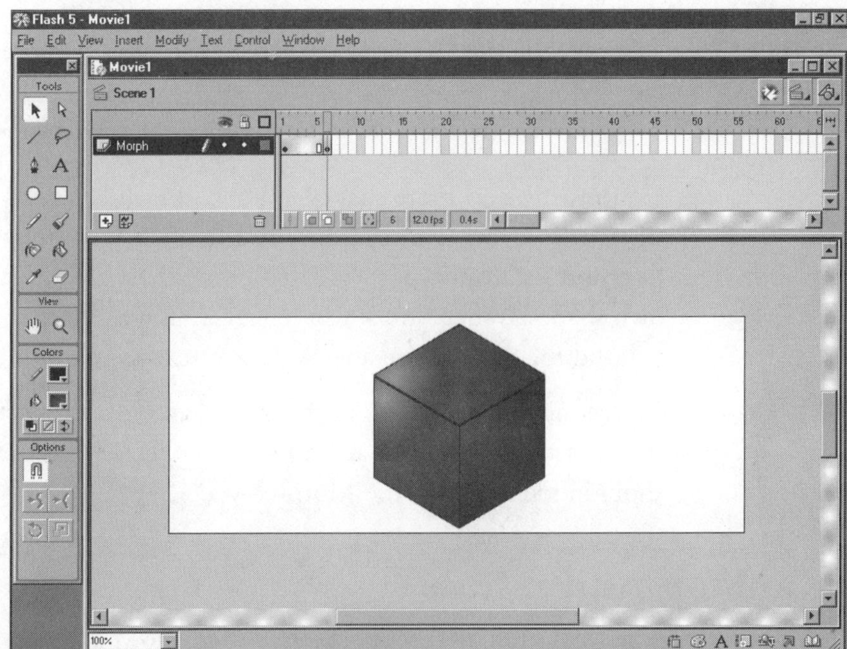

Figure 7.23

A 3D cube

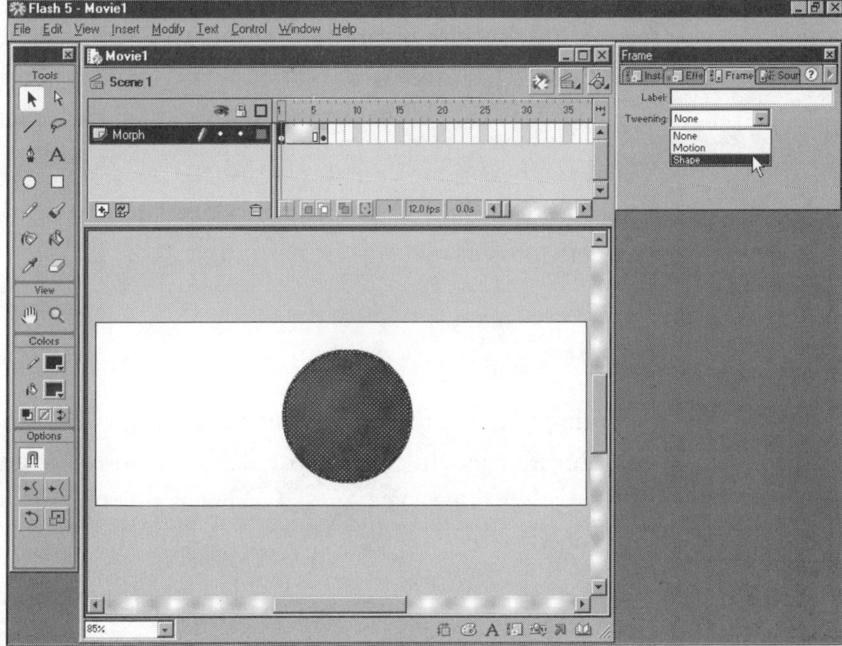

Figure 7.24

Creating the shape tween

If the morphing effect isn't what you were looking for, you can add shape hints to adjust the tweening.

Continue to add more shapes to your Morph layer. Try to come up with three or four other transitions. You might try to draw a globe, a smiley face, and a starburst, as in the final_project.fla file, or you can design your own shapes. When you finish, create a movie clip from the animation as you did for the Biplane and Welcome text animations.

Before moving on to the next section save your project file to your hard drive. If you choose to use this same file for the next animation you should hide and lock the Morph layer.

Slideshow Animation

The final animated sequence is a slide show. The exact contents of the animation are up to you. The final_project.fla shows a cartoon character in a number of locations, reminiscent of vacation photos. You can try to recreate these slides or produce an original sequence. Use your imagination! Be sure to leave a few frames between each slide and the next. That way your viewers will have time to appreciate each picture.

When you have your slideshow finished, create a movie clip from the animation as you did for the others. Before moving on to the next section, save your project file to your hard drive.

Take a Break

Now that you've finished all four movie clips, step away from the computer for a little while. Treat yourself to a smoothie and relax—the bulk of the work is done. Next, you'll create a control panel to link your movie clips together.

The Control Panel

Your movie needs a user interface—viewers of your movie need to be able to switch between movie clips. For this you will create a control panel. The control panel consists of a background and four control buttons. The following section will walk you through creating a simple control panel, but if you're feeling creative you can use your own design.

The Panel Background

The background is the graphic that will hold your control buttons and the movie clips. You can create a quick background using the Rectangle tool and the Fill Panel.

Open a new movie and use the Movie Properties dialog box to set the stage width to 550 and the height to 300. Leave the frame rate at 12 fps. Create a new graphic symbol named Background Panel by pressing Ctrl+F8 (Command+F8 on the Mac).

Since the control panel will hold the movie clips it needs to be a bit larger.

To create the control panel background, follow these steps:

1. Rename layer 1 **Silver Base**.
2. Use the Rectangle tool to create a rectangle with a thin gray stroke. The rectangle should fill the bottom of the movie, but should not be more than one-third high.
3. Open the Fill Panel and construct a linear gradient that alternates light grays, dark grays, and whites.
4. Use the Paint Bucket tool to give the rectangle a metallic look.

TIP You can use the Transform Fill option of the Paint Bucket tool to angle the gradient (see Figure 7.25). This will give a more reflective look.

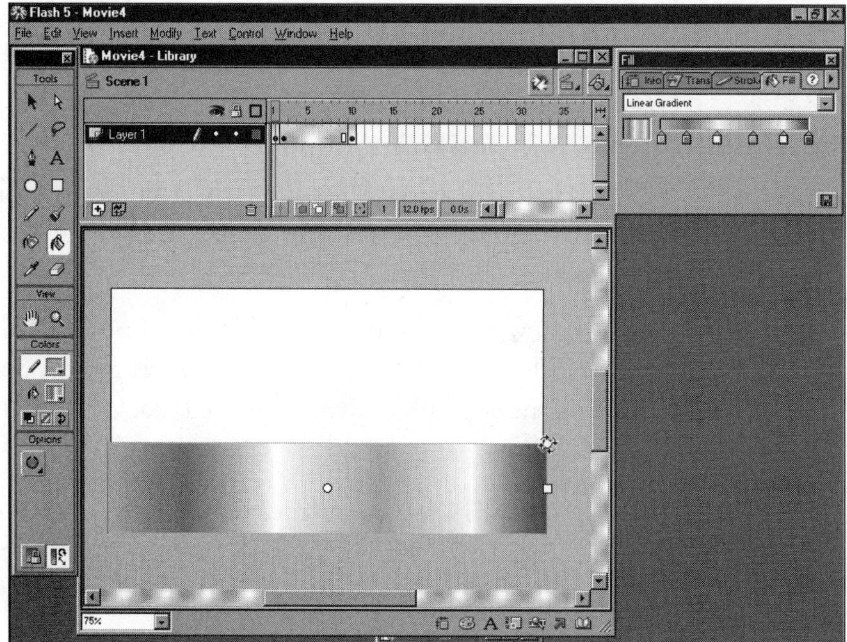

Figure 7.25

Angling the gradient

5. Select the Arrow tool and grab the top edge of the box, pulling it down into a concave curve.
6. Add a new layer and name it **Blue Panel**.
7. Drag the Blue Panel layer below the Silver Base layer in the Layers Panel.
8. Draw another rectangle—this time a blue one. Make it slightly smaller than the last.

9. Make a nice dark blue or medium blue radial gradient in the Fill Panel.
10. With the Paint Bucket tool, click on the blue rectangle.
11. Use the Arrow tool to curve the top edge of the rectangle upward (see Figure 7.26).

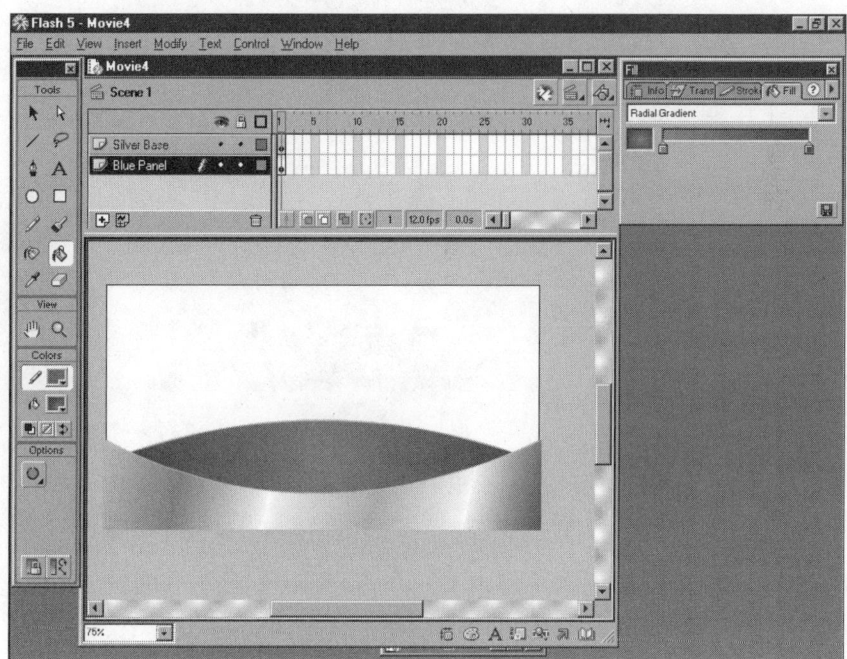

Figure 7.26

The blue gradient

12. Create a new layer named **Screen**.
13. Drag the Screen layer below the Blue Panel Layer.
14. Draw a large rectangle that fills the entire stage.
15. Give the rectangle a pale yellow, white, sky blue radial gradient for a sun effect (see Figure 7.27).

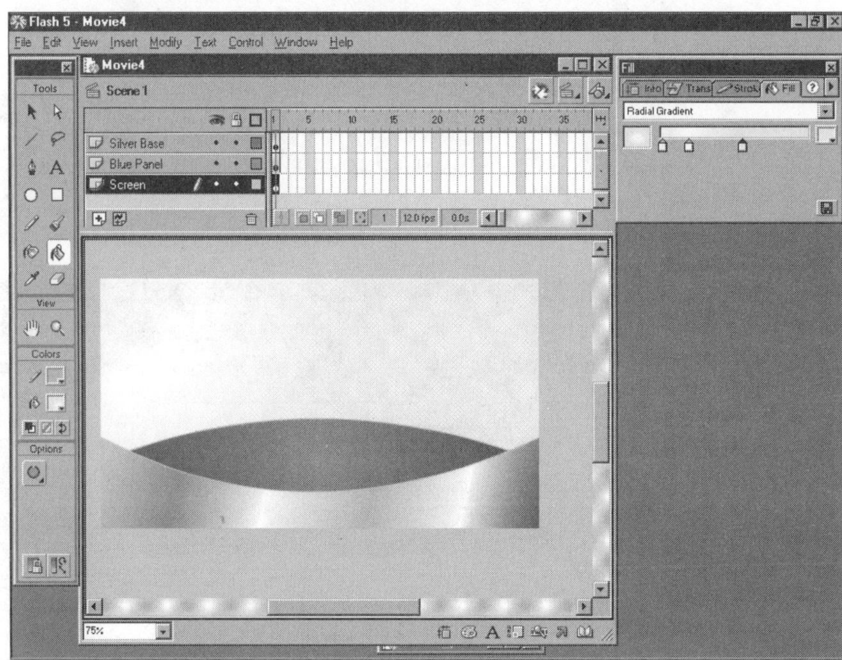

Figure 7.27

The finished panel

Adding the Background Panel symbol to the stage is easy:

1. Select Edit, Edit movie from the menu bar.
2. Rename layer 1 **Background**.
3. Drag the Background Panel symbol to the stage.

Before moving on to the next section, save your project file to your hard drive.

The Basic Button

You have four movie clips, so you will need four buttons. Recognizable buttons are an important part of any interface design. The movie viewers will need buttons that show a graphical representation of their use. A bunch of buttons numbered 1 through 4 just won't work.

To create a basic button, follow these steps:

1. Press Ctrl+F8 (Command+F8 on the Mac) to create a new button symbol.
2. Name the symbol **Basic Button** and select Button as the behavior.
3. Click OK.
4. Rename Layer 1 **Oval**.
5. Draw a circle filled with a green radial gradient—the gradient should go from light in the center to dark at the edges.
6. Open the Transform Panel by selecting Window, Panels, Transform in the menu bar.
7. Uncheck Constrain and adjust the height to 75%.
8. Press Enter (Return on the Mac) to apply the change. Figure 7.28 shows the result.

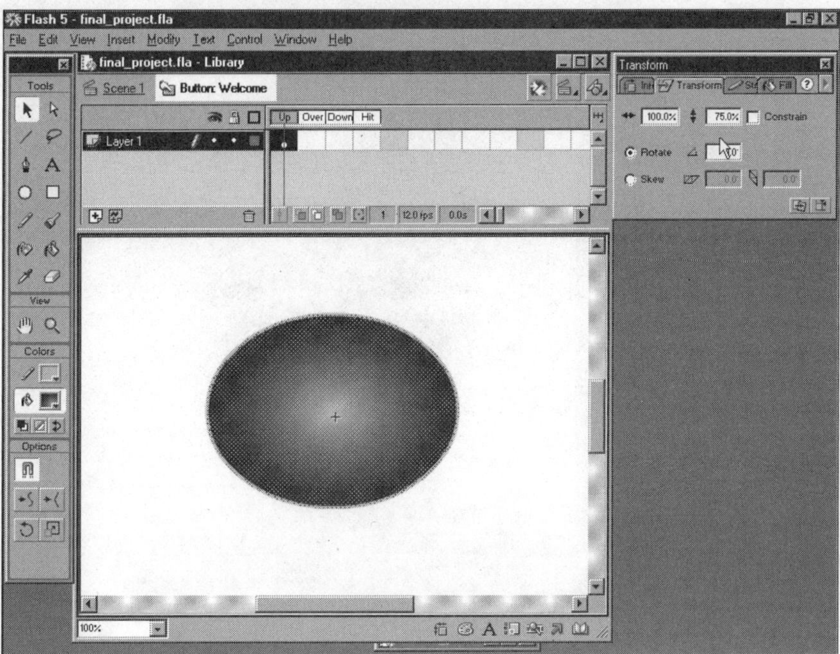

Figure 7.28

An oval with a nice gradient

Flattening a circle into an oval after applying a gradient produces a more realistic effect than applying a radial gradient directly to an oval.

9. Add a new layer named **Base** below your Oval Layer.
10. Draw an oval on the stage filled with an alternating light gray, dark gray linear gradient.
11. Position the gray oval behind the green one on the stage (see Figure 7.29).
12. Create a keyframe in the Over state of the Oval layer.
13. In the Fill Panel, move the light green slider to the right slightly. The fill of the oval changes to match the new gradient.

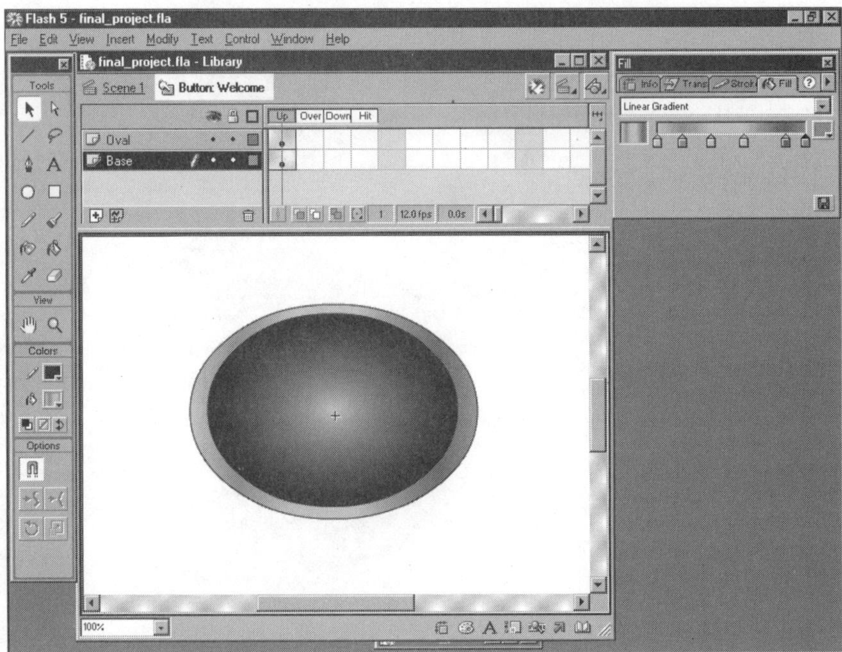

Figure 7.29

The Up state of the basic button

14. Create a keyframe in the Down state of the Oval layer and move the gradient slider even farther right (see Figure 7.30).
15. Create keyframes in the Down state of the Base layer and the Hit state of the Oval Layer.

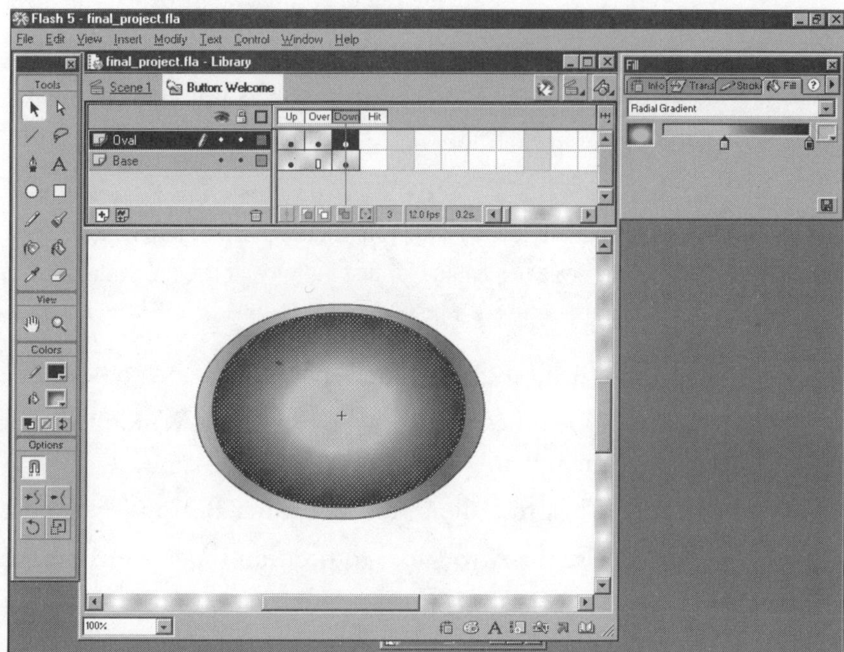

Figure 7.30

The Down state gradient

Now that you have the template for your buttons, you can copy the Basic Button symbol for each movie clip and add graphics or text to distinguish them. The final_project.fla file uses a combination of words and images on the control buttons. You can copy those, or create your own.

Adding Controls to the Buttons

Now make it so that each button will have an action that will move the animation to a different scene. But first, place the buttons on the control panel:

1. If you closed the background panel movie file, open it again.
2. Add a new layer at the top of the Layers Panel and name it **Buttons**.
3. Open the Library Panel, if it is not already open.
4. Drag each button onto the stage.

TIP If the buttons are too large you can use the Transform Panel to scale them down. Remember the scale percentage for first button and use the same value for the other three.

5. Click the Buttons Layer. All of the buttons will be selected.
6. Open the Align Panel by selecting Window, Panels, Align from the menu bar.
7. Click the Align Vertical Center Button (see Figure 7.31).
8. Use the Arrow tool to position the buttons on the control panel.
9. Deselect the buttons.

Adding controls to the buttons is simply a matter of assigning a Go To action for each. To add an action to the buttons, follow these steps:

1. Right-click (Ctrl+click on the Mac) on the Welcome Button and select Actions.
2. Click + and select Basic Actions, Go To from the menu.
3. Type **Welcome** in the Scene field (see Figure 7.32).

NOTE You'll create the Welcome Scene and all of the others in the next section.

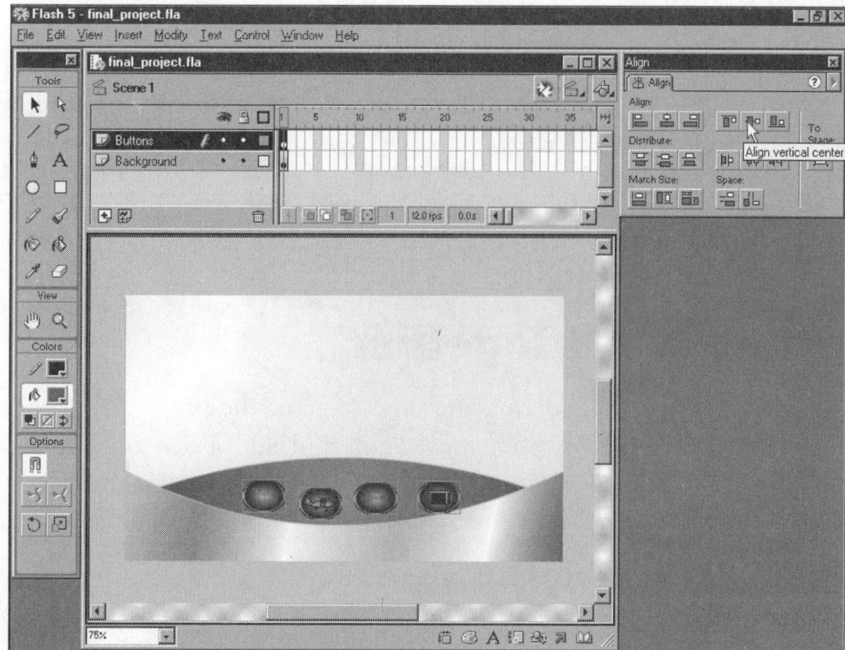

Figure 7.31

Aligning the buttons

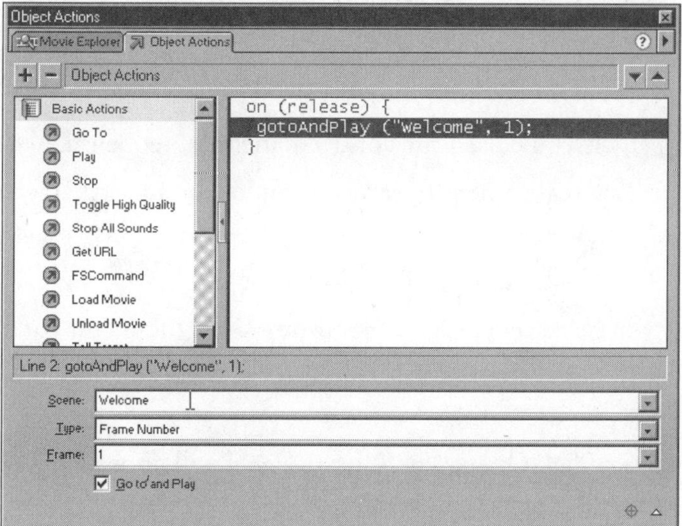

Figure 7.32

Activating the Welcome Scene

4. Close the Action Panel.
5. Repeat this procedure for each button. The Morph button should go to the Morph scene, Biplane to Biplane, and Slideshow to Slideshow.

Before moving on to the next section, save your project file to your hard drive.

Putting It All Together

You're entering the final stage of the project. All that's left is to create a scene for each movie clip and add a few final touches. It's all coming together!

Adding the Movie Clips

You spent a lot of time on the four movie clips; it's about time to add them to your movie. Each movie clip will get its own scene. This not only helps you organize the movie, but it makes it easy to add more movie clips later on, too.

To add a movie clip to your movie, follow these steps:

1. If you closed the control panel file, reopen it.
2. Create a new layer at the top of the Layers Panel and name it **Movie**.
3. Click frame 1 of the Movie layer.
4. Select File, Open As Library from the menu bar.
5. Select the file that contains the Welcome movie clip (see Figure 7.32).
6. Click Open. The Library Panel will appear.

Figure 7.32

Opening a movie file as a library

7. Drag the Welcome Movie Clip to the stage.
8. Use the Arrow tool to position the movie at the top of the control panel.

TIP

You can press Ctrl+Enter (Command+Return on the Mac) to see the movie clip in action. This will make it easier to properly position the animation.

Creating the Rest of the Scenes

You will need a scene for the each of the other three movie clips. To create the rest of the scenes for your move, follow these steps:

1. Select Window, Panels, Scene from the menu bar to open the Scene Panel.
2. Double-click scene 1.
3. Type **Welcome**.
4. Press Enter (Return on the Mac). This renames the scene.
5. Click the Duplicate Scene button (see Figure 7.33).
6. Rename the scene **Biplane**.
7. Create two more duplicate scenes named **Morph** and **Slideshow**.

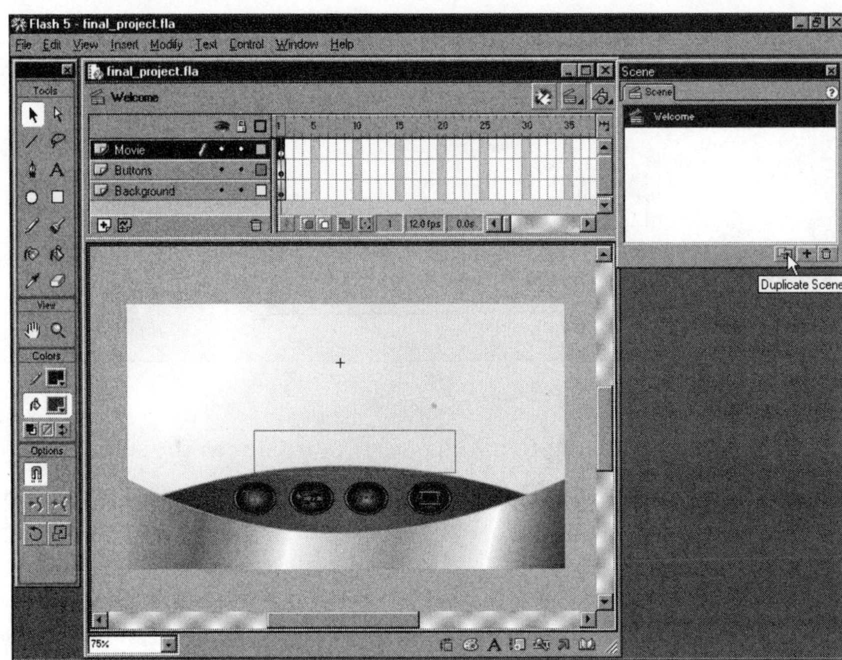

Figure 7.33

Duplicating the Welcome scene

You still have three more movie clips to add. To add the remaining movie clips, follow these steps:

1. Click the Biplane scene.
2. Select the Movie layer.
3. Press Delete to remove the Welcome movie clip.
4. Select File, Open As Library from the menu bar.
5. Select the file that contains the Biplane movie clip.
6. Click Open. The Library Panel appears.
7. Drag the Biplane movie clip to the stage (see Figure 7.34).
8. Use the Arrow tool to position the movie at the top of the control panel.

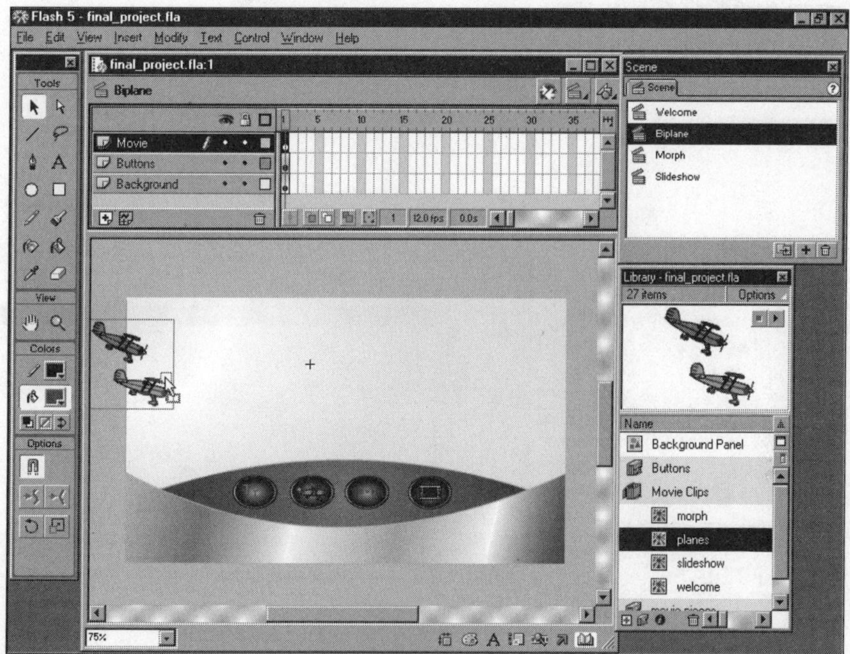

Figure 7.34

Adding the Biplane Movie Clip

You won't be able to use the Test Movie function to test the Biplane movie clip. Instead, use Test Scene by pressing Ctrl+Alt+Enter (Command+Option+Return on the Mac).

9. Repeat this procedure for the Morph and Slideshow movie clips.

Remember how to add controls to the buttons? You do it by assigning a Go To action for each.

1. Select the Welcome scene.
2. Right-click (Ctrl+click on the Mac) on the Biplane Button and select Actions.

3. Click + and select Basic Actions, Go To from the menu. The Object Actions Panel will open.
4. Type **Biplane** in the Scene field (see Figure 7.35).

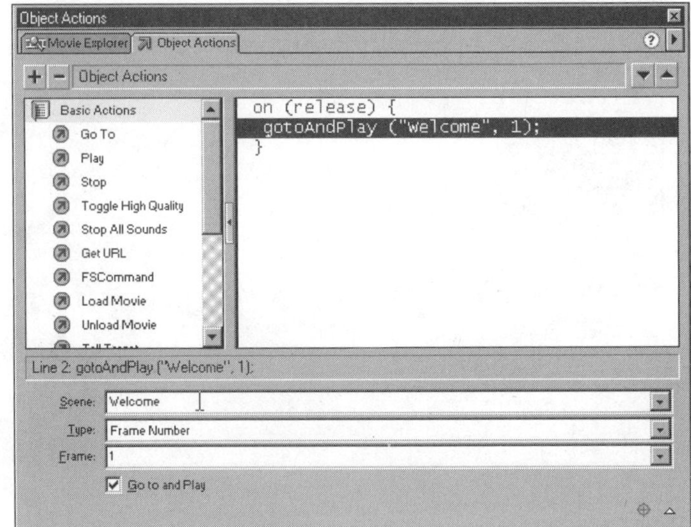

Figure 7.35

Activating the Welcome scene in the Object Actions Panel

5. Close the Action Panel.
6. Repeat this procedure for the Morph and Slideshow buttons. The Morph button should go to the Morph scene, and Slideshow to Slideshow.

Follow these guidelines to add the Go To action on the buttons in the other scenes. For each scene you should only add actions to three buttons. A button should not have an action on its own layer. In other words, don't add a Go To Slideshow action on the Slideshow button in the Slideshow scene.

Finishing Touches

Go ahead and test your movie as it is now. Notice something wrong? The animations run on top of one another. Here's what's going on: Flash automatically moves to the next scene when the first ends. Because your movie only has one frame on each scene, the four scenes fly by without giving the user a chance to appreciate the animations.

Luckily, there's a quick solution. You can add an action to the movie that will stop Flash from advancing to the next scene. To add this Stop action to your movie, do the following:

1. Select the Welcome scene in the Scene Panel.
2. Right-click (Ctrl+click on the Mac) on frame 1 of the Movie layer.
3. Select Actions from the menu. The Frame Actions dialog box will open.

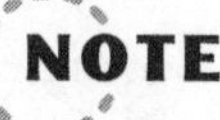

Many of Flash 5 actions don't have to be associated with buttons. They can be placed directly on a keyframe. When the timeline reaches a frame with an action, it triggers the command.

4. Click + and select Basic Actions, Stop from the menu (see Figure 7.36).
5. Close the Actions Panel.
6. Repeat this process for the other three scenes.

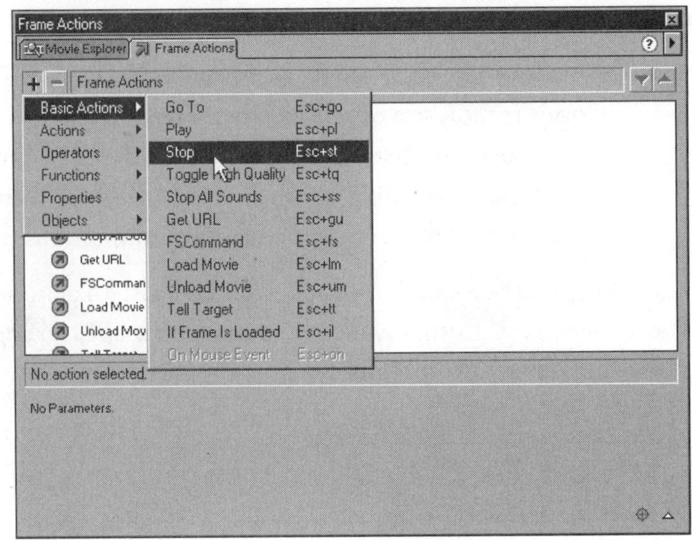

Figure 7.36

Adding the Stop action to the Welcome Scene

Test your movie now. It works! One last thing before publishing: you can have your movie take up the whole screen by doing the following:

1. Select the Welcome Scene in the Scene Panel.
2. Right-click (Ctrl+click on the Mac) on frame 1 of the Movie layer.
3. Select Actions from the menu that appears.
4. Click + and select Basic Actions, FSCommand from the menu.
5. Select Fullscreen from the list of commands for standalone player. The movie will take up the entire screen (see Figure 7.37).
6. Close the Actions Panel.

Publishing Your Final Project

Now you can publish your project! To create a stand-alone player for your movie, follow these steps:

Figure 7.37

The full-screen effect

1. Save your file.
2. Select File, Publish Settings from the menu bar. The Publish Settings dialog box will appear (see Figure 7.38).
3. Check Windows Projector and Macintosh projector as the Type.

If you don't need a Macintosh version, you may leave that option unchecked—and the same goes for the Windows version.

4. Click Publish.

Congratulations! In only one weekend, you've learned how to create your own Flash 5 movies from scratch. You can e-mail your finished movie to your friends and family. Show them all the cool skills you've developed!

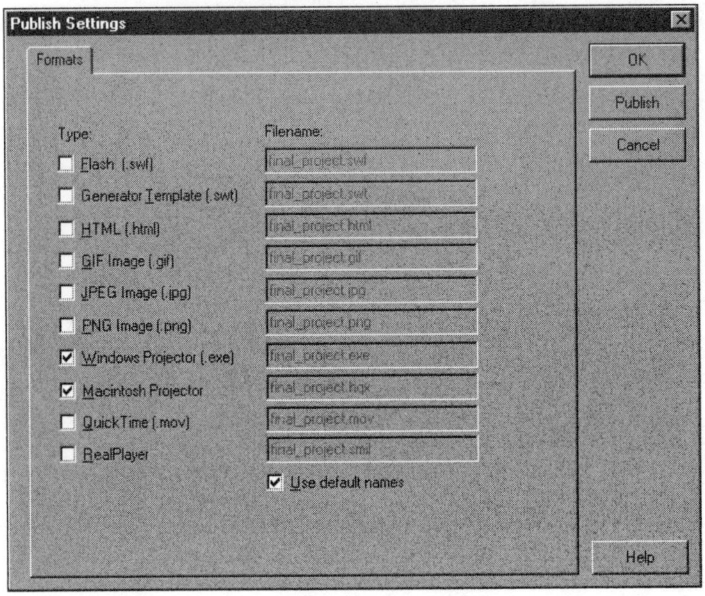

Figure 7.38

Publishing your movie

What's Next

You've only touched the surface of what Macromedia Flash 5 can do. If you want to learn more you can pick up a more advanced book or try an online tutorial. Appendix D of this book includes a number of Web sites where you can go to learn more about Flash 5. I've also included a bonus chapter explaining a few advanced topics, including adding sound to Flash 5 movies and converting bitmaps into vector graphics. Good luck!

APPENDIX A

Bonus Session: Beyond the Basics

As you've probably noticed, there's more to Flash 5 than can be learned in a single weekend. This book gives you a good introduction to the application, showing you just what you need to create Flash movies. This special bonus session introduces two advanced features of Flash 5: adding sound and using raster images. When you finish you'll be ready to explore the rest of the application on your own. There's a lot more it can do!

Adding Sound to Flash

Sound and animation have been together ever since America's favorite mouse first stepped onto a steamboat. No doubt you've noticed that your Flash 5 movies are a little quiet. It's time to change that.

There are two ways to add sound to your movie. You can add the sound files directly to the timeline or you can activate them with buttons. Sounds in the timeline will play in a predefined sequence based on the timing of the movie as a whole. Sounds linked to a button are activated based on the viewer's actions.

Adding Sounds to the Timeline

Importing sounds into your Flash movie is much the same as importing images. The only difference is that you select a sound file rather than a graphic.

To import a sound file into your movie, follow these steps:

1. Open a new movie and use the Movie Properties dialog box to adjust the stage to fit comfortably on your monitor.
2. Select File, Import from the menu bar. The Import dialog box will open (see Figure A.1).
3. Navigate to the sound file you want to import and click Open. Flash will add the sound file to the Library. I've included a number of freeware sound files courtesy of Prosonica Sound Design in the "bonus" folder on the CD-ROM.

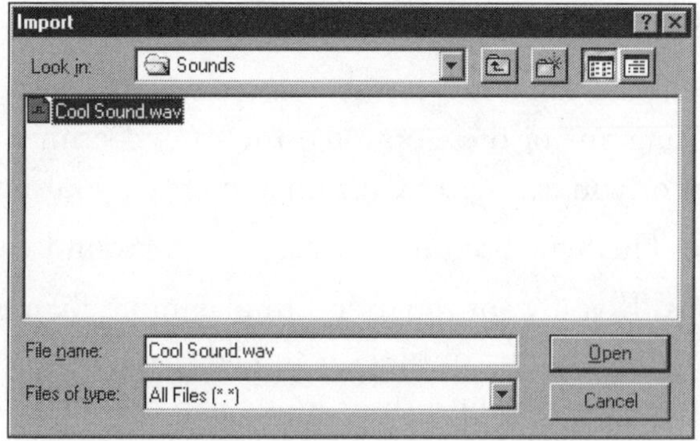

Figure A.1

Importing a .wav file

NOTE

Flash 5 will allow you to import many types of sound files: WAV (Windows only), AIFF (Macintosh only), and MP3 (either platform). If you have QuickTime installed, you can also import these sound file formats: Sound Designer II (Macintosh only), Sound Only QuickTime Movies (Windows or Macintosh), Sun AU (Windows or Macintosh), System 7 Sounds (Macintosh only), and WAV (Windows or Macintosh).

You can use the Sound Panel to add sounds to the timeline. To add a sound to your movie, do the following:

1. Create a keyframe where you would like the sound to play.
2. Select Window, Panels, Sound from the menu bar to open the Sound Panel.
3. Select your sound in the Sound Panel (see Figure A.2).
4. Choose Start as the Sync type. The sound will now play when the timeline reaches this keyframe.

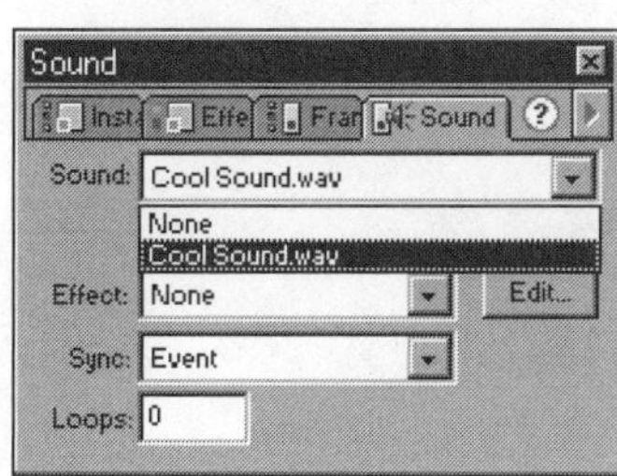

Figure A.2

Adding a sound to the timeline

There are a number of options available on the Sound Panel:

- **Effect.** You can add a number of special effects to your sound by choosing one of these options. You can experiment to find the best effect or you can select Custom and create your own.
- **Sync**. The Sync option controls how the sound will play.
- **Loops.** If you want the sound to play more than once you can designate the number of times it should play. Background music can be added by looping a short music clip.

Stopping a Sound

Stopping a sound is just as easy as adding one. To make a sound stop playing, follow these steps:

1. Create a keyframe where you would like the sound to stop.
2. Open the Sound Panel, if it is not already open.
3. Select the sound you wish to stop playing.
4. Choose Stop as the Sync type (see Figure A.3).

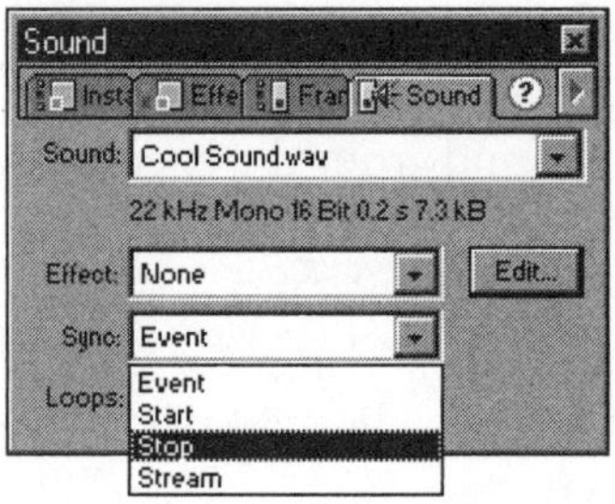

Figure A.3

Stopping a sound

Adding Sounds to Buttons

Nothing says "button" more than a nice, crisp click. Flash 5 allows you to add sound effects to button actions. As with any sound effect, though, be careful not to overdo it. Sound can make your movie pop, but if overused, it can be annoying and cumbersome.

To play a sound effect when the user clicks a button, follow these steps:

1. Open the Library Panel, if it is not already open.
2. Double-click a button symbol to edit the button.
3. Add a new layer to the button and name it **Sound**.
4. Create a keyframe on the Sound layer in the Down state (see Figure A.4).

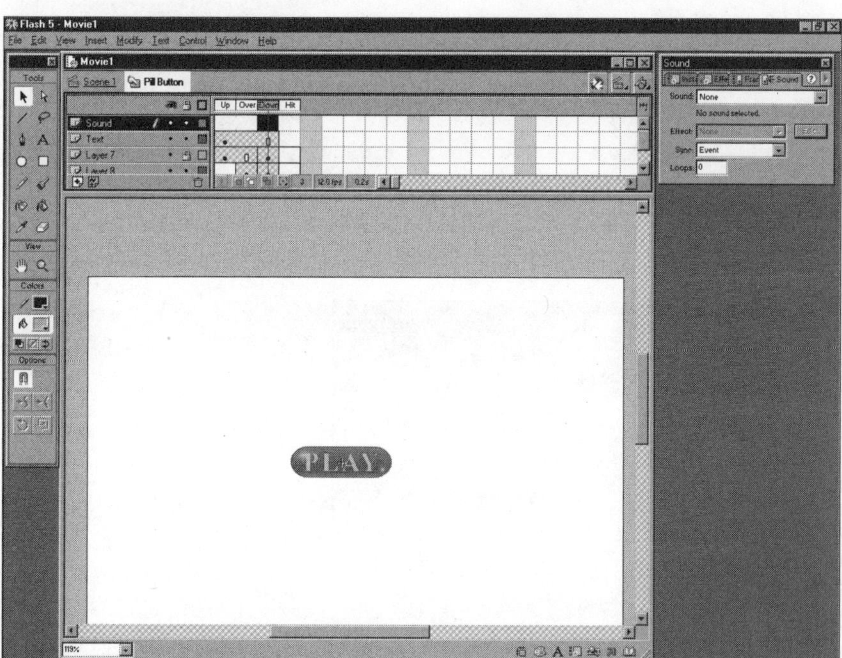

Figure A.4

Adding sound to a button

5. Open the Sound Panel, if it is not already open.
6. Select the sound you want to play.
7. Choose Event as the Sync type.

Creating a Mouseover Sound

You can also play a sound when the viewer moves the mouse pointer over a button. To create a mouseover sound, follow these steps:

1. Open the Library Panel, if it is not already open.
2. Double-click a button symbol to edit the button.
3. Add a new layer to the button and name it **Sound**.
4. Create a keyframe on the Sound layer in the Over state.
5. Open the Sound Panel, if it is not already open.
6. Select the sound you want to play.
7. Choose Event as the Sync type (see Figure A.5).

NOTE You can have sounds on both the Down and Over states.

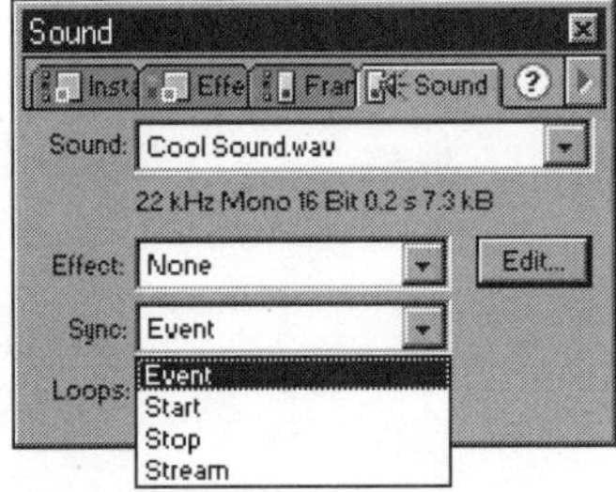

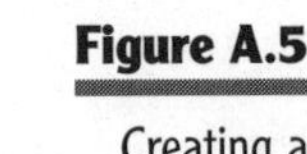

Figure A.5

Creating a mouseover sound

Stopping All Sounds

Not everyone will appreciate the sounds in your movie. Some people may have bad speakers or older sound cards, or may just prefer to watch the movie without sound. Most Flash animators, as a courtesy to their viewers, provide a way to turn off the sound. You should probably add a button that turns off the sound in your movie too.

To turn off all the sounds, follow these steps:

1. Add a new button on the stage. The button should have a graphic or text that explains to the viewer that it will turn off the sound.
2. Right-click (Command+click on the Mac) the button on the stage and select Actions to open the Actions Panel.
3. Click + and select Basic Actions, Stop All Sounds from the menu (see Figure A.6).
4. Close the Actions Panel.

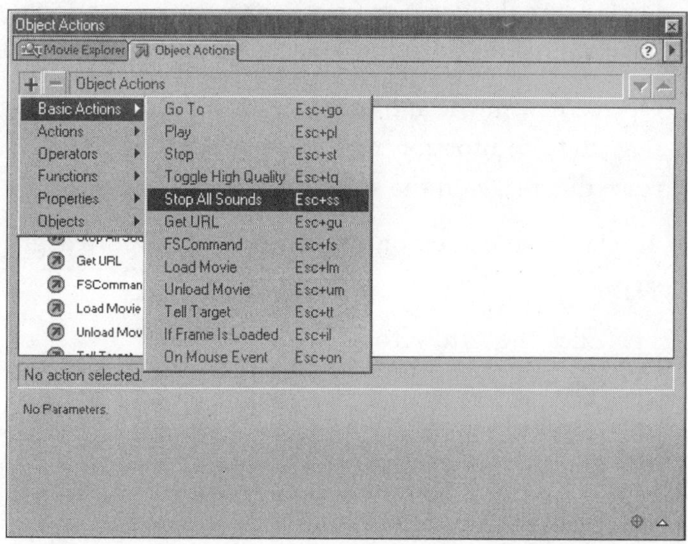

Figure A.6

Stopping all sounds

Using Raster Images in Flash

Flash 5 is a great drawing program, but there are a few things that can be done better or are just easier in other applications. As you saw in Sunday Afternoon's session, fluid animation often calls for imported graphics. Other times you might want to add photographs or scanned images into your movie. For these reasons, you should know how to handle raster images in Flash.

As you learned in Saturday evening's session, Flash 5 uses mathematical calculations, or vector graphics, to draw its images. This keeps the file size of Flash movies very low. Bitmaps, or raster images, are drawn in other imaging programs such as Photoshop or PaintShopPro. Raster images are defined pixel-by-pixel. This makes raster images far larger in size, but also more versatile than vector graphics.

Manipulating Raster Images

Flash won't allow you to create shape tweens or apply gradients to raster images, but you can still change a number of their image properties.

Open a new movie and use the Movie Properties dialog box to adjust the stage to fit comfortably on your monitor. Import an image into Flash and place the image on the stage.

To change the rotation and size of an imported graphic, follow these steps:

1. Click the Arrow Tool.
2. Select the Scale option.
3. Drag the handles until the image is the size you desire (see Figure A.7).
4. Click the Rotate option.
5. Drag the handles until the image is rotated to your liking.

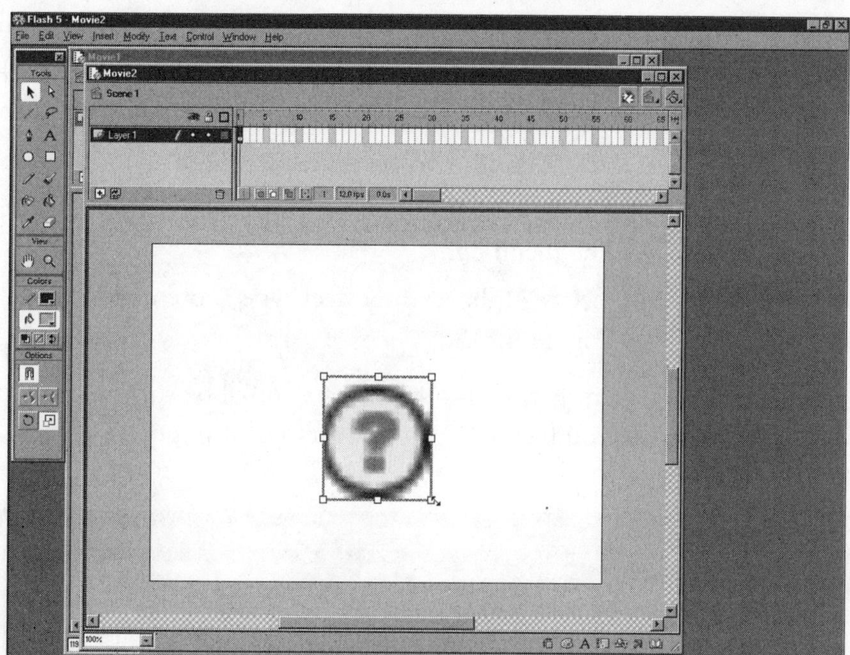

Figure A.7

Expanding a graphic

Expanding a raster graphic in Flash often produces a pixilated effect. To avoid this, use an image editing program, such as Photoshop, to resize the image before importing it into Flash. Alternatively, you can use the trace bitmap process described later in this session.

You can also create motion tweens using imported graphics. To create a motion tween, follow these steps:

1. Create a keyframe at frame 10.
2. Move the graphic to another position on the stage.
3. Click frame 1.
4. Select Insert, Create Motion Tween from the menu bar.

You can add effects to the tween just as you would with drawings created in Flash. To change the opacity of an imported graphic, follow these steps:

1. Click frame 1 in the timeline.
2. Open the Effect Panel by selecting Window, Panels, Effects from the menu bar.
3. Select Alpha as the Effect type and enter 20 as the percentage (see Figure A.8).

Experiment with other effects. You'll be surprised by the amount of control you have over the appearance of imported graphics.

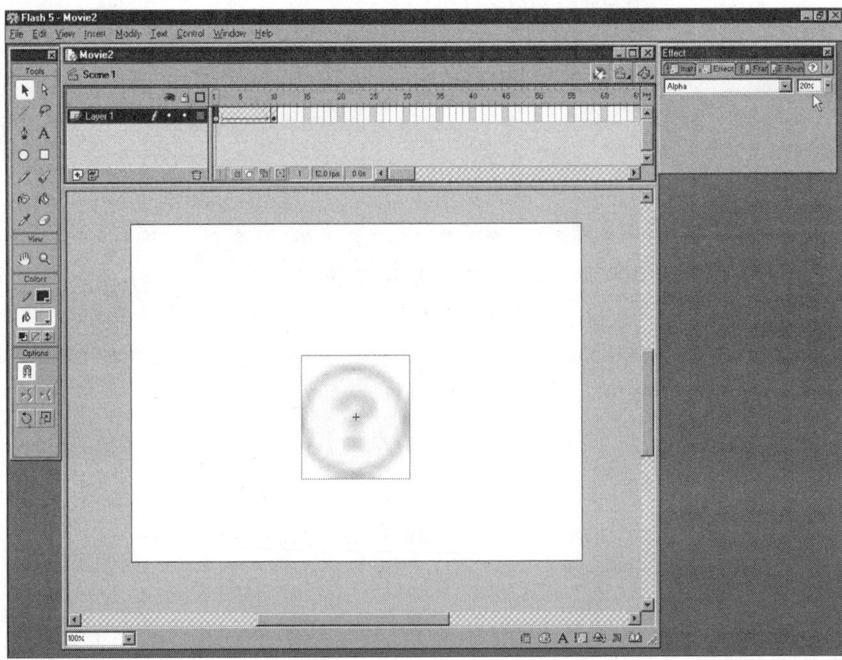

Figure A.8

A semitransparent graphic

Compression Issues

File size is always an important issue to your viewers, so it should be to you as well. One of the reasons Flash is so popular is because it can produce great images and animation without taking up a lot of disk space. Flash graphics are very small. Imported graphics, however, can be quite large. A good Flash designer should know the trade-offs in using imported graphics.

Flash can import three types of graphics: GIF, PNG, and JPEG. All three image formats are compressed, meaning that they take up less disk space than uncompressed formats. GIF and PNG files use a type of compression called *lossless,* where the files do not lose any clarity as they are compressed. The JPEG format uses *lossy* compression. This means that the more the image is compressed, the poorer the quality of the graphic.

When you add JPEG files to your movies you should keep in mind this trade off between file size and image quality. Flash 5 offers you a way to control the compression of imported JPEG images.

To change the compression of JPEG files in your movie, follow these steps:

1. Select File, Publish Settings. The Publish Settings dialog box will appear.
2. Click the Flash tab.
3. Adjust the JPEG compression by moving the JPEG Quality Slider or by typing a percentage in the text field (see Figure A.9). The higher the percentage the better the image will look, but the larger the file size will be.
4. Click OK.

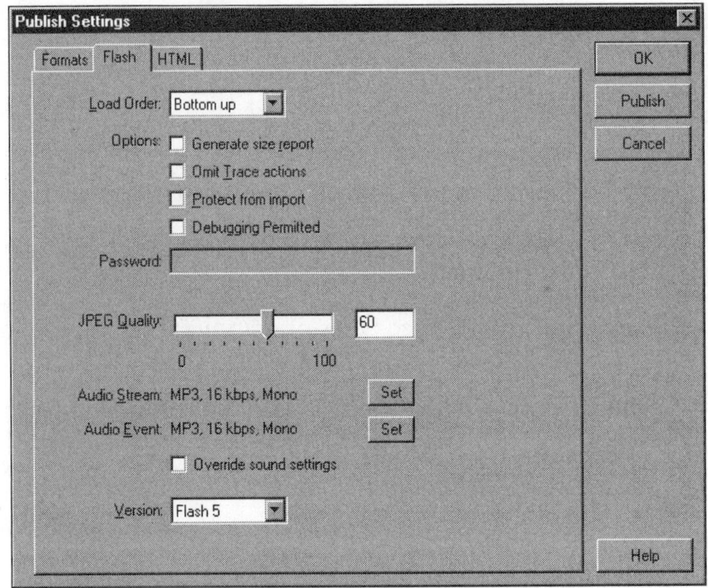

Figure A.9

Adjusting the JPEG compression

TIP

There are a number of image optimization programs available, such as Adobe's ImageReady or Macromedia Fireworks. If you have one of these programs, you should compress the file first, using that program, then import the graphic into your movie. Because the image has already been compressed you can set the Flash 5 compression to 100 percent.

Tracing Raster Images

Another option for dealing with large JPEG images is to convert them to vector drawings. This process is called *tracing*. A bonus advantage to tracing is that the image can then be treated like any other Flash drawing. You can create shape tweens, use the Stroke and Fill Panels to add colors or gradients, and change the shape using the Arrow tool.

To understand the tracing options available, you need to know how Flash converts a raster image into a vector drawing. When you tell the application to trace a raster image, the program looks at each pixel in the graphic individually. It records the color of the pixel and moves to the next. When it's done, the application can compare how the colors in the image relate to each other. It then uses this information to create a vector drawing. There are a number of options that let you change the way Flash uses the color information:

- **Color Threshold**. Controls how different two colors must be before Flash recognizes them as being different. As you increase the threshold value, you decrease the number of colors in the vector drawing.
- **Minimum Area.** Sets the number of surrounding pixels to consider when assigning a color to a pixel. A large minimum area will cause Flash to blend the colors.
- **Curve Fit**. Determines how smoothly Flash will draw curves.
- **Corner Threshold**. Determines how sharp Flash will draw the corners.

To trace a raster image, follow these steps:

1. Select the image on the stage.
2. Select Modify, Trace Bitmap from the menu bar. The Trace Bitmap dialog box will appear.
3. Enter the desired values into the dialog box (see Figure A.10).
4. Click OK.

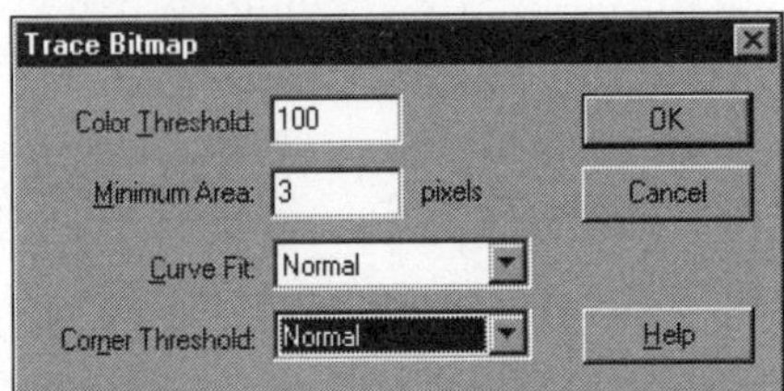

Figure A.10

Tracing an image

You can experiment with the settings to produce the effect you desire. For more information about tracing raster files try one of the additional resources listed in Appendix D.

Be careful about tracing bitmaps; at the highest settings traced graphics can be just as large as some compressed JPEGs. If size is your main concern, you may be better off using the raster image itself.

APPENDIX B

Installing Flash 5

Installing Flash on your PC

Following are the steps for installing the Flash 5 30-Day Trial on your PC:

1. Insert the CD-ROM in this book into your computer's CD-ROM drive.
2. Double-click the My Computer Icon.
3. Double-click the icon representing your CD-ROM drive.
4. Double-click the Flash 5 folder.
5. Double-click flash5-trial.exe.
6. Click Next to continue the installation program.
7. Read the license agreement and click OK if you accept the terms (see Figure B.1).

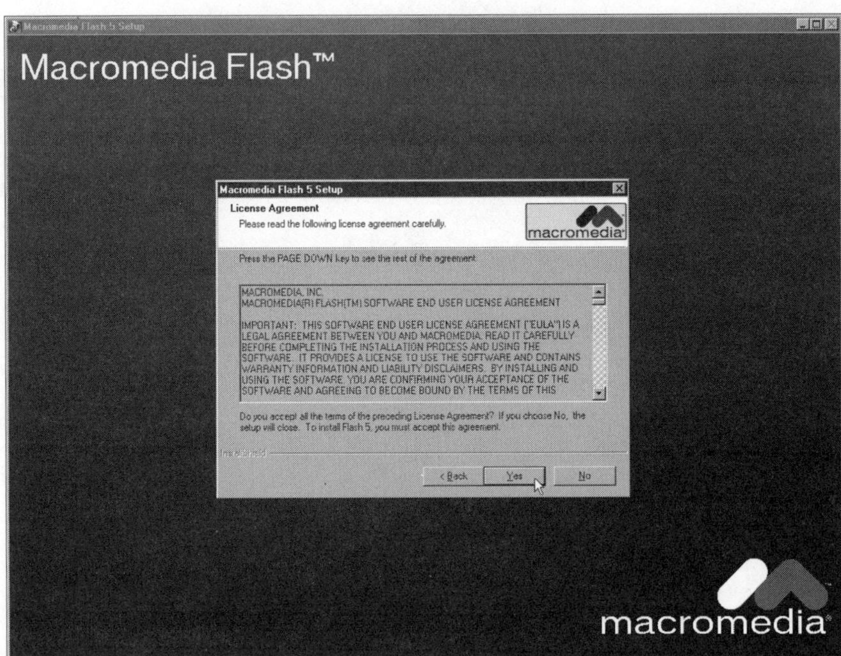

Figure B.1

The Flash 5 license agreement

8. If you want Flash 5 to be installed in the default folder, go on to step 9. Otherwise, click Browse to select the location in which you would like Flash to be installed, and then click Next.
9. Select Typical as the installation type and click Next.
10. Select the name of the programs folder in which you would like the Flash 5 Shortcut to be placed.
11. Select the Flash plug-ins for the browsers on your computer (see Figure B.2), and then click Next.

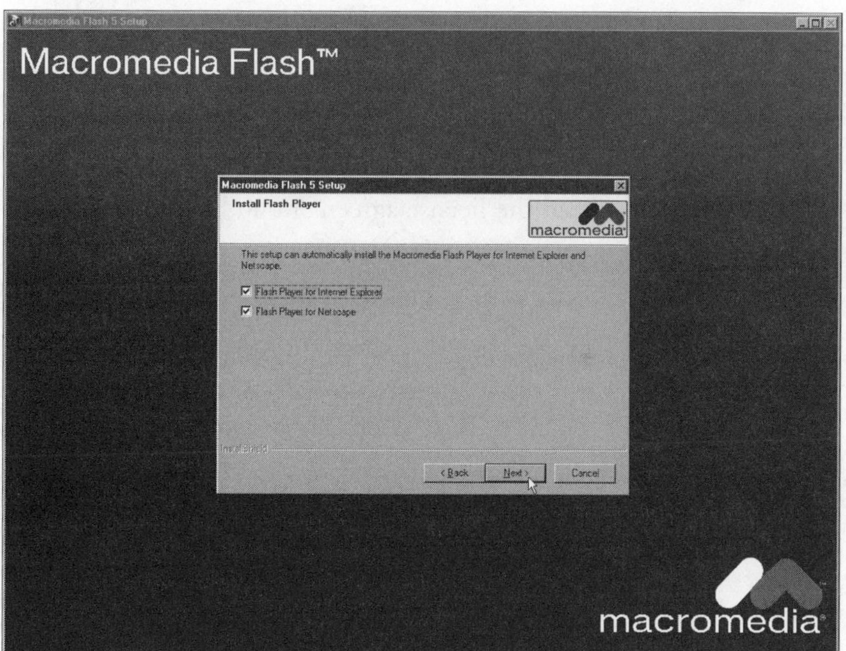

Figure B.2

Installing the plug-ins

12. Click Browse and navigate to the appropriate Plug-Ins folder (that is, Netscape if you selected the Netscape Plug-In) and click Next.
13. Read the installation settings, and if they are correct click Next.

FIND IT ON THE WEB

You can also download the trial version directly from Macromedia's Web site, at http://www.macromedia.com/software/flash/trial/

Installing Flash on Your Mac

To install the Flash 5 30-Day Trial on your Mac, follow these steps:

1. Insert the CD-ROM in this book into your computer.
2. Double-click the CD-ROM icon on your desktop.
3. Double-click the Flash 5 folder.
4. Double-click Flash 5 Mac.
5. Click Continue to complete the installation program.
6. Read the license agreement and click OK if you accept the terms.
7. Click Select Folder to select the location in which you would like Flash to be installed, and then click Install.

APPENDIX C

Keyboard Shortcuts

Listed here are some of the more common keyboard shortcuts for Macromedia Flash 5. You can also assign your own custom shortcuts by selecting Edit, Keyboard Shortcuts from the menu bar.

PC and Macintosh Keyboard Shortcuts		
To Accomplish This	**Do This (Windows)**	**Do This (Macintosh)**
New Movie	Ctrl+N	Command+N
Open Movie	Ctrl+O	Command+O
Save Movie	Ctrl+S	Command+S
Save Movie As	Ctrl+Shift+S	Command+Shift+S
Close Movie	Ctrl+W	Command+W
Undo Last	Ctrl+Z	Command+Z
Redo Last	Ctrl+Y	Command+Y
Copy Selected	Ctrl+C	Command+C
Cut Selected	Ctrl+X	Command+X
Paste Clipboard	Ctrl+V	Command+V
Clear Selected	Backspace	Delete
Select All	Ctrl+A	Command+A
Deselect All	Ctrl+Shift+A	Command+Shift+A
Copy Frames	Ctrl+Alt+C	Command+Option+C
Cut Frames	Ctrl+Alt+X	Command+Option+X
Paste Frames	Ctrl+Alt+V	Command+Option+V

PC and Macintosh Keyboard Shortcuts (Continued)

To Accomplish This	Do This (Windows)	Do This (Macintosh)
Insert Frame	F5	F5
Remove Frame	Shift+F5	Shift+F5
Insert Keyframe	F6	F6
Insert Blank Keyframe	F7	F7
Clear Keyframe	Shift+F6	Shift+F6
Group Objects	Ctrl+G	Command+G
Ungroup	Ctrl+Shift+G	Command+Shift+G
Break Apart	Ctrl+B	Command+B
Play Movie	Enter	Return
Test Movie	Ctrl+Enter	Command+Return
Test Scene	Ctrl+Alt+Enter	Command+Option+Return
Library Panel	Ctrl+L	Command+L
Character Panel	Ctrl+T	Command+T
Align Panel	Ctrl+K	Command+K
Arrow Tool	V	V
Subselect Tool	A	A
Pen Tool	P	P
Text Tool	T	T

PC and Macintosh Keyboard Shortcuts (Continued)		
To Accomplish This	Do This (Windows)	Do This (Macintosh)
Oval Tool	O	O
Rectangle Tool	R	R
Pencil Tool	Y	Y
Paint Bucket Tool	K	K
Help	F1	F1
Quit	Ctrl+Q	Command+Q

APPENDIX D

Additional Resources

This appendix lists additional resources. You can use them to go beyond the topics covered in this book or as sources of inspiration, utilities, or samples.

Additional Reading

Epic Software, *Macromedia Flash 5 Design: From Concept to Creation.* Rocklin, CA: Prima, 2001.

This is a great tutorial for intermediate-to-advanced users. It not only teaches you about some of the more complex Flash 5 functions, but it also provides numerous real-world examples of robust Flash technology that a Flash developer can put to instant use! The book demonstrates the creation of more than 20 sample animations.

Hillman Curtis, *Flash Web* Design: The v5 Remix. Indianapolis, IN: New Riders Publishing, 2001.

This book is a must for anyone seriously considering creating effective and interesting Flash Web pages. As well as teaching the mechanics, the book demonstrates the importance of conceptualizing the clients' needs and how to preplan and storyboard projects.

David J. Emberton and J. Scott Hamlin, *Flash 5 Magic: With Action-Script.* Indianapolis, IN: New Riders Publishing, January 2001.

If you're interested in learning more about ActionScript, I recommend this book. It is targeted at Web developers who want to make more effective use of Flash, and its authors have gone to great lengths to ensure that the projects are real and relevant.

Flash 5 Web Sites

Macromedia
http://www.macromedia.com/

Macromedia, the developer of Flash 5, describes its other great Internet and graphics applications on this site.

Flash 5
http://www.macromedia.com/flash/

The homepage for Flash 5. Check here for product news, updates, and patches.

Flash 5 Support Center
http://www.macromedia.com/support/flash/

Macromedia has one of the best online support structures on the Web today. The support center includes tutorials, technical notes, FAQs, newsgroups, mailing lists, and message boards.

Online Tutorials

Macromedia University
http://www.macromedia.com/university/

Online classes ranging from basic to advanced skill levels.

Webmonkey
http://hotwired.lycos.com/webmonkey/multimedia/shockwave_flash/

Webmonkey has a number of short tutorials on Flash.

We're Here Forums
http://www.were-here.com/forum/tutorials/

This site has a number of tutorials, mostly intermediate to advanced.

Virtual-FX
http://www.virtual-fx.net/tutorials/

This site has quite a few detailed tutorials.

Phong
http://www.phong.com/tutorials/

Phong walks you through creating some spectacular graphics—mostly with Photoshop, but it includes a few Flash tutorials as well.

Moock
http://www.moock.org/webdesign/flash/

Moock has a number of techniques for creating complex Flash animations.

Flashheaven
http://www.flashheaven.de/englisch.htm

This site has some advice on creating really cool Flash effects.

Designs By Mark
http://www.designsbymark.com/flashtut/

Mark has a large number of easy-to-follow tutorials.

Flash Movies
Macromedia's Site of the Day
http://www.macromedia.com/showcase/

Macromedia spotlights a different Flash or Shockwave site every day.

Hotwired's Animation Express
http://hotwired.lycos.com/animation/archive/

Here's a large collection of movies; most of them were created in Flash.

Todaystoon
http://todaystoon.com/

This collection of movies is updated daily, from the best Flash animations on the Web.

Cartoovie
http://www.cartoovie.com/

Cartoovie has a number of good cartoonish Flash movies.

2Darcade
http://www.sess.net/

You can find a bunch of really cool Flash games at this website.

Flash Resources

Macromedia Exchange
http://www.macromedia.com/exchange/flash/

When you need Flash resources, start at the source.

Flash Kit
http://www.flashkit.com/

This site has collected hundreds of sounds, movies, fonts, and tutorials from all over the Web.

Virtual-FX
http://www.virtual-fx.net/

This is another site that has an abundance of Flash resources.

Sound Files

Prosonica
http://www.prosonica.co.uk/

This good-looking site has lots of free sound files. They can also create custom sound effects.

Wave Bomb
http://www.wavebomb.com/

Another sound effect company. Wave Bomb also has free sound files.

APPENDIX E

Using the CD

The CD that accompanies this book contains 30-day trial versions of Macromedia Flash 5 and Freehand 9. Freehand is a popular drawing program that can create vector graphics that can be easily imported into Flash. You'll also find links to Flash 5 related Websites including those listed in Appendix C. The CD also contains the sample movie files used throughout the book, and a bonus folder with a few extra treats.

Running the CD with Windows

Insert the CD into your CD-Rom drive and do the following:

1. Double-click on the My Computer icon on your desktop.
2. Double-click on the icon representing your CD-ROM drive.
3. Double-click start_here.html. A browser window will open containing the license agreement.
4. Click "I Agree" if you accept the agreement. The Create Macromedia Flash Movies In a Weekend interface will appear.
5. Use the navigation buttons on the top of the window to move through the interface.

You will need to install the Flash 5 plugin before exploring the CD interface. Appendix B explains how to install Flash 5 and the plugins.

Running the CD with MacOS

Insert the CD into your CD-Rom drive and do the following:

1. Double-click on the icon representing your CD-ROM drive.
2. Double-click start_here.html. A browser window will open containing the license agreement.
3. Click "I Agree" if you accept the agreement. The Create Macromedia Flash Movies In a Weekend interface will appear.
4. Use the navigation buttons on the top of the window to move through the interface.

Some older browsers (3.0 and older) may not be able to view the interface correctly. If you are having difficulties, double-click on the flash.html file. If you are still unable to view the interface you can download an updated browser from Microsoft (http://www.microsoft.com/ie/) or Netscape (http://www.netscape.com/browsers).

INDEX

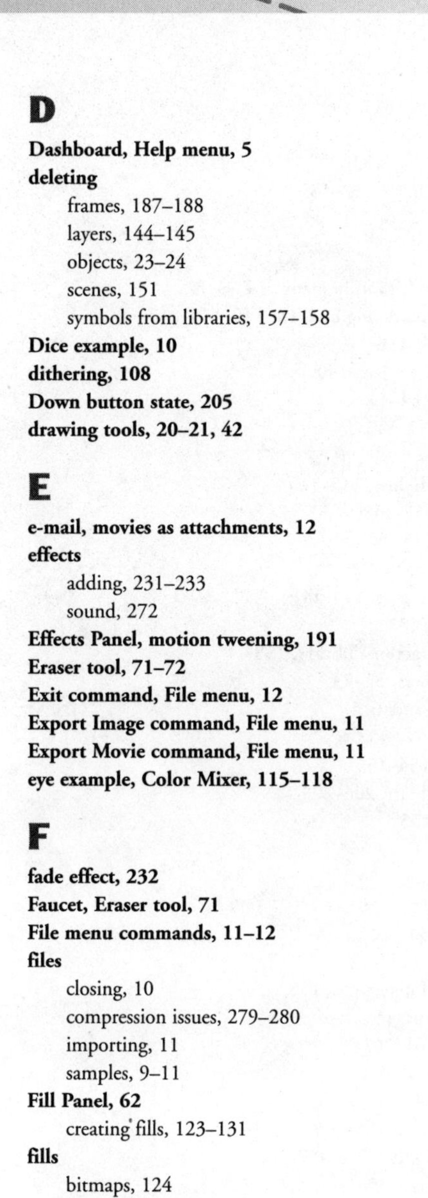

D

E

F

G

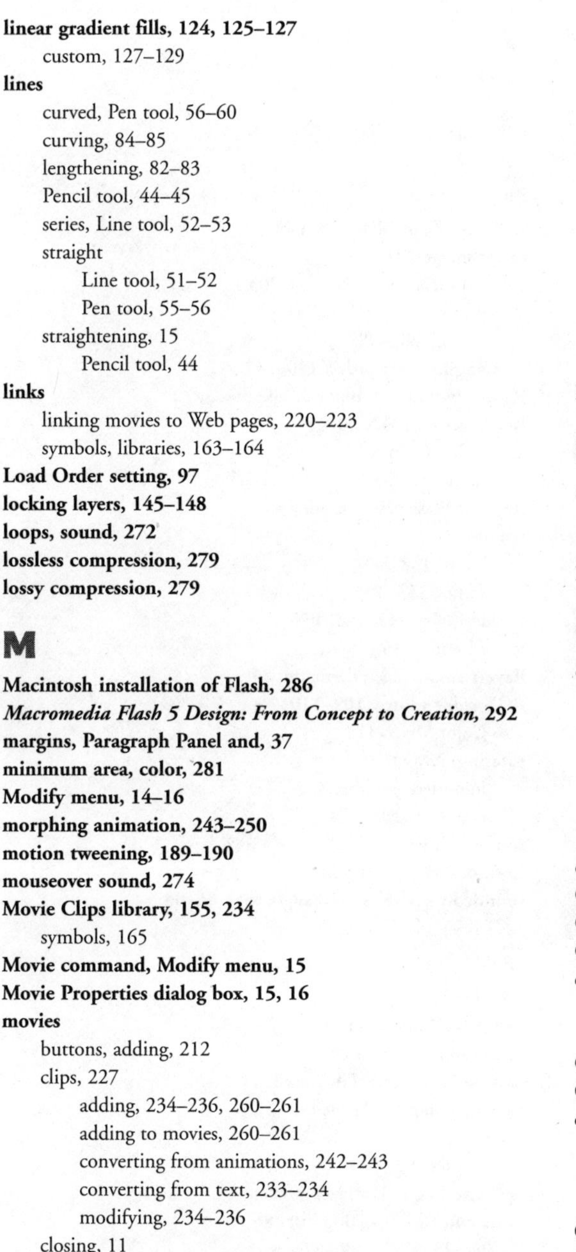

M

N

O

P

Q

R

S

T

U

V

W

Z

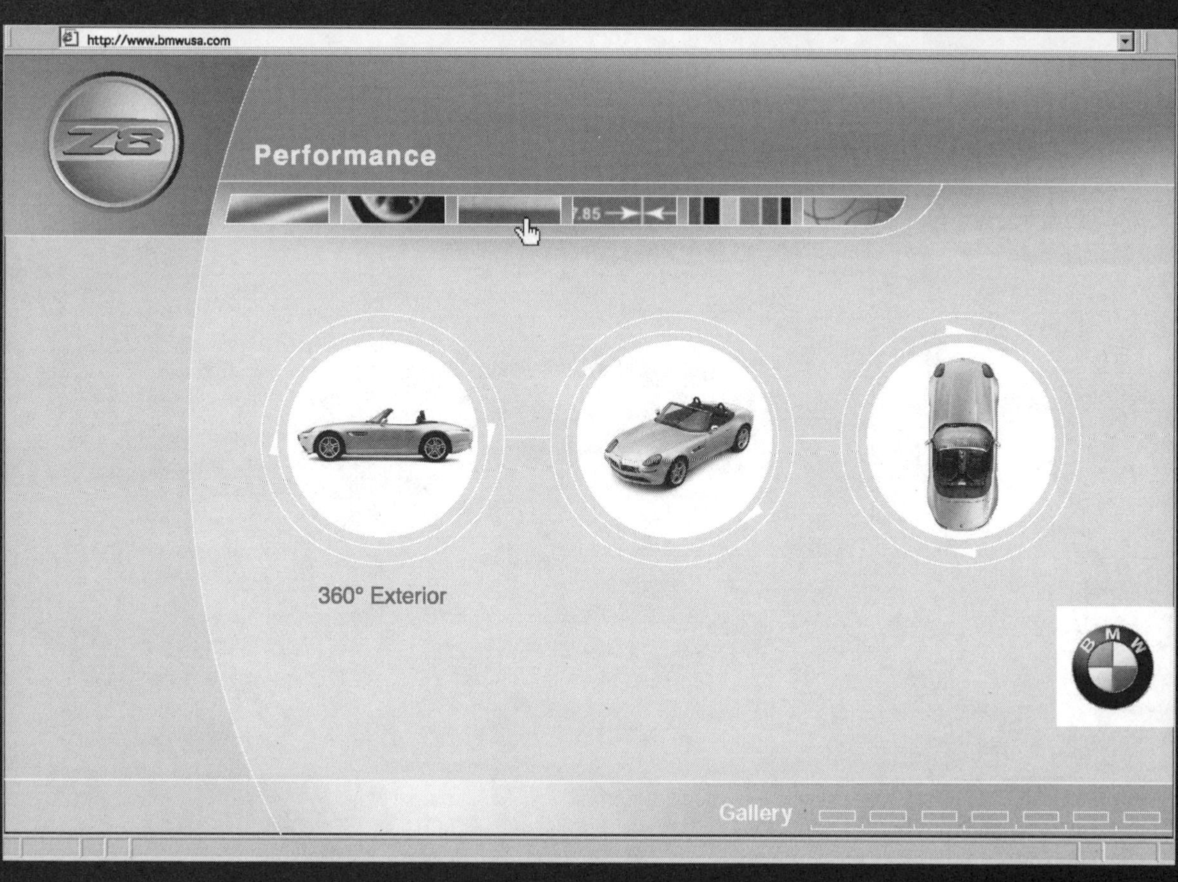

fast&easy® web development

Less Time. Less Effort. More Development.

Don't spend your time leafing through lengthy manuals looking for the information you need. Spend it doing what you do best—Web development. PRIMA TECH's *fast & easy*® *web development* series leads the way with step-by-step instructions and real screen shots to help you grasp concepts and master skills quickly and easily.

Adobe® LiveMotion™
Fast & Easy®
Web Development
0-7615-3254-4 ▪ CD Included
$29.99 U.S. ▪ $44.95 Can. ▪ £21.99 U.K.

ASP 3 *Fast & Easy®*
Web Development
0-7615-2854-7 ▪ CD Included
$24.99 U.S. ▪ $37.95 Can. ▪ £18.99 U.K.

CGI *Fast & Easy®*
Web Development
0-7615-2938-1 ▪ CD Included
$24.99 U.S. ▪ $37.95 Can. ▪ £18.99 U.K.

ColdFusion® *Fast & Easy®*
Web Development
0-7615-3016-9 ▪ CD Included
$24.99 U.S. ▪ $37.95 Can. ▪ £18.99 U.K.

Macromedia®
Director® 8 and Lingo™
Fast & Easy®
Web Development
0-7615-3049-5 ▪ CD Included
$24.99 U.S. ▪ $37.95 Can. ▪ £18.99 U.K.

Macromedia®
Dreamweaver® 4
Fast & Easy®
Web Development
0-7615-3518-7 ▪ CD Included
$29.99 U.S. ▪ $44.95 Can. ▪ £21.99 U.K.

Macromedia®
Dreamweaver® UltraDev™ 4
Fast & Easy®
Web Development
0-7615-3517-9 ▪ CD Included
$29.99 U.S. ▪ $44.95 Can. ▪ £21.99 U.K.

Macromedia®
Fireworks® 4 *Fast & Easy®*
Web Development
0-7615-3519-5 ▪ CD Included
$29.99 U.S. ▪ $44.95 Can. ▪ £21.99 U.K.

Macromedia®
Flash™ 5 *Fast & Easy®*
Web Development
0-7615-2930-6 ▪ CD Included
$24.99 U.S. ▪ $37.95 Can. ▪ £18.99 U.K.

HomeSite™ 4.5 *Fast & Easy®*
Web Development
0-7615-3182-3 ▪ CD Included
$29.99 U.S. ▪ $44.95 Can. ▪ £21.99 U.K.

Java™ 2 *Fast & Easy®*
Web Development
0-7615-3056-8 ▪ CD Included
$24.99 U.S. ▪ $37.95 Can. ▪ £18.99 U.K.

JavaServer Pages™
Fast & Easy®
Web Development
0-7615-3428-8 ▪ CD Included
$29.99 U.S. ▪ $44.95 Can. ▪ £21.99 U.K.

PHP *Fast & Easy®*
Web Development
0-7615-3055-x ▪ CD Included
$24.99 U.S. ▪ $37.95 Can. ▪ £18.99 U.K.

XHTML *Fast & Easy®*
Web Development
0-7615-2785-0 ▪ CD Included
$24.99 U.S. ▪ $37.95 Can. ▪ £18.99 U.K.

PRIMA TECH
A Division of Prima Publishing
www.prima-tech.com

Call now to order!
1.800.632.8676, ext. 4444

License Agreement/Notice of Limited Warranty

By opening the sealed disc container in this book, you agree to the following terms and conditions. If, upon reading the following license agreement and notice of limited warranty, you cannot agree to the terms and conditions set forth, return the unused book with unopened disc to the place where you purchased it for a refund.

License:

The enclosed software is copyrighted by the copyright holder(s) indicated on the software disc. You are licensed to copy the software onto a single computer for use by a single concurrent user and to a backup disc. You may not reproduce, make copies, or distribute copies or rent or lease the software in whole or in part, except with written permission of the copyright holder(s). You may transfer the enclosed disc only together with this license, and only if you destroy all other copies of the software and the transferee agrees to the terms of the license. You may not decompile, reverse assemble, or reverse engineer the software.

Notice of Limited Warranty:

The enclosed disc is warranted by Prima Publishing to be free of physical defects in materials and workmanship for a period of sixty (60) days from end user's purchase of the book/disc combination. During the sixty-day term of the limited warranty, Prima will provide a replacement disc upon the return of a defective disc.

Limited Liability:

THE SOLE REMEDY FOR BREACH OF THIS LIMITED WARRANTY SHALL CONSIST ENTIRELY OF REPLACEMENT OF THE DEFECTIVE DISC. IN NO EVENT SHALL PRIMA OR THE AUTHORS BE LIABLE FOR ANY OTHER DAMAGES, INCLUDING LOSS OR CORRUPTION OF DATA, CHANGES IN THE FUNCTIONAL CHARACTERISTICS OF THE HARDWARE OR OPERATING SYSTEM, DELETERIOUS INTERACTION WITH OTHER SOFTWARE, OR ANY OTHER SPECIAL, INCIDENTAL, OR CONSEQUENTIAL DAMAGES THAT MAY ARISE, EVEN IF PRIMA AND/OR THE AUTHOR HAVE PREVIOUSLY BEEN NOTIFIED THAT THE POSSIBILITY OF SUCH DAMAGES EXISTS.

Disclaimer of Warranties:

PRIMA AND THE AUTHORS SPECIFICALLY DISCLAIM ANY AND ALL OTHER WARRANTIES, EITHER EXPRESS OR IMPLIED, INCLUDING WARRANTIES OF MERCHANTABILITY, SUITABILITY TO A PARTICULAR TASK OR PURPOSE, OR FREEDOM FROM ERRORS. SOME STATES DO NOT ALLOW FOR EXCLUSION OF IMPLIED WARRANTIES OR LIMITATION OF INCIDENTAL OR CONSEQUENTIAL DAMAGES, SO THESE LIMITATIONS MAY NOT APPLY TO YOU.

Other:

This Agreement is governed by the laws of the State of California without regard to choice of law principles. The United Convention of Contracts for the International Sale of Goods is specifically disclaimed. This Agreement constitutes the entire agreement between you and Prima Publishing regarding use of the software.